Eight Fingers and Eight Toes

Accepting Life's Challenges

Debbie Jorde

Debbie Jorde

Columbine Press

ISBN-10: 0-615-39616-X
ISBN-13: 9780615396163

Columbine Press

Cover design and photo: Logan Madsen
Back Cover Photo: Melissa Papaj
www.debbiejorde.com

First American Paperback Edition

Printed in the United States of America

Dedicated to my loving husband, Lynn,
and my amazing children, Heather and Logan.

Acknowledgements

As I thought about all that I've learned from being Heather and Logan's mother, I realized that I didn't want to die one day and have all the valuable lessons die with me. So I wrote my story, partly from memory and partly as events were happening. When I completed the first draft, I asked a few people to read my manuscript and offer feedback. Some of my readers were anonymous, but I would like to thank the readers I know—my beautiful daughter, Heather Madsen, not only shared her experiences and contributed her insightful writings, but read and edited each draft; my sister, Kathy Cherrett, read the first manuscript from start to finish and supported me through the book's completion; my sister, Shelli Lether, not only supported my book from start to finish, but validated and honored me by viewing me as her role model and teacher; my friend, Kathy Newton, whose praise and support helped me believe in my ability to write the book. She gave feedback throughout the process and edited the final proof for errors. Kathy also gave my manuscript to Annette Haws, an English teacher, who edited and made helpful suggestions. Thank you Carolyn Green and Sara Brozovsky for editing.

After I finished writing my first drafts, I knew I needed an editor to make it read better. I am deeply grateful to my amazing husband, Lynn Jorde, who financed the professional editing that achieved this goal. Thank you, Lynn for your love, patience and support through the years of writing my book. My appreciation to Jayne Pupek (www.jaynepupek.com), the writer who edited my manuscript. Jayne is the author of three books: "Tomato Girl," a novel, and two poetry collections: "Forms of Intercession" and "The Livelihood of Crows." Thank you, Dr. John Carey, for writing the beautiful foreword to this book. I asked Dr. Carey ten years ago if he would write a foreword for my book. He agreed, and when the time came, he wrote a foreword which exceeded my expectations.

My story would not have been published without understanding, insights and encouragement from my creative and witty son, Logan Madsen. The theme and design for the cover of the book are Logan's ideas and he shot the photos for the cover and for some interior pictures. Logan is an artist www.loganmadsen-fineart.com. He paints with acrylics and oils, has an associate degree in graphic design and has an artistic eye with photography.

I would like to thank my brother, Shaun Lether, for designing my website, sharing his marketing knowledge and skills, and for encouraging me to publish my book. Thank you to my mom and my dad for loving me and being proud of my successes. Thank you to my brother, Cloyd Hepworth, for his love and support. Cloyd's daughter, my talented, niece and award winning photographer Melissa Papaj, took some photos for the book, photos for my website and personal use, and edited the black and white photos for the interior of the book. Her website is www.melissapapaj.com Thank you, Melissa. Thank you, Uncle Willis, for reading my book and giving me many fine suggestions. I would also like to thank my niece, Desi. for reading my manuscript.

I would like to offer a special acknowledgement to Terry Madsen, Heather's and Logan's father, who shared the early days of fear and uncertainty with me and later gave support during some tough times.

My gratitude to Rubin St. James, Heather's loving partner for the past five years. Having him as a member of our family and a loving partner to Heather is invaluable. Thank you, Rubin.

My appreciation and admiration to the researchers at the University of Washington and the University of Utah, and other institutions, who participated in finding the genes responsible for Miller syndrome and the primary ciliary dyskinesia. Finally knowing "Why" has given our family closure.

I'm grateful to both Margaret Hogan, founder of the Foundation for Nager and Miller syndrome (www.fnms.net), and DeDe Van Quill, for their ongoing support in making the FNMS a successful organization that supports families affected by these syndromes. And a heartfelt thanks to the financial donors who make it possible for the families to come together from all over the world every two years, and to all the people who help make those conferences a success.

I would also like to thank the staff at the University of Utah Behavioral Home Program for the excellent medical care they give to Heather and Logan.

A heartfelt thanks to all my customers and my good friends. Your support through life's many challenges over the past thirty-five years has been invaluable. My gratitude also goes to the many people who have supported me and touched my life, but whose names are not mentioned here.

I've had many experiences to share with limited space in which to include them. In choosing the stories I've included, I've left out others. All the people involved in this story would tell something different from what I have chosen. One day, I hope Heather and Logan will tell their own stories. Responsibility for errors or omissions is mine. If I have misrepresented anyone in any way, I apologize. For the sake of privacy, I changed many names.

Eight Fingers and Eight Toes

Eight Toes

Accepting Life's Challenges

Foreword

"They have disabilities, but they are not their disabilities."

When Debbie Jorde asked me to write the foreword to "Eight Fingers and Eight Toes: Accepting Life's Challenges," I was truly honored and humbled. I had known Debbie for almost three decades, having met her shortly after my arrival at the University of Utah as a junior faculty member and just after the birth of Logan, the second of her two children with Miller syndrome. This condition, named for the author who first published a description of the syndrome (which is also referred to as postaxial acrofacial dysostosis), consists of birth defects of the face and limbs. It is a very rare disease, with only about 30 individuals documented in the entire medical literature.

At the time of Logan's birth, one of my colleagues, a medical geneticist, was caring for Logan's older sister, Heather. When Logan was admitted to Primary Children's Hospital as an infant, my colleague invited me to "take a look" at him. As a young and recently trained clinical geneticist, I reviewed the medical chart and appreciated the experience of seeing a child with this rare syndrome. Soon thereafter, I was introduced to Debbie, and I was immediately struck by her poise and composure. I wondered how she – as the mother of two children with this rare, poorly understood, and visibly obvious syndrome – was really coping. Over the ensuing 10 years I would run into Debbie at the Children's Hospital with Heather, Logan, or both, as she orchestrated, in her words, the "maze" of specialists' visits.

Years later Debbie met and married Lynn Jorde, another long-time associate of mine, and I recall the happiness I felt that two people whom I admired were together. Afterwards, at University social events, I would greet Debbie with Lynn and receive updates about Heather and Logan.

On one occasion I attended a talk that Debbie delivered to the first-year medical students, relating her story of raising two children with this medically overwhelming condition. Later, with my clinician's tape recorder in place, I reflected on my impression of a mother who had accomplished so much: rearing her children with this rare disease as a single parent and coping well with its many complications.

Then I read "Eight Fingers and Eight Toes ..."

Throughout the pages I was struck with how little we as physicians (and, I am certain, other health professionals) are in touch with the actual lives and day-to-day stories of our patients and their families. We provide "news" of the diagnosis, we obtain snapshots of progress at clinic visits, we talk among ourselves about "coping," "acceptance," "feelings," maybe even "celebrating differences" – all noble themes – but do we really *know*? Perusing this narrative taught me that we do not. We intellectualize about so-called narrative medicine, we theorize about a parent's (or "patient's") coping mechanisms, we try to be in "their shoes," we even strive to empathize–all with good intentions– but we don't really know: we only observe the surface layer.

Debbie Jorde has created a masterful piece that exemplifies what is now an emerging genre: parents telling the story of their children and family, not as an anthropologist investigating a medical culture or as a counseling student performing a qualitative study, but rather through their own unique lens. In "Eight Finger and Toes: Accepting Life's Challenges," we witness and experience the true-to-life account of how one deals with seemingly endless challenges: the news of the birth of an infant whose condition is highly visible but poorly understood, the chronic medical problems requiring many surgeries and regular visits to multiple specialists, and the existential dilemma–the assault on the meaning and essence of parenthood–of the condition's genetic nature. And while these are the centerpieces of the story, the edges of the account–the outer rim of its circle–include divorce, single motherhood, an eating disorder, a chronic lung disorder in Heather and Logan (that mimicked cystic fibrosis and is not even a typical component of Miller syndrome), depression, and autism spectrum disorder. From this emerges resilience, self-doubt, inspiration, pain, authenticity, trials, self-esteem, differences, creativity, wisdom, and real quality in life: not simply "accepting" life's challenges but embracing them.

The story "Eight Fingers and Eight Toes..." has not concluded; life proceeds for Debbie, Heather and Logan. We read the story, are touched much of the time, inspired most of the time, ponder the events all of the time, but meanwhile "life's challenges" continue while we are reading these words.

The story's postscript and our understanding of Miller syndrome was enriched recently by the identification of the gene that, when mutated, causes the syndrome. Researchers at the University of Washington, the University of Utah, and other institutions published articles characterizing the gene discovery in the prestigious scientific journals, *Nature Genetics* and *Science*, in 2010. One of the insights provided by the research, which brought some clarity to Heather, Logan and Debbie, was the discovery that they had changes in two very different genes: the recently discovered Miller syndrome gene and alterations of a completely separate gene for lung disease. This explained their unusual chronic lung disease, which is not a typical feature of Miller syndrome.

"Eight Fingers and Eight Toes ..." should be read by all who care for persons with medically complex and rare conditions. While it covers many themes, the book's most stirring message is captured in Debbie's own words in Chapter 12: "They have disabilities, but they are not their disabilities."

John C. Carey, MD, MPH
Professor and Vice-Chair,
Dept of Pediatrics,
University of Utah School of Medicine

Photos

Chapter 1

My first baby was finally coming. The large round mirror mounted on the ceiling of the delivery room was positioned at a perfect angle to give me a good view of the birth. At this time ultrasounds were not routinely performed, so we had no idea of the baby's gender or health. As my husband, Terry, sat next to me, I was filled with anticipation and curiosity, wondering whether we would have a boy or girl, imagining which of us the baby would resemble.

Outside, the Utah landscape was white and pristine with last night's snow, but inside the hospital, the world was a sea of stainless steel and blue-green surgical scrubs. The room pulsed with a sense of excitement.

I looked at Terry, whose face revealed his own expectancy and wonder, and then back at the mirror.

As the baby pushed out of my body, I spotted the crown. The swatch of dark hair pleased me; it meant that my baby wasn't bald. The presence or absence of hair seems a small matter now, but I was young and naive. Nothing in my experience as a twenty year old woman had prepared me for the reality of what was to come.

When the baby's head emerged, the doctor used a small suctioning bulb to remove fluids from its nose and mouth. I wasn't worried: This was a routine procedure performed on newborns. Besides, Dr. Kirk had been delivering babies for many years; he had delivered my brother, Cloyd, eighteen years earlier.

When he finished suctioning, he helped ease the baby's shoulders out. Once freed, the rest of the body slid out, wet and slippery, and the doctor exclaimed, "You have a girl!"

Terry leaned closer and squeezed my hand. I wasn't worried that he might be disappointed not to have a boy. Throughout my pregnancy, whenever he was asked if he wanted a boy or a girl, he had responded that it didn't matter as long as the baby had ten fingers and ten toes.

Suddenly my eyes caught sight of our baby's body. She looked strange to me, nothing like I expected. Her skin was a pale blue and coated with a creamy substance. Was that normal? My eyes flashed to Terry, whose brown eyes revealed his own uncertainty. My eyes quickly darted to Dr. Kirk, but his focused expression revealed little. My attention finally settled back to my daughter.

She didn't seem to be moving. I was frightened. Was she alive? Panic coursed through me. I had heard the term stillborn before, but had never imagined that something could go wrong with my baby. I was young and healthy. So was Terry. Nothing could be wrong with our child, could it?

As the doctor placed the baby on my abdomen, her body flopped like a rag doll. Was she breathing? I couldn't tell. My heart pounded wildly inside my chest.

A pair of nurses moved nearby, but my attention was focused on my small motionless baby and the doctor who was busy clearing more fluids from her nose, mouth and throat. The word breathe was like a chant inside my head: Breathe, breathe, breathe.

Finally, after long and excruciating moments, gurgling sounds arose from her mouth. She made noises that sounded like muffled cries. Her arms and legs moved frantically, as if she had the sensation of falling. Yes! She was very much alive. I was relieved. My eyes moistened with tears.

And then I saw her arms; really saw her arms.

Something was wrong. These were not normal arms; not normal hands.

Now I was the one struggling to breathe.

My pulse raced as I tried to make sense of what I was seeing. Her small bluish arms looked abnormally short and were severely bent at the wrists. Her hands and fingers looked really small—too small even for a newborn.

Just as quickly as my eyes absorbed the images, my mind worked to deny them. This wasn't supposed to happen, not to us. My mind raced. Her arms were fine. She had simply been cramped inside the birth canal, she would look differently in a few hours; she just needed a little time in a less confined space. What else could explain her odd appearance? Nothing was wrong with my baby. She was normal. She had to be. I had to make my denial real. I whispered out loud, "No, her arms aren't bent,"

I blinked to clear my vision, but that did nothing to correct the distorted arms on my baby's body. A lump was forming in my throat. I could feel the muscles in my face strain from the fear and worry that consumed me. My voice was like a prayer inside my mind: "Oh please, let her arms be all right. This can't be happening. This isn't real. I need to know that what I'm seeing isn't the truth."

And then I heard Terry's voice. "Something's wrong with her arms," he said. The certainty in his voice hit me like a fist.

At that moment, I knew that what I thought I was seeing was true. Those words reverberated inside my head: Something's wrong with her arms.

"Is everything else all right? I mean, besides her arms?" I asked. I barely managed to form the words, but I needed some kind of reassurance, some good news.

Dr. Kirk, who was in his sixties and had undoubtedly comforted other new mothers in difficult situations, placed his hand gently on my shoulder. The expression on his lined, porous face softened as he spoke. "Well, Debbie, this isn't the kind of baby I anticipated for you."

My heart sank. This wasn't the kind of baby I had anticipated either.

Chapter 2

Our baby had eight fingers and eight toes. Not ten. Eight.

As I gazed at her deformed arms and hands, all I knew was that I wanted to leave the delivery room and pretend that I hadn't given birth, not to her, not to a baby like this. I wanted to start all over. I told myself that I would just go home and get pregnant again.

I would have a different baby. I didn't want this one.

After the birth, Dr. Kirk took the baby to another area to examine her. A nurse wheeled me into the recovery room and took care of me, cleansing my body and dressing me in a fresh gown.

Terry had left my side briefly to telephone his parents, but returned a short time later. As he sat next to me, I stared at the ceiling and wondered what to say, what to do. I was afraid to put my feelings into words. I didn't know how Terry would respond if I admitted the truth. How would he react if I said out loud that I didn't want the baby? Would he be hurt? Angry? I wasn't sure. This was his child, too. I studied his face for clues and saw the same stunned and confused expression I'd seen in the delivery room when he'd first noticed her arms.

Finally, I found the courage to say what I was feeling. "I don't think I want this baby."

"I don't either," he replied, his voice sounding tense. "What are we going to do?"

I didn't have an answer, at least not a practical one. I wanted to get dressed and leave the hospital. I wanted to pretend that this had only been a bad dream. I knew we couldn't just walk away, but I wanted to go far away from this hospital.

None of this was supposed to be happening. It had all started out so differently.

Approximately four months before the wedding, I had been late for my monthly cycle. That coupled with recent bouts of nausea prompted fears that I might be pregnant. I couldn't get my mind off of the changes that were happening to my body. I kept trying to deny the evidence because I didn't want to be pregnant, not yet. That only happened to other girls, not to me. I continued to look and hope for physical signs that my suspicions were wrong, and every day I was disappointed.

Finally, six or seven weeks later, I had to know the truth. I had made an appointment with a doctor to have the necessary tests done to find out if my suspicions were correct. I was so scared. I timidly walked into the doctor's office and checked in. I felt like I didn't belong there. I sat down and looked around the room at all the pregnant women. I couldn't believe I was there. I opened a magazine, only to shut it again. I got up and paced around the small, plain office and then sat down again. At last, the nurse called my name. My heart jumped as I rose and walked to the office.

The nurse drew my blood and excused me to the waiting area to wait for the results. I looked at the clock; the black hands seemed frozen, as if time had stopped. How long would I have to wait? A woman seated nearby cradled her bulging abdomen. I kept looking for magazines to read to take my mind off what was happening and why I was there, but all the magazines had something to do with pregnancy or motherhood. I wanted to run. Would this ever end? The nurse called my name again and I walked to the desk. My knees trembled.

"The test is positive. You are pregnant," the nurse said, her voice as flat and steady as rain.

I scheduled a future appointment and left the doctor's office in a daze. Overhead the sun broke through dismal clouds.

As I drove away from the narrow brown building, I considered the life growing inside me. "Are you really in there?" I asked and patted my abdomen. I was afraid and filled with disbelief, but at the same time, I felt the first twinges of maternal love. When I thought about telling Terry the news, I wondered what I was going to say. I wondered even more about how he might react to the news. Neither of us had counted on this.

I fought the urge to call him. Instead, I waited until later in the evening when we were alone. "I went to the doctor today and found out that I'm pregnant."

There, I had said it.

Silence.

"Well? What do you think?"

"What is there to think?" he said, and shrugged his shoulders.

Neither of us seemed to know what to say. I had the whole day to begin getting used to our new reality, but the news was fresh for him, and he seemed dazed, as I had been earlier.

"Well, I'm glad that we already set our wedding date, so people can't say that we had to get married." I was worried about what people would think of me. "Let's not tell anyone until after the wedding."

We kept our secret. After our wedding, I continued working at the hair salon as a licensed cosmetologist. Eventually, I started growing out of my clothes. The time came to announce that we were expecting. I cut words out of the newspaper and pasted them in a card to make the sentence: "We are going to have a baby." I passed the letter around at a family gathering. Everyone was very happy for us.

How did our beautiful dream become a nightmare? How could a baby like this belong to Terry and me?

A short time after the delivery, an orderly wheeled me into a room in the maternity ward. Overhead the florescent lights seemed harsh and unkind. I felt like a stranger in my own life. None of this was supposed to happen to us.

When we arrived in the small room, Terry's parents were standing there, waiting for us. They both smiled, trying their best to be optimistic and reassuring. They hugged Terry and leaned to kiss me on the cheek.

The sky in the window was dark and starless. I could have stared into the void for hours. I didn't feel like talking.

After a few awkward moments when none of us seemed to know what to say, Terry's father finally spoke. "You have to remember there's a perfect spirit inside that little body," he said. His wife nodded and took the seat Terry offered.

Terry's parents were devout Mormons, and I knew those words were intended to comfort and reassure me. Instead I felt ashamed. I, too, had been raised a Mormon, but I rarely attended church anymore and believed I had disappointed everyone by becoming pregnant before marriage. I also knew what our church taught about children with disabilities, and how the parents of such children were chosen by God. I knew, too, that a mother's love was supposed to be unconditional. What kind of mother doesn't want her own child?

I tried to force a smile, but even that was too much effort. I could not accept that the baby in the delivery room belonged to me. I didn't want to hear about her perfect soul. I didn't want to hear about her at all.

Chapter 3

Soon after Terry's family left, my mother and my older sister, Kathy, walked into my room. Mom carried a beautiful bouquet of flowers and handed them to me. "These flowers reminded me of a Heather," she said.

"Oh yeah, I was going to name the baby Heather if it was a girl," I murmured under my breath. I wasn't even sure that I wanted to name her, because in some way, to give her a name was to claim her. And yet, the flowers somehow made it easier. Of course we would call her Heather.

My sister, Kathy, sobbed into a tissue as she sat next to my bed. "This shouldn't have happened to you. It should have happened to me. You should have had Brandon," she said. Brandon was Kathy's eighteen-month-old son, a beautiful and healthy little boy. (We would sadly learn later that Brandon had cystic fibrosis and would die prematurely.) As a teenager, Kathy was rebellious and adventurous; she constantly challenged authority and broke the rules. By contrast, I was always trying to be "perfect." I did what I was told, studied hard, got good grades, always did my chores at home and rarely got in trouble. I went to church and tried to do the things I was taught were right. Kathy may have felt that I didn't deserve a baby with problems.

Mom and Kathy had been to the nursery to see Heather before coming to see me. They said the doctor told them she had a cleft palate. I was disappointed to hear that news.

While we were talking, the pediatrician came in. He was a tall man, mid-forties, with a receding hairline and glasses. After a brief introduction, he explained that he had examined my daughter. He told me about her cleft palate and explained that the baby couldn't get any suction to nurse or suck on a bottle because she had a hole in the roof of her mouth. I had planned to nurse my baby. I felt numb and overloaded.

The doctor went on to say something was different about her eyes too. "Her lower eyelids slope downward, as if there isn't enough skin for lower eyelids but I'm not sure because they are still swollen from the birth." He paused, and then added something he seemed to find positive. "At least everything is symmetrical."

"Symmetrical? What is that?"

"Everything is the same on both sides. Her ears are small and cup-shaped, her forearms are both short, both of her wrists bend down ninety degrees putting her hands below her wrists with her palms facing each other. Both hands are smaller than normal and missing the little finger. Her six other fingers are unable to straighten. Her feet are the same on both sides; turning in slightly and missing the little toe."

"Is symmetrical the best thing you can tell me about my baby? Is she able to hear?"

"Well, her ear canals are so small we can't see ear drums. We'll have to wait and see."

"What about her vision?"

"Her eyes are still adjusting. We don't have any reason to think that she can't, but again we'll have to wait and see."

When he had answered my questions and given me all the information that he could, he left. I leaned my head against the pillow and felt overwhelmed by all the problems we faced. This was more than we had bargained for; how could these things be happening to us?

Soon all our family members had gone, and Terry and I were left alone. We didn't discuss our feelings about not wanting the baby. We were numb with exhaustion, fear and disbelief. Like any young couple, we had small disagreements in the past, but there had never been this long, awkward silence between us. Until now.

Terry went home and I was left alone for the first time since giving birth. A few doors down, our newborn daughter spent her first night in the care of nurses. Perhaps the only saving grace was that she was too young to know that her parents did not want her.

That was one of the hardest nights of my life.

Sleep didn't come easily, even though I was exhausted. My eyes finally closed and I drifted into a deep sleep. When my eyes opened, I felt an intense, deep sense of fear, unhappiness and gloom. It was as if I had been awakened by a nightmare, only this nightmare was real. I had a baby who wasn't normal. I couldn't make the problems go away and I didn't know what to do. I'd never experienced such emotional pain. I sobbed uncontrollably. "I can't believe this is happening. I don't want this to be real. Please God, make this go away."

I cried myself back to sleep, only to awaken over and over throughout the night, repeating the same experience. I felt so helpless, so out of control. There was nothing I could do to change what was happening. I couldn't make it go away and I didn't know how to accept it.

When I awoke early the next morning, I wasn't ready to deal with the reality that I was facing. I asked the nurse to stop all my phone calls. I didn't want to talk to anyone. I couldn't bear to hear people say, "I'm so sorry." Hearing those words would force me to admit what was happening was real and I couldn't. Not yet. I just wanted to be left alone.

Terry came to the hospital that morning so he could be with me. Over and over we both said, "I can't believe this is happening. What are we going to do?" We didn't have any answers.

We were curious about the baby, even though we were in denial and disbelief, so we called the nursery and asked the nurse to bring Heather to our room. The nurse left her with us so we could be alone with her. We sat beside her little clear box, which served as a bassinet, and just looked at her. I noticed the little pink bow in her hair. She was asleep, eyes still swollen closed from birth. The pink undershirt she was wearing had long sleeves and her arms were too short to fill them. The sleeves just hung off her arms, the way a shirt might fit a scarecrow.

"She's so little. I can't believe she's our baby," I said.

Terry nodded, but said nothing. Neither of us touched her.

Our eyes roamed over her little face and her body. She was sleeping, and we just looked at her, curiously studying every feature we laid our eyes on. When she was asleep, we couldn't see the downward sloping eyelids, but we noticed that her chin receded more than normal, and we could see her small, cup-shaped ears. Her wrists were so bent that her hands looked strange where they were and her little fingers wouldn't straighten out making them look like a garden claw. Soon the pain of our new reality was unbearable, and we'd had all we could handle. We called the nurse and asked her to come get Heather. We didn't know what to think, because we were numb from all the emotions. Out of habit and not knowing what else to do, Terry decided to go to work.

I cried all morning long. I thought I would never stop. I didn't want to see the baby, and I didn't want to talk to anyone. I just wanted the whole experience to end. I kept thinking, "I can't stand this."

I heard a knock at my door. A nurse walked into my room. "Do you mind if I come in and talk with you a minute?" she asked.

I didn't feel like talking, but I didn't have the energy to come up with a good excuse. I smoothed the front of my hospital gown and nodded for her to come in.

She smiled, introduced herself, and sat on the chair next to my bed. She was dressed in white and had kind gentle eyes. She knew about our baby and wanted to share her experience as the mother of a child with Down syndrome. I knew she wanted to help me, but I couldn't relate to her, and her story didn't mean anything to me personally. I just wanted her to go away. I felt numb as she spoke. I wasn't ready to face the reality of being the mother of a disabled child, and nothing about her story brought me any comfort. Her intentions were good, but the timing was all wrong.

After she left, I wore myself out crying and thinking, and then I slept some more.

When I awakened, I couldn't cry anymore. I started to feel curious about the baby again. Maybe maternal instincts were setting in; I didn't have any other explanation for why I wanted to see her.

I climbed out of bed, put on my robe and slippers, and walked to the nursery. I stood outside the window looking in at all the bassinets. Every bassinet was empty, except for one, the one holding my baby. I knew what this meant: All the other babies were with their mothers. My heart ached for that little baby. I thought, "That baby is all alone because her mother doesn't want her, and I'm her mother!"

Tears filled my eyes and began to stream down my cheeks. I was on the edge of losing control of my emotions. Suddenly, I felt a warm arm wrap gently around my waist, and a nurse spoke. "Do you want to hold her?" she asked.

I nodded through my tears and allowed her to take my hand. She lead me into a small, windowless room where she helped me put on a sanitary gown and scrub my hands.

I felt like a robot programmed to do what I was told. I followed the nurse's directions because I didn't know what to do on my own. When I finished scrubbing, we went into a little room in the back of the nursery. The nurse disappeared for a few minutes and I was left alone, feeling afraid and uncertain. Part of me wanted to get up and leave the area before she returned, but somehow I managed to stay put.

When the nurse returned, Heather was lying in her arms, wrapped in a small pink blanket like the ones I had seen when I first arrived at the hospital. Another nurse accompanied her. She asked me if I wanted to watch them feed Heather. I nodded passively, not knowing what to expect but not knowing what else to do. She repeated the same information that the doctor had given me right after Heather's birth, that with a cleft palate the baby can't get enough suction to suck the nipple on a bottle or a breast, so they had to use a special feeder called a Breck-feeder. It looked a bit like a turkey baster and was composed of a large glass syringe, about two inches in diameter, with a rubber ball on one end and a quarter inch tube, approximately four inches in length, on the other end.

One nurse propped Heather into a seated position, while the other nurse inserted the tube into Heather's mouth, far enough to direct the formula down her throat without gagging her. Then she lightly squeezed the ball to squirt the formula through the Breck-feeder. As the liquid was released, it began to stream out of Heather's nose and mouth. She was gulping uncomfortably, as if she might be drowning. Her strange looking arms were flailing. They looked as if the hands had been cut off at the wrist and then glued back on in the wrong place under the wrist pointing down to the floor. I felt as if my heart would break. Everything I was seeing made me feel terribly sad. Heather looked so helpless. Few things are more difficult to watch than a newborn struggling to feed or breathe, especially when that newborn is your own.

When the nurses finished feeding and cleaning Heather's milky face and chest, one of them asked me if I wanted to hold her. I didn't know what I wanted, but I didn't feel like I could, or should, say no. "Yeah, I guess," I said.

Before I had the chance to change my mind, she gently placed Heather in my arms. Both nurses left the room. I was alone with my new baby. As I rocked Heather, I studied everything about her. She was so small. I stroked her dark hair, which was the color of my own. I gently touched her face, lightly grazing her closed eyelids with my finger tips. I observed her downward sloping lower eyelids. I could see the red tissue inside the lower lid as the doctor had described to me soon after her birth. I ran my finger along the edge of her small cup-shaped ears, and moved my hand downward to caress her little forearms. In a soft whisper, I quietly counted her fingers and toes. I placed my thumb in her little hand. Her three bent fingers curved around my thumb. I gently caressed her fingers to see if I could straighten them. They didn't straighten at all; as if they had no knuckle but were formed bent. My tears fell on her arm as I cried, wondering how this little girl would be able to do anything in this world with arms and hands like this. I could hardly believe that this was the baby that had been inside my body for ten months; the one I felt kicking and moving and the same one I talked to from the moment I found out I was pregnant. Even though she had all these problems, I was in awe, thinking that I helped create this little human being. I was marveling at the miracle of creating a human life.

The pediatrician came and offered his assessment. "It's possible that this condition could be genetic." He went on to explain about recessive and dominant genes. He was suggesting that perhaps this condition could occur again with another pregnancy. I couldn't believe what he was saying.

All I knew was that I didn't want this to happen again. I reacted instinctively by saying, "I'm getting fixed. I'm not having any more babies if this can happen again."

He didn't have any conclusive answers for me and suggested that I talk with a geneticist. I still couldn't believe that this was all real, or that it was all happening to us.

Later that day, I decided I was ready to have the baby in my room. I nervously dialed the nursery. "Could someone bring Heather Madsen to me?"

Just as they wheeled Heather's bed into my room, Terry's mother walked in. Hospital policy prohibited newborns from being around anyone except the mother and father, so the nurse took Heather back to the nursery. I felt disappointed. I still wasn't sure I wanted this baby, so my disappointment surprised me.

After visiting with Terry's mother, I received another guest: my dad. He kissed my cheek and sat in the chair beside my bed. As I looked at him, I thought about the baby's dark hair and how her coloring was like my father's, and like mine.

He didn't know anything about how I felt when Heather was born. No one knew about my feelings of not wanting the baby except Terry, so I was surprised when he said, "You don't have to worry about anything. I've made some arrangements to have the baby cared for if you don't want her."

My emotions were still unsettled. On some level, I felt grateful that he wanted to take care of this problem for me. Another part of me was disturbed by the offer.

I knew my father's offer was real. He had always tried to make things right for me. When I was in the fifth grade, my father made my dream of having a horse come true. He knew I loved horses because I collected all kinds of plastic horses and read novels about horses and their owners. He gave us an Appaloosa mare and colt for Christmas. Another gift from my dad was braces for my teeth. I really needed them because I had sucked my thumb for thirteen years, and my front teeth protruded. Besides being self-conscious about my height – at six feet tall I towered over other girls – I was very self-conscious about my overbite, so when I smiled, I tried to keep my teeth covered with my lips. I was so grateful to have straight teeth when my braces were removed two years later.

All I had to say was thank you, and my father would see to it that I did not have to mother the deformed child I had given birth to. But something had begun to shift inside me, and my father's offer forced me to make a choice. I could either accept this baby as she was and do my best to care for her, or I could walk away, relinquishing her care to strangers.

"It's all right, Dad, I want to keep her," I said, and my eyes filled with tears. I wasn't quite sure how I would be a mother to this baby, but I wanted to try. I could not abandon her. She was mine.

"Do you want to go to the nursery to see her?" I asked.

We walked down to the nursery together and looked into the viewing window. A nurse held Heather up to the window. She was wrapped tightly in a pink blanket so we couldn't see her arms and hands. She looked beautiful to me. Her dark hair was combed up into a curl, and a pink bow placed there. Her skin had the olive coloring that my dad's and mine had. She tried to open her eyes a little bit. I smiled. It was strange the way time was helping me adjust to my new reality, and at that moment I felt like a proud mother, full of love for her first child.

After I went back to my room and said goodbye to my father, I changed into a clean gown and brushed my teeth. I stood at the bathroom mirror and looked at my face. My eyes were red and swollen from too little sleep and too many tears. This strained and exhausted face belonged to someone else. I was not this person. I had watched my mother's face grow weary over the years, as if all her battles had taken their toll on the very cells that made up her skin. I didn't want to become someone weary of her own life. I had been a mother for all of one day, but already the strain was visible. Any of the radiance I had shown during pregnancy had somehow evaporated into thin air. I flipped off the light and stepped back into my room.

I missed Terry and wanted him here with me. I climbed into the hospital bed and rested my head against the pillow. As the moments ticked by, I thought about our baby in the nursery. I wanted to hold her again.

When Terry arrived, I suggested having Heather brought to us, but he shook his head. "I'm not ready yet," he said.

I respected his feelings and assumed that he needed more time to get used to everything that was happening. He'd been at work all day and probably had very little time alone during the day to sort through his feelings. I had spent many hours alone thinking of little else.

We ate dinner in my room, a special meal prepared by the hospital to mark the birth of our child. The cafeteria staff had grilled steaks for us and served them with baked potatoes and steamed broccoli. They had also made a white cake and decorated it with a little pink plastic baby to celebrate the arrival of our new baby girl. The festive cake was a sad reminder of all the things that were wrong with our daughter.

While we were eating, there was a knock at the door, and a team of doctors walked into the room. I lost count of them, but remember feeling as if a herd of white coats had overtaken the small space. They informed us that Heather had taken a turn for the worse.

"Your baby's in trouble," one doctor explained. A stethoscope hung around his neck; another jutted from his coat pocket. "She has a heart murmur and she's aspirating. She also has jaundice."

My breath caught in my throat. I wondered if her jaundice explained the olive coloring of her skin.

"I was about to sit down and have my dinner at home when my phone rang," the specialist continued. "It was Heather's doctor, informing me about all the problems she was having. For a moment I wondered why the doctor bothered to call me because it sounded like this baby had so many problems it seemed obvious that she probably wouldn't live. But I just couldn't eat my dinner knowing I hadn't tried." His voice and manner were kind as he explained that he was going to have Heather transferred to Primary Children's Hospital in Salt Lake City, where they would perform a procedure called a heart catheter. The results would help determine what was causing the murmur. He asked us to sign the release forms giving them permission to do the surgery.

He also asked us to sign a form giving them permission to do an autopsy.

Terry and I looked at each other, but didn't speak. Autopsy? The word was like a door slamming inside a quiet cathedral.

I felt numb as I signed the necessary forms. The doctor said he would call when he finished the procedure. He told us we could go see her before they transported her.

Together Terry and I walked to the nursery. We had to scrub our hands and put on sanitary gowns before we could go in. As we entered, I immediately saw Heather under bright lights, in an open hospital crib, hooked up to several plugs and wires. They were attached to her stomach and heart, and her skin color looked a sickly yellow. Her chest and stomach heaved rapidly as she fought for each breath.

As the blood rushed from my face, I turned away and almost fainted. I had expected to see the beautiful little baby girl shown to my father and me through the window earlier that day. Terry and the nurse had to hold me on my feet until we could find a chair. I wasn't prepared for this.

"I'm so sorry, I should have warned you," the nurse said.

I sat there, numb and shaken. When I was able to stand, Terry and I slowly walked back to my room. Neither of us could find the words to express what we felt. We stared ahead like zombies, unable to process the events unfolding before us.

We didn't know how long the operation was going to take. Terry was restless and didn't know what to do with himself, and I didn't know what I wanted him to do. He had a basketball game scheduled that night, and he robotically felt compelled to go play. I felt empty and paralyzed, so I told him he might as well go. As I said it, I felt hollow, like my mouth was just saying the words. I was drained and exhausted. He kissed me goodbye and walked out of the room.

Almost immediately, he stepped back inside the room and sat next to me. "I can't believe I was just going to go play basketball and leave you here alone waiting for a phone call that will tell us if our baby is going to live or die," he said.

While we waited, we discussed the probability of Heather's dying. After all, they wouldn't have had us sign papers giving permission for an autopsy if she were going to live. We started to adjust to the idea that she would die. We thought maybe it would be for the best. We didn't know if her life would be worth living, and we didn't know how to take care of her.

I started to feel a sense of relief, but it was bittersweet. I felt sad about her dying before friends and family got to see her. She looked so beautiful to me that afternoon, and I worried that when people heard about all her problems, they would picture a monster. I didn't like that idea. But I didn't feel so worried about the future now, because this would probably be over soon. I believed that Terry felt the same mixture of sorrow and relief.

We waited for hours for a telephone call that night, but instead of a phone call, the doctor came to our room in person. His broad smile told me that our baby was still alive. I wasn't sure if I felt relieved or disappointed.

"If I had known her heart looked this good I wouldn't have done anything," he said. He sat down and drew a picture of Heather's heart as he explained that a valve that usually closed at birth hadn't closed yet and was causing the murmur. He said usually the valve closes by itself within the first year.

For a split second, I felt genuine disappointment as the fear welled up inside me again. I had already accepted the possibility that Heather wouldn't suffer in this life, and I believed that was for the best. Now I had to readjust my thinking again. I felt like a ping-pong ball being batted back and forth between two equally difficult realties.

After everyone was gone, I slept fitfully and cried all through the night.

I didn't know what was going to happen to Heather or my life. I didn't know how Terry and I would manage a baby who needed so much.

During the night, a woman who had just given birth was brought into my room. Until then, I had been fortunate to have the room to myself.

A voice woke me later that night. I forced my eyes open and saw a nurse. She held a baby in her arms. "I have your baby for you," she said.

I was startled and confused, and then overwhelmed. The baby belonged to the woman in the next bed. This was the way it was supposed to be, but my experience had been nothing like that. "That's not my baby, my baby's at Primary Children's Hospital, and I don't know if she will live or die," I said, my voice breaking as I tried to explain.

The nurse gasped and apologized. She gave the baby to its mother and paused beside my bed to ask how my baby was doing.

"I don't really know. She has so many problems, and she's so little." My eyes moistened with tears. I had cried more in the last day than at any time in my life, and still there were more tears.

Before she left, the nurse apologized again. "I hope your baby is all right."

"Me, too," I said, although I was too numb and overwhelmed to know what I hoped.

I didn't feel it necessary to stay in the hospital the three days that was typical after giving birth. I wanted to see Heather. I got dressed, packed my bags and waited to be released.

Throughout my pregnancy, I pictured my baby dressed in the little yellow and white sweater, booties and cap I crocheted while she kicked inside me, and wrapped in the yellow gingham blanket I tied with my friends at my baby shower for this special day. As I imagined Terry carrying our new baby out to the car to take it home to the new nursery, I was consumed with sadness and disappointment. The nurse placed some tissues in my hand to wipe my tears. I was leaving the hospital with empty arms.

The nurses made me ride in a wheelchair to the car. I didn't want to, but they insisted. As I was being wheeled down the hall, I kept thinking about the way this day was supposed to be. Instead of carrying my baby, I held the flowers my mother gave me in one hand and a tissue in the other. Terry walked ahead to pull up the car near the exit.

I tried to shake my feelings of despair by focusing on one thing: getting to Primary Children's Hospital to see Heather.

When Terry and I arrived at PCH, we were directed to the intensive care unit. A thin nurse with auburn hair guided us to the section where Heather was being cared for in a clear, plastic box called an isolette. The nurse explained that our baby was receiving oxygen and warmth.

Terry and I stared at Heather inside her little cubicle. She looked so small and fragile, lying on her stomach with her head turned toward us. She was asleep but without lower eyelids to close her eyes, they looked open. Her short, little arms were lying by her sides, bent at the elbow exposing her strange bent wrist and small hand. I felt a surge of love for her. She looked so helpless and alone, and I wanted to hold and protect her. For the moment, all we could do was look at her.

Another newborn slept in the isolette next to Heather. This baby had a completely healthy torso, neck and head, but didn't have any arms or legs. Hands extended from the shoulders where arms should have been and feet extended from the pelvis where legs belonged. The parents seemed to be healthy like Terry and me, and this was their first baby. For the first time, I felt grateful for the little arms that Heather had; at least she had arms, and she had legs, too. That was my first experience appreciating the problems I faced, because I could see that there would always be someone whose situation was more difficult.

My first night at home without a baby was painful. Terry tried to cheer me up, but when I flipped on the light in the nursery, I was heartbroken. My gaze moved over the white canopy crib and the yellow gingham quilt, the rocking chair with matching yellow gingham cushions, the window draped with matching curtains, all sewn with my own hands during the long pregnancy, then across the room to the changing table that held a stack of small diapers and talcum powder. I still didn't know if I would have a baby at all. The feelings of emptiness were unbearable.

As I lay in bed that night, I looked down at my flat stomach where my baby had been. I felt empty and alone. The baby had been with me for the past ten months and now it was gone. I sobbed uncontrollably. I couldn't understand why this happened. I felt helpless.

Terry and I gravitated to traditional roles while Heather was a newborn and still hospitalized. I rose early, showered and dressed and we drove to the hospital in separate cars so I could spend my day with Heather. Terry spent some time with us and then headed to work. In the evening, when Terry and I talked, most of our conversations focused on our disbelief that this was happening to us. We were constantly worried about whether our daughter would survive.

Seeing my baby, spending the day at the hospital where she was, and learning all that I could about how to take care of her gave me some kind of sense of direction. It was nothing like what I had pictured, but it was a direction and purpose.

Because Heather was in ICU, there weren't many visitors. I quickly got used to spending the day there alone. It wasn't my nature to seek support and comfort from other people. As I had done most of my life, I accepted what was happening and did what was required to cope. Whenever difficult emotions surfaced, it was as if I had an internal switch that I could flip off to avoid those feelings. I could shut down at will, and I did. While Terry went to work, I spent every day for two weeks in the intensive care unit with Heather. I held her whenever the nurses would let me. I watched them feed her and take care of her. I grew impatient because I wanted to take her home and be her mother. I didn't care anymore that she wasn't a perfect baby. She was mine. I loved her and wanted to take care of her.

Terry felt nervous about my attachment because we still didn't know if Heather was going to live. "I don't want to see you get hurt. We still don't know how this will turn out," he cautioned me.

The doctor was concerned because Heather wasn't getting enough to eat. Her cleft palate made it difficult to get enough nutrition. The formula just flowed out of her nose and mouth; very little went into her stomach. The doctor didn't know the prognosis on Heather's life expectancy, and they still didn't know what syndrome she had. The uncertainty was hard to accept.

I had planned to nurse, but Heather's cleft palate made it impossible. I felt very sad and disappointed that I couldn't nurse, and when the doctor gave me medication that would dry up my milk, I was very upset. The milk came in anyway, so I rented a breast pump and took milk to the hospital for Heather. Pumping my milk wasn't very easy; after a couple of weeks I decided it wasn't working out. The doctor said the baby would be fine without the mother's milk and not to worry about it.

After two long weeks, the doctor said that if I could learn to tube feed Heather, I could take her home. I was nervous about intubating Heather; if the tube went into her lungs instead of her stomach, she would drown. The doctor assured me that we could test for that situation before putting the formula into the tube. The tube was placed into a cup of water and if there were continuous bubbles, then the tube was in the lungs. No bubbles meant it was in the stomach. The time came for me to try intubating Heather myself. I was scared, but it went smoothly, and I felt like I could do it at home if I had to. I would do my best to feed Heather with the Breck feeder, so I wouldn't have to intubate her, but at least I knew I could do it if necessary.

One of the nurses brought in a lamb's nipple; a big black nipple approximately four inches long. She replaced the tube on the feeder with the nipple.

She cut a bigger hole in the end so that when she squeezed the ball on the other end of the bottle, the formula squirted down Heather's throat. This worked much better than the tube, and it gave Heather something to suck on. With this important procedure learned, the doctor felt comfortable releasing Heather to our care.

I carefully dressed Heather in the new yellow and white sweater outfit I crocheted before she was born and wrapped her in the yellow gingham quilt that I tied during my pregnancy. Walking out of that hospital was exciting and scary. I didn't know what the future held for us, but I was ready to try to handle whatever it would be. I was finally taking my baby home.

Chapter 4

"So, what's her problem?" the plastic surgeon asked on my first visit to his office to see about a cleft palate repair for Heather. His tone of voice sent a chill through my body. This was one of our first doctor appointments after bringing Heather home from the hospital and I was a nervous new mother.

I'd heard some doctors described as "cold and clinical" and he came across that way. I didn't feel any warmth or connection. "The doctors think she has a syndrome called Treacher Collins," I offered.

"Well, that isn't the only thing wrong with this baby." He pushed his glasses up on his nose and stared at me.

I wanted to cry. Instead, I stayed put and tried to remain composed. I didn't want to show my feelings or lose control. For the past few weeks, I had been staying at home as a full-time mother with my beautiful baby girl. I was so happy to have her and was grateful that she was alive. I had brought her to the doctor's office for one reason: to see what he could do to help my baby. I resented that he spoke about my daughter as if she was an object and not a person. He didn't seem to care that he was talking to the child's mother. Maybe she did have multiple problems, but she was my daughter.

"Did you do drugs?" he asked.

"Of course not." I held more tightly to Heather. She wriggled in my arms.

"Did the father do drugs?"

"No, absolutely not." I felt accused, as if he thought Terry or I had caused Heather's birth defect. I had come here for help, not judgment. I had not expected his calloused demeanor. It was all I could manage to keep myself together while he explained what he could do for my child.

He informed me that he could close the cleft in her hard palate when Heather was six weeks old, and then at two years, he would complete the repair.

I was very upset when I left the office. When the time came for Heather's surgery, I would not let that doctor operate on her. I had made up my mind that I would have his associate do the surgery.

As I walked across the parking lot to my car, my eyes overflowed with tears. A deep sadness came over me. In the safety of my car, I rested my head on the steering wheel and sobbed. I couldn't believe how that doctor had acted toward my baby and me, but even more than his awful bedside manner, I was frightened by the reality of all Heather's problems and a future of surgeries. We were only at the beginning of this, and already it seemed that the problems would never end.

While I was at home, I could relish the roles of wife and mother. I didn't have to deal with opinions, decisions and the cruel realities of surgeries and health problems. Every doctor's visit was another confrontation with a reality that overwhelmed me. Each time I felt as if I had been blasted with a dose of cold air. I was terrified by all the problems my little girl had, and I felt unprepared to handle them. I loved my daughter and wanted to do the very best for her, but would my best be good enough? Nothing in my childhood or earlier life had prepared me for this.

I was born in Henderson, Nevada in 1956. Because my dad was in the Air Force, we lived in a home provided by the military at the time of my birth. Soon after, we moved to Salt Lake City and lived in a basement apartment in a big home on Wilson Ave. The house was a two story, yellow wood-frame house with a pitched roof. The house faced south, which meant the frequent and abundant snow melted off the driveway on warm winter days. The driveway at the west of the house lead to my maternal grandfather's machine shop. That is where he built his trains.

My maternal aunt, Minnie, and her husband, Willis, lived downstairs. Aunt Minnie took care of my older sister, Kathy, for two months at the time of my birth because a newborn baby and a toddler were too much for my mother to manage with her sensitive health issues. Minnie reminded me of Aunt Bea from the Andy Griffith Show. She was like a mother to the three of us: my sister, Kathy, my younger brother, Cloyd, and me. We loved her so much and knew she loved us.

Aunt Minnie cleaned my grandma's house, took her to get her hair done and bought her groceries every week. She taught us we could depend on her if we needed help. My grandmother never learned to drive, but was a perfectionist with her house.

By contrast my mother said she didn't even know how to boil an egg when she left home to get married. She said Grandma wanted everything done perfectly so she didn't even allow her to make her own bed. Her time was spent taking piano and ballet lessons.

Dad, strikingly handsome, looked like a tall Elvis Presley. He worked for my grandpa in the machine business. Later he started his own tool and die business and bought his own building. Long after we moved, we stayed with my aunt and uncle every summer for a week. We always looked forward to that visit. Our aunt bought all our favorite sugared cold cereals, made the best spaghetti in town, served great bologna sandwiches and offered us buttered bread covered with Dutch chocolates.

My mother's entire family is Dutch. My mom, Elizabeth, is a beautiful woman. She looks like Elizabeth Taylor. She was the last child born in a family with seven children. She and the two children before her were the only three born in the United States. Her father and mother became Mormons and migrated to Salt Lake City from Holland. My grandfather was very committed to the Mormon religion. He paid us all five dollars to read the Book of Mormon when we were children. When he bore his testimony in church on Fast Sundays, we stood and bore our testimony, too, which involved standing before the congregation to declare that the church is true and Joseph Smith is a true prophet of God.

My mother loves flowers. She was always arranging flowers to put around our home. We lived in a green cinder block house until I was in the middle of second grade. There was a clump of red river birch in the back yard. My dad would put a blindfold on and chase us around that clump of trees while he growled like a monster. The game was called blind man's bluff and we loved it. When he was busy working, we spent many hours playing in the sandbox and playhouse. The playhouse was a little rectangle building built of cinderblocks and was painted green to match our house.

Kathy and I played house a lot with our dolls and doll furniture. Even then, I loved assuming the role of the mother. I knew from early on that I would someday be a mother. It was something I never questioned.

I got a beautiful doll for Christmas when I was five. She wore blue make-up on her eyes and had short curly, pale blonde hair. I took her to kindergarten for show and tell. I was so proud to show off my doll. She was perfect, just like I longed to be.

There was a red brick house next door. Mrs. Nell, who lived there, invited us over for chocolate cake. She had a big metal swing set in her backyard, so we could play on her swings any time we wanted. She left her key on her window sill in case we needed to get in if our mother wasn't home.

One day a boy babysat Kathy and me at Mrs. Nell's house. I was in kinder-garten and Kathy in the first grade. He made us take off our clothes and run around the house naked. He didn't touch us that I can remember. I felt strange, but did it anyway. I only remember that happening one time. I don't think we told our mother. Already she was starting to display mood swings and outbursts that would become more prevalent over time. We learned early on not to upset her.

I sucked my thumb a lot, so much, I had worms. I received a black cat as a gift from my dad to stop sucking my thumb, but I couldn't quite kick the thumb, not for many years and after acquiring a pronounced overbite. The cat's name was Sambo, and he used the sandbox as a litter box. I played in the sandbox and sucked my thumb, so I got worms. The itching felt awful, as if it would never stop.

That was the house we lived in when my parents were fighting and divorced.

Sometime between the age of four and six years old I saw my mother lying on the living room floor with my dad sitting on top of her. He was straddling her. Her arms were over her head and he was holding both her wrists firmly to the floor as she was sobbing and screaming while throwing her head from side to side. I think he was holding her down so she wouldn't throw things the way she sometimes did when she was mad. She was begging me to run to the neighbor's house and tell them to call the police. My whole body was shaking with fear. All I could do was suck my thumb.

Another time, my brother, Cloyd, was sitting in his high chair. My mother was spoon-feeding him. He was spitting out his food. I watched my mother shoving the spoonfuls of food into his little mouth with shaking hands as her anger increased. I felt the familiar tightening in the pit of my stomach and the fear ris-ing inside my body. I started sucking my thumb as I watched. My mother's voice sent shivers through my body as she screamed bad words and continued to force the spoonfuls of food towards his mouth. The food ended up all over his face as he continued to spit out each bite. The high chair tipped over and my brother's head hit the floor. His head split, and I watched as blood spread over his face and make a puddle on the floor. Cloyd's fussing turned to screaming and my mother began sobbing as she tried to untangle his little body from the chair.

My maternal grandparents brought us groceries every Saturday. They always had frozen ice cream bars covered with chocolate and peanuts for us. They also brought us Twinkies. My grandmother's short plump body would climb out of her dark blue Cadillac. She wore a navy blue dress, thick flesh colored support hose, and plain comfortable shoes for her old knotty feet. Her black hair was in tight waves close to her head and covered with a thin hairnet like a spider's web. Sometimes she wore a small round box hat with a feather or a fancy net that matched her dress. My grandpa was a large man with a bald head on top and silver hair around the edges. He wore wire framed glasses and always had a big smile on his face. I loved to run up to him and give him a big hug. His arms embraced me as he picked me up and put me on his shoulders. He took little steps up on his toes and down again to make us go up and down like a train on a rickety track as he said, "Toot, Toot, Toot," over and over.

Grandma and grandpa knew my mother needed extra help, especially after she and my dad were divorced. When we were young, Grandpa would come to our house early in the morning before we went to school to cook our breakfast. He would boil the water on the stove and add cracked wheat. It cooked until it was thick and creamy. I waited and watched him pour the hot cereal into my bowl. I dipped a big spoon into the golden honey and filled it to the rim. I slowly poured the sweet sticky honey over my cereal, making swirls and designs. My grandpa poured enough milk onto the hot cereal to make it cool down so I could eat it. I felt so warm and cozy when my grandpa was there.

When my mother had her bad moods, her face turned a bright red, and she screamed really scary, mean things. "I wish you would all run out in front of a car, get run over and die!" she screamed. We knew she didn't mean it but it was still scary.

I would flip my magic switch when I felt the familiar scary, shaky sensation crawl over my body. I would put my thumb in my mouth and go away as fast as I could go. I don't know what I would have done without my thumb. It allowed me to find comfort when there was no other comfort to be found.

After she calmed down, our mother would sob her apologies. Sometimes she would turn into the happy mommy and bring us donuts or treats to show how sorry she was. My friends thought I had the best mommy in the world because she was the happy, friendly mommy when they were around. I loved her so much.

She never physically abused us. When she was the angriest, after screaming mean and bad words at us, she would start banging her head against the wall or slamming the receiver of the phone on her head. Her face was twisted with agony as she wailed words that I couldn't always understand. She pounded her head with her fists as she collapsed in tears on the floor yelling, "One day you will come home from school and find me hanging from the rafters."

I always feared that day would come. The dread of it lived inside me like those worms.

One dark, cold, rainy night before I was in first grade, my mother loaded us into the car. I knew she was very angry because she spoke through her teeth in a low voice, words that I couldn't understand. As she drove, her hands were gripping the steering wheel as if she were wringing a wet wash cloth. Her foot was going up and down on the foot peddle, making us sway forward and backward a little when the car sped up and slowed down in a rocking motion. I huddled in the back seat with my brother and sister, sucking my thumb, as we exchanged fearful looks. Would she get in a car accident and kill us all?

I knew my mother was angry at my dad because I would hear his name through her mumbling words. We were soon parallel parked outside a building. I figured that my dad was in the building because my mother told us to stay in the car while she talked to him. The first thing I saw when she came out of the building was her sobbing, red face. She was running back to the car. She opened the door and fumbled around to start the engine. Once the car started, she put it into reverse and crashed into the car parked behind us. Then she flipped the car into drive and slammed into the car in front of us.

I flipped the switch inside myself and felt nothing.

To compensate for her terrible mood swings, my mother tried to make amends. She would bring home donuts and sweet treats to say she was sorry. My favorite was chocolate donuts. Sometimes she would load my brother, sister and me in the car, then drive us to the mountains to our favorite spot. We called it "The Laughing Place." It was located in Salt Lake City, Utah where we lived, in a canyon called Big Cottonwood Canyon. We drove twenty minutes from our home which was located close to the mouth of the canyon. The mountains rose high on both sides of the car. They were covered with scrub oak trees, cottonwood trees, and bushes of many varieties. Sometimes we stopped to pick chokecherries and mom later made chokecherry syrup and jam. During these special times I felt happy, but unfortunately, the happy times never lasted for long.

Chapter 5

As a baby, Heather seemed to respond to her environment the way she was expected to. When we first brought her home from the hospital, Terry and I weren't sure if she could hear. Her ears were small; half the size of normal ears, and formed like cups, having no flatness around the outer edges. The doctor said that her ear canals were so small that he couldn't see her eardrums. He didn't say that she couldn't hear, he just said that we would have to wait and see as she progressed.

Terry and I would get big pans out of the cupboard and bang them together behind Heather's back where she couldn't see us. When she jumped, we were delighted because we knew she could hear loud noises. But we weren't sure that her hearing was normal.

As she grew we could see that she could hear, but the doctors still couldn't see into her inner ear. Her ear, nose and throat doctor, (ENT), suggested doing a surgery that would open her ear canal. It sounded simple enough. The date was made for the surgery.

After going through all the pre-operation steps, Heather was wheeled into the operating room and I was left to wait. I was told that the surgery would take two hours or so. After three hours had passed, I inquired and was told that Heather's facial nerve didn't run in the same pattern as the average facial nerve so the surgery was going to take longer. The doctor had to test every tissue before he cut anything so that he wouldn't damage the facial nerve. They explained that if the facial nerve were damaged, Heather would be left paralyzed on that side of her face.

I was a nervous wreck. What if the surgery left her more impaired?

After five hours, I was becoming really scared. Unable to stay seated, I paced outside the operating room doors, waiting to hear any news. I was too upset to remain in the waiting area any longer. The clock ticked by the minutes and hours.

After eight long hours, the surgery was over and Heather was moved to recovery. The doctor directed me into his office to discuss what he had done, and what he had discovered.

He told me that he didn't think he hit the facial nerve, but to know for sure we would have to wait and see when Heather woke up. He continued to tell me that when he had opened the canal and was able to see into her inner ear, he discovered that Heather had a tumor in her ear. He said it was quite large and it had to be removed. It wasn't a cancerous tumor, but the type of tumor that forms from accumulated dead skin cells that have sloughed off.

He went on to tell me that the small bones in the inner ear that help conduct hearing—the hammer, anvil and stirrup—weren't working at all in Heather's ear, so he took them out. He held up a bottle that contained the three small bones. I felt a little bit sick to think that he took out bones that were necessary to help conduct hearing. All I could do was trust that doctor and believe that he did the best thing possible for Heather.

I'll never forget seeing those small bones in that bottle. Now, I wish I had asked him if I could have them.

To determine if Heather was developing along a normal path, a public health nurse came to our home and gave her tests once a month. Heather smiled, reached for toys, rolled over and made sounds at the expected times for her age, as if trying to communicate when we were talking to her. Heather was considered to be on or above her age level in almost every area, based on the results of the tests and observations.

However, there was a natural reflex that Heather was missing. It was the reflex of reaching out with her arms to protect herself if she was falling. To test that reflex, the nurse held her by her ankles, upside down and moved her toward the floor. Heather didn't reach toward the floor automatically. She needed help developing that reaction.

The nurse had a large orange ball approximately three feet in diameter. Heather was placed on her abdomen on the ball and a toy was placed on the floor in front of the ball. The ball was rolled forward, with Heather on the ball and someone holding her ankles, as we encouraged her to reach for the toy as her head moved toward the floor. I helped Heather do this exercise daily. When the nurse returned each month she would test Heather's development. And for the most part, Heather reached developmental milestones on time. Her crawling had been impaired because of her short arms and bent wrists, but she adapted by developing her own method of locomotion. She mostly scooted around on her bottom using her legs to pull and push her along the floor. She also developed incredibly strong abdominal muscles and could go from a lying position to a sitting position without the use of her arms with no difficulty when someone held her ankles, similar to traditional abdominal crunches.

Heather developed her own unique methods for doing things with her hands. She held toys pressed between her wrists when she wanted to put them in her mouth. Even though her hands weren't positioned normally at the ends of her forearm, but instead attached under her wrist with palms facing each other, she could grip a rattle in her hands when it was placed in her hand. At the appropriate age she could reach for the rattle, grasp it herself, and shake it to make noise. Later she could pick up colorful plastic shapes and put them in the matching shaped holes in the plastic box and play normally with other toys designed for her age.

As Heather was developing, I noticed that she was very focused on whatever she was doing at the time and didn't get distracted easily. Perhaps she needed to concentrate more than the average child to figure out how she was going to do something because her arms and hands made doing everything challenging. It was difficult to distract her at all. She could be playing with the dishes in the dishwasher, putting blocks of various shapes into the designated holes or putting a dress on a doll, and she was literally lost in concentration. It was hard to know which behaviors to be concerned about, because this was our first child and Heather had not yet started school. Until we had the opportunity to see her alongside other children her age, we did not know what to make of some of her peculiar behaviors. She was an easy child to parent. She always wanted to do what she was expected and told to do. She rarely refused to follow the rules or routines. She was content to entertain herself and rarely came to me to be entertained. She laid down for a nap when I said it was time. She didn't resist what she was told to do. She always found something in her environment to entertain herself. Whether I was working in the yard, cutting someone's hair, or cleaning the house, Heather was close by quietly entertaining herself. Much later she would be diagnosed with high-functioning autism, and only then would we understand these behaviors.

Heather's wrists were surgically straightened out, one at a time, at the age of two. Before the surgery she had a little finger dexterity but afterward she had even less. She still had the opposing force of her thumb so she used her pincer movement for everything. She pressed her thumb to the side of her bent forefinger and did everything with only her pincers.

Going back to work full-time was out of the question for me now that I had a baby with so many complicated physical needs. I would do a few haircuts in my home, but Terry would be the sole breadwinner in a household that would soon be drowning in medical bills.

Caring for any infant is exhausting. There is a constant sequence of feeding, diaper changes, bathing, and holding the baby. In between caring for the infant's needs, the stay-at-home mother usually has to fit in household chores, laundry, and meal preparation. That was true for me as well, except I had a baby who required special feeding techniques that consumed much of the day. I spent hours situated in the brown leather rocking chair where I fed Heather and watched soap operas. The house was never as clean as I wanted and I had no time for myself, but I was keeping our daughter fed.

I was so relieved when I figured out I could thin baby cereal to feed to Heather. I cut a big hole in a regular nipple and used a plastic bottle I could squeeze to feed her the cereal. She wasn't sleeping through the night, and I was always tired. After starting the cereal, she slept better. Each small accomplishment gave me confidence that I could take care of my baby. For months, the single most important goal for my day was making sure that I got enough nutrition into her.

When Terry arrived home from work, I had dinner ready for him. I started eating less, trying to lose weight. I usually just had a portion of meat with a salad and grapefruit. I weighed almost two hundred pounds when I delivered Heather, which was fifty pounds over my usual weight, and I was determined to slim down.

I followed a very low carbohydrate diet. All the eggs and bacon I wanted for breakfast with half a grapefruit. All the salad and no carbohydrate veggies I wanted with oil and vinegar dressing, meat and grapefruit for lunch and dinner. I snacked occasionally on cottage cheese and peanuts, but I never broke the diet for three months. Maybe it gave me something I could control. The rest of my life seemed too overwhelming, but I could control what I ate.

I went to an exercise class in the evenings and Terry tended Heather. He was always good about watching her for me. For the most part, he was a homebody who liked to watch television, drink Pepsi and eat pretzels, so he did not mind tending to the baby.

Sometimes my younger siblings, Shaun and Shelli, came to our house to spend the night. They weren't old enough to babysit on their own yet, but they played with Heather and gave me a break.

Terry was active in sport leagues playing basketball, baseball, and volleyball. I took Heather and went with him to the games where I could talk with the other

wives. These were some of the first outings with Heather, and my first experiences noticing how people reacted to her differences. Our families had accepted
her and treated her with love. In public there were more stares and awkward
moments as people tried to make sense of her deformed arms. I learned to
ignore people's reactions, with the understanding that I too was curious when I
saw someone who looked different. Terry and I never talked about how it felt to
have strangers stare at our baby as if she were freakish or odd. Maybe we should
have.

Sometimes I wanted him to go do something special with me on weekends,
but he rarely wanted to leave his television. He would encourage me to go while
he tended to Heather, but all I wanted to do was be with him. I didn't have much
sense of myself. I was Terry's wife and Heather's mother. They were my whole
world.

After Heather was born, we went to church occasionally, but not regularly
as we had when we were first married. Taking care of her needs preempted
everything else.

My first Mother's Day was not what I expected. We visited his mother and
my mother, but Terry didn't wish me a happy Mother's Day. I was devastated by
his indifference, especially after all we had been through with our baby. I held my
feelings inside until that night, when I asked him why he didn't give me anything
or even acknowledge me. He replied simply that I was not his mother.

I was dumbfounded and hurt. Maybe another woman would have stormed
out or expressed her anger, but not me. I shut down to avoid the full brunt of
my emotions. I had seen my mother lose control and go on tirades. That would
never be me. I simply said, "I am the mother of your child, and she can't get me
anything." And then, I let it go.

After the disappointment of a missed birthday and Mother's Day, I started
planning all my future holidays. I found items I wanted that were on sale and I
bought them. I said, "You don't have to buy me anything for Christmas because
I already found what I want." To this day, I still get presents for myself, choosing
to make my own holidays special without relying on someone else to do it. When
I receive an unexpected surprise, I'm delighted.

It didn't really occur to me to voice my anger or argue my points. My
approach to conflict was to avoid it. Instead I adapted to Terry's behaviors. I
learned to stay home and watch television, including football and basketball
games, not because that was how I wanted to spend my time, but because I
wanted to be with my husband. I conformed to his likes and dislikes, and in the

process, lost a little more of myself as the weeks and months passed by. I took pride in the fact that Terry and I never argued. I didn't see or admit to myself that the lack of arguments was not a sign of a perfect marriage, but a sign of a marriage in trouble. The quietness did not indicate contentment, but was instead, the quiet that precedes a storm.

Chapter 6

I wanted a second child, but naturally Terry and I feared having another baby with problems similar to Heather's.

Before deciding to get pregnant again, we sought the advice of a geneticist. "One in a million. Probably even less risk than that because it has already happened." These were the words the geneticist used when Terry and I went for counseling

"It was a chain mutation," the geneticist continued. "When the cells were dividing, they mutated somewhere in early development, and that began the chain of divisions that caused Heather's condition. It's unlikely to happen again."

I was happy with the information and didn't question it. I had made my decision. I was going to have another baby. If I got pregnant during the next few months, Heather would be more than three years old and out of diapers when the baby was born. Terry was concerned about having another baby and worried that there would be more problems, but he reluctantly agreed.

When I thought about having another child, I felt life would be easier for Heather if we had a boy. I was concerned that if we had a healthy girl, Heather would always make comparisons. She wouldn't be able to do many of the things a person with normal arms and hands could do. If a sister was interested in activities such as cheerleading, Heather's self-esteem could take a beating; she would constantly be reminded of her limitations.

One day I read an article about choosing the sex of your baby. It had interesting suggestions for steps to take to have a boy. The article seemed questionable, but I thought the ideas were worth a try. I followed the rules and prayed for a boy.

When I was praying, I started to question myself. "Who was I to tell God what was best for Heather?" I started asking God to give me the baby that would be best for Heather.

Soon I had strong feelings that I was pregnant and was excited when I got the positive results.

Right on schedule, I got morning sickness again. I took the drug Bendectin because it had helped during my pregnancy with Heather. I was relieved when my nausea subsided after four months, but I continued the medication throughout the pregnancy.

When I was seven months pregnant, I wanted to get an ultrasound to see if the baby was developing normally. I thought that because Heather's arms were bent at a ninety-degree angle at the wrist, the ultrasound would show if the baby had the same problems. I really didn't expect there to be any problems. I had faith and was optimistic by nature. I knew that if there were any problems, I didn't plan on doing anything about them like terminating the pregnancy or giving the baby away. I just wanted to be prepared before the birth.

I could see the picture on the screen. The technicians said the baby looked like a girl. They also said the arms looked normal. I thought I could see a healthy fist in the picture. I smiled at the little hand, convinced that my baby was normal.

My due date was near the end of March. As the date came and went, I was concerned that this would be another ten-month pregnancy like Heather's. After a couple weeks past the due date, the day finally came. Terry and I drove Heather to my mom's house on the way to the hospital. It was April Fools' Day, and I remarked about all the jokes this baby would have to endure because it had been born on April Fools' Day.

"Hey, we ought to play a joke on everyone and tell them the baby is just like Heather," I said.

Terry frowned at the idea. "No, that would be cruel."

When we arrived at my mom's house, I told her about my idea. She just laughed. She agreed that it wouldn't be a good joke to play on people.

When we arrived at the hospital, the nurses settled me in my room. I stared at the pale walls and held Terry's hand. This time everything would be different.

I had an epidural and was relieved that I wouldn't be in so much pain. My doctor came in and broke my water so my labor would progress more quickly. The time came and I was wheeled into the delivery room. The only other people in the room were Terry, the doctor and the nurse. All of us were very quiet. I think you could have heard a pin drop in that delivery room. We were heavy with anticipation. Everyone had the same question: Would this baby be normal? After all, this was the same doctor who had delivered Heather and the memory of her birth was fresh in all our minds.

When he pulled the baby out of my body, I stared first at the reddish patch of hair, and then I saw the baby's arms.

They were small and bent, just like Heather's.

"Son of a bitch!" Terry exclaimed. His voice didn't sound angry, but was more like an expression of disbelief.

"It's a boy," the doctor added.

I was stunned that this had happened, but not overwhelmed as I had been the first time. Heather was three years old by then; we knew more, and she was doing well. We loved her so much that we didn't feel the kind of shock during Logan's birth that we had during her birth. We just had a very strong reaction of disbelief.

"Does he have a cleft palate, too?" I really wanted to nurse. I had sewn a big cape that I was going to wear when I nursed in public. It read, "Out to Lunch."

The doctor told me that he did have a cleft palate, so I was disappointed. The doctor then sent the baby to an area where they could see to his needs.

While I was in the recovery room, the pediatrician who was taking care of Heather came in to see me. He slapped me on the leg and said, "Congratulations, you just made medical history!"

Well, yes, this was technically true, but I wasn't sure how I felt about his comment.

He told me about Logan's condition. Our baby was having a hard time breathing, but holding his own.

"Can I hold him for a few minutes?" I desperately wanted to. He said I could, but only for a minute. As I held Logan, I looked into his beautiful little face and felt so much love for him that my eyes filled with tears. He was my little boy, and I desperately wanted him to live.

Our son was having difficulty breathing, so I gave him to the nurse to take back to the nursery. The doctor said that Logan would have to go into intensive care until his breathing stabilized. I was frightened. Since they were keeping Logan in the same hospital that I was in, I decided to stay the three days allowed by our insurance. I walked down to the nursery regularly to see Logan. He needed oxygen and close monitoring, so I couldn't bring him to my room.

When I wasn't at the nursery, I was in my room resting from the birth. I didn't want my friends to find out about Logan through the grapevine, so I decided to call them myself. I called my friend Pam.

"I had a boy, and he's just like Heather," I said.

There was silence. Then she said, "April Fools'!"

"No really, he has arms and missing fingers just like Heather except he has red hair." I told her I was fine and that I loved him very much. "Everything is going to be all right."

Terry brought Heather to the hospital to see me. We showed her Logan through the window. She waved at him and squealed, delighted to have a little brother.

We were desperate to take Logan home, but he had to stay in the hospital because he kept aspirating on the formula. I pumped my breast milk and took it to the hospital for him during the two weeks that he was in there. It wasn't much, but the doctor said every little bit helped.

Two long and difficult weeks passed, and the day finally came to take Logan home.

I had bought a new rubber baby doll for Heather so she would have a new baby, too. We both walked out of the hospital carrying our new babies. Heather hugged her new baby to her chest. When I fed Logan, Heather fed her baby. When I bathed Logan, Heather bathed her baby.

One night, about five days after bringing Logan home, I was feeding him with the same lamb's nipple that I had used for Heather. Suddenly, he began to make gurgling sounds, and I knew he had aspirated on some of the formula. His little face turned red as he struggled to breathe. I screamed for Terry, who was in the next room. When he saw what had happened, he scooped up Heather and told me to take the baby to the car. We had to get to the hospital or our son would die.

Terry and I were filled with terror as we drove him to Primary Children's Hospital. The whole time we drove, I held Logan and stared at his little face. I knew he was getting very little air, and the sight of him struggling to breathe made me feel afraid and helpless. I glanced over at Terry, whose gaze was fixed on the road. His knuckles on the steering wheel were bone white.

The doctors worked quickly to try to save our son. They put an intravenous line into his head and placed a paper cup over it so it wouldn't get bumped. They ran tests to find out what was wrong.

Logan's doctor was out of town at the time. Our son's needs were so specialized, and his condition so serious, we were distressed to have new doctors on the scene. They didn't know Logan, and it seemed like they were trying all sorts of invasive treatments because they weren't sure which would work. We felt like our child was being used for experiments; it was excruciating to witness.

We had to leave Logan at the hospital that night in order for the medical staff to monitor his breathing. Walking through those hospital doors without my baby was absolute agony. I folded my empty arms and stared across the parking lot.

During the drive home, Heather slept in the back seat. Terry and I were crying. We were tired, frightened, and overwhelmed. Caring for two small children is taxing on any young couple, but we had two special needs children under three years of age. We had little reserve left. The thought of losing our little boy was simply unbearable.

"It just isn't fair. How could God let this happen?" Terry's voice and face were full of pain. It broke my heart to see him this way. Having Logan sick was hard on both of us, but Terry seemed tortured beyond his limits.

After Heather was born, Terry and I used to discuss how much easier it was because she was a girl. We thought it would be harder for a boy to have the same problems because a boy might be more athletic, and with the physical limitations, he wouldn't be able to participate in sports. Males were also considered the stronger sex, expected to protect women and children. Going through life as a physically weak man seemed like it would be a greater challenge. Terry was a gifted athlete, so he identified very strongly with the problems a boy would have, and I agreed with him. Being male and physically impaired would be an ongoing battle, and it seemed unfair.

Maybe thoughts like these were the reason it was so hard for us to see Logan go through all the doctors, needles and other invasions that he had to endure that night. Our faith in God was shaken.

Religion had always been a part of my life. Before our children arrived, Terry and I usually went to church on Sundays. Afterward, we rarely went. It was no longer a priority. We were busy feeding Logan and taking care of Heather.

I believed in the Mormon religion; it was all I knew. I felt guilty that I didn't go to church or read scriptures. I learned that temple marriage was important, so I always felt a sense of unhappiness that I hadn't taken the necessary steps to make that happen.

After Logan's birth, our faith was challenged.

Logan came home a few days later. The doctors determined that he had developed aspiration pneumonia because he kept inhaling his formula. I was so afraid that this would happen again that I decided to start feeding him through a tube that was threaded through his nose, down his throat and into his stomach.

I learned that if he sucked on a pacifier while I was intubating him, he didn't gag while the tube was going down. After it was in place, I taped the end of it to his cheek. I fed him that way for the first six months of his life.

I got used to the procedure. Sometimes I just left the tube in throughout the day so I wouldn't have to intubate him again. When I left him with a baby-sitter,

I showed her how to hook up the syringe of formula to the tube and let it drain down the tube using gravity. When the formula was gone, we just unhooked the syringe and closed the lid to the tube. It became a normal part of every day.

Heather had a tube and syringe for her baby doll, too. She put her doll in her cradle, taped the tube to the dolls face and let her baby tube-feed. She was such a busy little mother and big sister. She loved her new brother.

Chapter 7

I had a husband who loved me, our children were home from the hospital and used to our routines of hospitals and doctors. Even though our finances were tight, we were able to buy a home of our own. It was the house of my dreams, complete with a stone fireplace and a yard where the children could play. Terry had also bought a black motorcycle and a black car, completing dreams of his own.

In the middle of our domestic comforts, medical bills began to accumulate faster than we could pay them. Both Heather and Logan required multiple surgeries. They saw numerous doctors and specialists, and even though we had insurance, we were still responsible for a portion of each bill. We did not have the resources to pay what seemed like an endless string of hospital bills. When Heather was born, we didn't have any insurance and we didn't have much income, therefore, the government paid for most of the medical bills. When Logan was born, we had insurance, and our income was too high to qualify for Medicaid. Before long, we were sinking deeper and deeper into debt. Terry hated owing doctors, so he took out a second mortgage on our home.

Most of my day was spent tube feeding Logan, adjusting the splints on and off his little arms preparing him for surgery and caring for Heather, which left little time for me to work, other than doing a few haircuts in my basement. Considering the seriousness of our children's health, we could not easily leave them with babysitters. With a second mortgage and more medical bills, we soon fell behind on everything.

When Heather was under four years old and Logan was not yet one year old, Terry got laid off at work. This terrified me, because we had so little, and I began to fear that we might lose the house. I had difficulty sleeping. My stomach was a constant knot of worry.

Terry got the idea that if we bought a dry cleaning company and floral company, we could make them successful, and then we would hire someone else to run them while he worked a regular job. So he borrowed money from his dad to buy the businesses. I was nervous about the plan, but couldn't see an alternative. At least he was doing something, which seemed better than sitting around while the bills kept coming in.

Terry took Heather to work with him at the dry cleaners. She was able to ride a Big Wheel so he took it along and she rode it around under the racks of clothes. She always found ways to entertain herself. I worked at the floral shop with Logan in a backpack. I was feeding him between making floral arrangements for customers. I'm not sure how long we tried living this way, but it soon became clear that it wasn't working. Neither the dry cleaners nor the florist were making any money, and we couldn't afford to hire someone to work the dry cleaning business so that Terry could get employment elsewhere. We didn't know what we were going to do.

One alternative looked possible and we decided to take it. Terry's grandparents lived in Springdale, about a five-hour drive from Salt Lake City. Their health wasn't good and they were considering hiring someone to live in and take care of them. Terry saw this as an opportunity for us. He wanted a clean start and saw this as the answer.

I was concerned. I knew that if we moved to Springdale, I would be the one driving the many miles back and forth to Primary Children's Hospital. My religion taught me that the husband was the head of the household and that I should always follow his desires, so I agreed to go. Besides, I didn't have another plan. Without children, I may have been able to go to work full-time myself, but that wasn't feasible anymore. I was reliant upon Terry.

Money had gotten to be such a problem that we could no longer make payments on our car or mortgage. Terry sold his motorcycle and our car got repossessed. When the man from the bank came to our home and drove our car away, my stomach churned. This was not about losing material possessions; this was about survival. We had two young children depending upon us to provide for them, a fact that seemed to magnify each loss.

Sadly the car was only the first of our losses. We knew we would never be able to keep up with the mortgage at this point, and we didn't need the house if we were going to live with Terry's relatives.

We were forced to sell our house. I was inconsolable.

We rented a truck and started loading up our belongings for the move to Springdale. While we were packing, Terry's grandmother telephoned to say that they couldn't wait for us; they had hired somebody else to take care of them. They were aware that they would have had to wait another month before we could have come. Heather was scheduled for surgery and we needed to stay in Salt Lake until after the surgery. They felt they couldn't wait.

I was so scared. I couldn't believe we didn't have anywhere to go. Our house had sold within a week. Now we no longer had a home. "What are we going to do? Where are we going to live?"Terry didn't know.

I couldn't stand how I felt, so I called my dad, who owned two duplexes on the same property. My sister, Kathy, lived in one of them and my dad said we could live in the other one. I couldn't spend time worrying too much about how Terry felt about me asking my father for help. If I hadn't asked him, we would've been homeless. I wasn't willing to sleep in the car with my children or live on the street.

Leaving my beautiful home felt like part of my flesh was being torn away. I had put so much work into the house to make it feel like home. I had wallpapered and painted the walls and spent hours decorating it to make it our own. As devastated as I felt, I had to pull myself out of my despair so I could keep handling my responsibilities. I didn't have the luxury of wallowing in my sorrow even for a day. I kept reminding myself that I had my husband and my children, and that was all that really mattered. There would be another house someday.

Our apartment was spacious, except for the kitchen, which was tiny and didn't have a dishwasher. But it was a home for the time, and I appreciated having a roof over our heads. I didn't want to think where we might be without my father's help.

Terry was unemployed, and because of our debts, he filed bankruptcy. He was withdrawn and quiet, but neither of us seemed to know how to approach each other to talk about what we were feeling. He didn't seem to want to bring up the subject of finances or how much we had lost. He didn't want to add more burdens to my life by unloading more problems on me, and I didn't want to make him feel like more of a failure by reminding him of all the material things we had lost. He felt hopeless about his job prospects. I felt helpless to do anything about our situation.

I was concerned about Terry's emotional state, but I was also worried because he was supposed to be looking for a job. Instead he sat around, making a latch hook rug, while watching television, eating pretzels and drinking Pepsi. What was he thinking?

I felt like he should work any job just to make some money, but he disagreed. He wanted to be able to use his time looking for the "right" job.

We just went on handling life as best we could in our own individual ways. I kept reminding myself that I was a good wife and mother, and I still had my family. I convinced myself that material things were unimportant, and I became more active in my religion. I also started exercising three days a week, which lifted my spirits.

Terry seemed to go through the motions of the day, and while I knew he was sad about our situation, I didn't know how deep his depression ran. He later told me that he was so depressed that he thought about suicide. Terry described waking up every morning and asking himself if that was the day he was going to end it all. His decision was to wait one more day. He would try to accomplish at least one task, even if it was just putting gas in the car. That strategy kept him alive.

We were a young couple trying to care for two small children with disabilities and handle the mounting debt that accumulated as a result of their medical care. We didn't have the experience or skills to talk through these problems. Relationships can withstand only so much strain, particularly when the people involved are young and inexperienced with communication and problem solving.

After what seemed like many weeks of unemployment, we received a phone call from a friend telling Terry about a job possibility. Terry followed the steps required to apply for the job and was happy when he got the news that he was hired. Having made the decision to stay alive and see how it went, he was able to start working again.

Since one of our cars had been repossessed, we had only one car, and Terry drove it to work, so I usually wasn't able to drive during the day. That was very hard for me. Some days I felt trapped at home. When I needed the car for a doctor appointment, I had to wake up early, pack up the kids and drive Terry to work. Then I would pick him up at the end of the day. It was a difficult time, both physically exhausting and emotionally draining.

Terry was working hard and making money, so some of our financial pressure eased up. I found a duplex that I liked which was available for rent. It was located one street east from where we were living. Terry said that he didn't really care where he lived, but if I really wanted to live there, we could move. He seemed despondent and aloof, as if something else weighed on his mind. Sometimes I caught him staring into space, but I hesitated to probe further. Maybe I was afraid of what I would find.

I was excited and busy packing for our move. When we owned the house, I had been giving haircuts in the basement to earn a little extra income; the new duplex had a spacious and well lit area in the basement where I could continue doing that. I never made much money, but I enjoyed interacting with my customers. Being at home with two small children didn't give me much chance for adult conversation, so I looked forward to the arrival of each customer.

After a while, Terry started coming home smelling of cigarette smoke. One night he came home with a pack of cigarettes in his pocket, so I asked him who they belonged to. He said that his boss had left them on the table after dinner so he had picked them up for him. It made sense and I wanted to believe him.

I felt the distance between us. There was too much silence, something that had never existed before. I didn't know how to articulate my fears, so I tried to ignore them. Instead, I poured my energies into Heather and Logan, and into making our house a home.

As a girl, I had often flipped the switch to my emotions as a way to cope with my mother's unpredictable behavior and outbursts. I used the same strategy when my stepfather molested me. As my relationship with my husband deteriorated, I shut down those emotions to avoid facing the painful truth.

Often our genetics doctor would see me at the hospital, and once or twice, we ran into each other at the grocery store. He would always first ask how the children were, and then he would ask how my marriage was. He informed me that, statistically, couples that had children with disabilities usually ended up divorced. His comments raised my hackles, and I resented the implication that he thought that would happen to us.

"We are not one of your statistics, Doctor. Terry and I are doing fine," I said. More than convince the doctor, I said those words to convince myself.

As it turned out, we were a long way from fine.

Chapter 8

Terry's secretary lived close by, so it only made sense for him to catch a ride to and from work with her. This meant that I could have the car during the day. Otherwise, I was stranded at home with two small children. On days that the children had doctor appointments, not having a car meant rising early to drive Terry to work so that I could keep the car.

I was concerned that a relationship might develop between Terry and Sally, but I tried not to worry. If there wasn't trust in our marriage, what kind of marriage did we have?

Once when I was searching for evidence of an affair, I found several check stubs that revealed he had gotten a raise many months before. I was crushed. I couldn't believe he would keep this information from me. My suspicions about him having an affair grew stronger. Eventually, my suspicions were confirmed.

Heather was only about five and a half years old, and Logan was about two and a half when Terry moved out. It must have been more traumatic for Heather than I knew. When she was talking to a school counselor who helped children deal with divorced parents, she drew a picture of me standing and shouting at her father to get out. Today, she still remembers that terrible day.

Six months later in June, 1983 my divorce was final. During my divorce, sadness and depression permeated my days. I lost interest in most things, including food. I would think that I was hungry, and I would make something to eat, but when I started eating, I would lose my appetite and be unable to eat. This went on for weeks.

I began to lose weight. I was already at my desired weight, which was thin for someone of my height. I just couldn't eat. Before long, I had lost sixteen pounds. My clothes were getting too big, and I couldn't afford to buy a new wardrobe.

Around Easter time, I was my thinnest ever. That weekend, I was making baskets filled with candy and goodies for Heather and Logan. Since I loved sugar, and had lost so much weight, I decided it wouldn't hurt to indulge in some candy myself. It made me feel better to treat myself to this small luxury, so I continued to buy and eat sweets. A few candy bars and cookies seemed like benign comfort.

Before long, I started gaining weight. I decided that the weight gain was all right, because after all, I had gotten too thin. Eventually I reached the weight that I had been before my divorce.

My small indulgence seemed to take over. I soon found myself in the habit of eating more than a few sweets. I craved potatoes, pasta, and other comfort foods. I couldn't seem to stop. My weight was higher than I liked.

I had always exercised, so I started walking five miles every day. I was exercising as much as I felt I could, physically, and as much as time would permit, but it wasn't enough to burn the amount of calories that I was consuming. I was worried. I felt out of control. I really didn't want to eat the foods that I was eating, but I couldn't seem to stop myself.

I had heard about Overeaters Anonymous on the radio and hoped I might find some answers there. I looked up the number in the phone book and went to a meeting held at a local library. I couldn't believe the stories that I was hearing. Some people spoke about binging on huge quantities of food and then throwing up. I recall an older woman who talked about her fear of gaining weight from her binging and purging. She spoke of her husband's comments concerning the changes in her body shape as she aged. Another woman spoke of eating a whole bucket of Kentucky Fried Chicken and then sticking her finger down her throat and throwing up. Their stories astounded me. I decided that my overindulgence wasn't so bad.

I went home vowing to lose weight. I managed to stick to a diet of twelve hundred calories a day for a few weeks, losing eight pounds in the process. I had succeeded in my goal, but thoughts of food started to creep into my mind daily. It was as if the more I deprived myself of food, the more I craved it.

I accepted an invitation to go to dinner with a man that I had golfed with a few times. He was considerably older than me, and not someone I wanted a romantic relationship with, but we were friends. I really didn't want to go out to dinner because I didn't want the temptation to eat too much or the wrong kinds of foods. I said yes anyway. I felt like I was out of control, because I said yes when I really wanted to say no. I ate dinner even though I didn't want to, and when I got home I felt terrible. I felt desperate because I had eaten too much. Why was it so hard to say no? Why was it so hard to push the plate away?

Although I had never done this before, I decided to stick my finger down my throat to see if I could make myself throw up. It was a very difficult thing to do.

My eyes were red and swollen by the time I finished, but I succeeded in throwing up. I felt guilty and exhausted, but I also felt that somehow I had regained control. I had not wanted to go out to eat, and by throwing up the food, I had somehow rectified my choice. I felt a sense of relief.

Later, when I was thinking about it, I couldn't believe that I had done what the people at the Overeaters Anonymous meeting had described. A couple of weeks went by and I purged again. For several months, I treated myself to all the food I wanted once every two weeks or so, and afterward, I purged. I felt like I had discovered this tremendous secret. I could eat fattening foods, but not gain weight. It gave me a sense of power. I wanted to eat the comfort foods and not pay the consequences of gaining weight. I didn't realize how the consequences of indulging in an eating disorder behavior had more severe consequences than gaining weight did.

I learned later that an eating disorder is a progressive illness, like alcoholism. A person starts out using their "drug of choice" as an occasional escape from their feelings, and soon they are using it all the time. After a while, it isn't their choice anymore. That time came for me. I felt completely out of control by the time I looked for help. I wasn't "choosing" when I would binge anymore. I felt as if my body had become a robot, walking to the cupboard or fridge, finding the food that I craved and then putting the food in my mouth without even considering whether I wanted to eat the food. After I had eaten the food, even though I didn't consciously want to, I thought, "Oh well, now I have to throw up, so I might as well make it worth it." So I would eat even more because I was only going to throw it up anyway. In a strange way, it seemed logical.

Sometimes I would wake up in the middle of the night, and almost like someone sleepwalking, I would go to the kitchen and make myself some pancakes with tons of maple syrup or Cream of Wheat loaded with brown sugar. I would sit down and eat until my stomach hurt, and even then, I couldn't stop thinking about what else I could eat. The only reason I stopped eating was because I literally couldn't fit any more food into my stomach. Then I would go into the bathroom and purge until I was exhausted. When I awoke in the morning, sometimes I wouldn't be sure if I dreamed of the binge or if it had really happened. When I realized that it did happen, I felt terrible about myself. The more depressed and ashamed I felt, the more I wanted food to comfort me and the release that came from purging.

At my most desperate, I found myself on the ground level of a local hospital, using the pay phone. I was calling the eating disorder clinic that was on the third floor of that hospital. I told them that I was downstairs, and they asked me to come up to the clinic to talk with them. After talking with them for a little while, the counselor wanted to hospitalize me so that I could get some help right away. I told her that I was a single mother of two children with disabilities, and I had to work to help support my children and myself, so there was no way I could be hospitalized.

She told me about a support group that met every Wednesday night at the hospital. The meeting was free. She also helped me find a therapist that I could talk with on a regular basis, one that would accept Medicaid Insurance as payment.

I talked with the psychiatrist every Friday. I also found an Overeaters Anonymous group that met every Sunday afternoon.

It was very hard for me to go to the Overeaters Anonymous meeting for the first time. It was held at an old building in a fairly run-down part of town, about twenty minutes from my home. I felt embarrassed and self conscious about being there. The Alcoholic Anonymous meetings were also held at that location. There were usually a few rough-looking people standing around the building and grounds, so I was a little nervous. How did someone like me end up in a place like this? I really had to humble myself to follow through with my plan to attend the meeting. Once inside, I found people that were welcoming, and they helped me feel more comfortable about being there.

Overeaters Anonymous is a twelve-step program like Alcoholics Anonymous. I learned acceptance through working the program. Whenever I find myself facing a difficult situation, I still say the familiar serenity prayer. (God, grant me the serenity to accept the things I cannot change, the courage to change the things I can and the wisdom to know the difference.)

Counseling also helped me deal with feelings buried in my past that were still affecting me. I talked about my childhood.

We had moved to a new house close to the mountains when I was in second grade. Here my mother met Ron, the man she would soon marry. He was ten years younger than her, skinny with very blond hair, and a red face from acne. Sometimes people would say, "I didn't know you had an older brother," or when they were speaking to my mom, some would ask if he was her son. She rented him a room in our unfinished basement for a while before she married him.

Ron was obsessive compulsive about having a clean house, just like my grandma. He made us do our chores over and over, criticizing everything we did or didn't do. He and my mother also had violent fights. I got that scared, shaky feeling inside my body every time they fought. I would start cleaning everything in sight because I knew having a very clean house would keep them from fighting so much. Sometimes I would do my brother and sister's chores because they refused to do them. I knew there would be a big fight when Ron got home from work if their chores weren't done. Between cleaning, I was sucking my thumb. Being busy and doing something that I thought would help solve the problem—these became my automatic reactions to stressful situations. I was always working to make everything all better. I flipped the magic switch to tune out the violent behaviors acted out by my family. The more I cleaned, the less aware I was of my pain and anger. So I kept cleaning, cleaning, cleaning.

I worked hard on being perfect in every way I could. "If I can be perfect, they won't fight so much," I said to myself. I would be perfect, just like my doll.

"God gave me you because He knew I needed you," my mother said to me.

I felt responsible for my mother's happiness and for her life. I believed I could keep her from committing suicide if I did everything right. I believed that if I didn't do everything my mother wanted me to do, she would kill herself.

My sister and I were both keeping a secret that came out when we were talking together around age ten or twelve. During that conversation, she told me that our stepfather was fondling her. He had been fondling me too. On our own, we may never have told what was happening to us. Having each other for strength and support, we gathered the courage to tell our mother what Ron had been doing to us.

She was upset and went to the bishop, who arranged for counseling for our whole family. Usually my mother and Ron ended up fighting, and I wasn't very cooperative in speaking up about any feelings that I was having. Eventually we quit going, and I just shoved all the unresolved issues into the back of my mind. The fondling stopped, but mild sexual harassment continued through junior high school and high school. I learned to block it out. Sometimes I had to threaten him with telling my mom, and that usually made him back off for a while; eventually he backed off all together.

I had many confusing emotions during this time. My stepfather obviously had a serious problem, and at some level I hated him, but he also did so much for our family. My mother had three children from her previous marriage, and Ron provided a beautiful home for us to live in. He bought a big boat and we went camping and water skiing as a family all through my childhood years, from ten years old through adulthood. We went on family picnics together, ate dinner together every night, and watched television programs together. When I graduated from high school, he gave me a little blue, convertible Fiat. He taught me how to drive a clutch.

Ron may have been a father figure, but he was not my father. My father and mother were divorced when I was around three years old, and ever since then, I experienced a constant longing to see my father. I missed him terribly. I got to see him sometimes, but it seemed like it was never enough. I worshiped him.

I didn't want to think about the sexual abuse by my stepfather, and I knew I was trying to forget that the abuse occurred. In counseling, I was able to tell someone my story and learn how those experiences had damaged my self-esteem.

Chapter 9

Dating was the last thing on my mind after my divorce. I had all I could manage taking care of both children while trying to cut hair in my basement to supplement the child support I received from Terry and the benefits I received as a low income mother with two dependent disabled children. My life had not turned out as I expected. When Terry and I married, I believed it would last forever. Now I was on my own and the notion of happily ever after seemed like a long time ago.

Eventually, I began to date, and after several months into a relationship, I wanted more commitment. The man I was dating was reluctant, even though we had grown close. I was outside walking by myself one night, thinking about my life, when I came to the realization that it was unlikely that a man would make a commitment to me given my situation. The medical bills, constant physical care after surgeries, and fears about the future of two disabled children were huge burdens. I was their mother and had to face the challenges ahead, but no one else had to face these issues with me. I knew in my heart that I could not leave my children. Sometimes I wanted to escape, but I loved Heather and Logan and would never abandon them. Leaving was a choice–it just wasn't one that I would make because I would be unable to live with myself. I was choosing to stay, even though the challenges were hard. I would never have chosen this life, but somehow it had chosen me. I could either face this or walk away, and I was not a woman who could walk away from her children. I was in this for the long haul.

When I arrived home after a walk one evening, I went into the bathroom, got on my knees, leaned on the toilet seat and cried. I felt desperately sad, trapped inside a life that I had never imagined. I couldn't leave my children, but by staying, I didn't think I could have what I really wanted in my life, which was a committed relationship. I wanted marriage. It had been a lifetime goal. I didn't know how to want anything else. I had to learn how to accept the reality of my life as a single mother with no real opportunity for more than that, at least not for many, many years. The future looked dismal, which made it even harder to pull myself out of the grief I felt.

Sometimes fighting a situation takes more energy than the simple act of acceptance. That lesson hasn't always come easily. Resisting the reality of something unwanted has always been automatic for me. But I have found that resisting only causes me unhappiness and pain, where acceptance brings eventual peace. Once I accept a situation, I don't have to try to change it anymore. Most of the time I would be trying to change the impossible anyway. For example, I have no choice but to accept that Heather and Logan's arms are short. That reality makes me sad. I wish they were longer, but wishing for the impossible only makes me unhappy. When I accept the reality that my children's arms are short, and they will always be short, and there is nothing that I can do about it, I can put those thoughts aside. I can let go of them. Sometimes I feel the sadness, but I don't dwell on it because it's useless.

That night, after sobbing in the bathroom while my children slept in their room, I accepted that I would be single until my youngest, Logan, was eighteen years old. The truth was painful, but simple: I needed help from the government to pay their medical bills. As a single, low-income parent, I could qualify for that help.

As much as I wanted to remarry and have a traditional life, I did not believe it was fair to expect any man to cover the expenses that treating the kids' disabilities could incur. If I married, the government would use my husband's income in their calculations to qualify for help, and we wouldn't qualify. The bills would be ours to pay.

The expenses would be more than a middle-class income could handle. My children had both gone through numerous surgeries before they even started school. There would be more surgeries and more hospital stays ahead. The bills for hospitals and specialists would consume any normal salary. I had already gone through this experience with Terry. We had loved each other, but mounting medical bills had placed so much stress on us. The resulting bankruptcy and infidelity had led to divorce. I didn't want to go through all that again. I chose to stay unmarried.

During the years as a single, unmarried mother I had many opportunities to grow personally. I could even say too many opportunities to grow, since I have discovered that sometimes I grow the most when I have difficult challenges. The results were worth the hard work, but there were many challenges that I wouldn't have consciously chosen.

Chapter 10

A friend of mine told me about a transformational seminar that she had recently attended and invited me to attend a meeting about the seminar. We would be invited to participate in a few exercises to experience a taste of the actual seminar should we choose to attend it. The exercises were called processes, and the purpose for them was to gain more knowledge of ourselves. The ideal situation was to be unprepared for the activities we were going to do, because then we would react spontaneously. We wouldn't be able to prepare our reactions like we do in many of our routine encounters.

We showed up at the presentation on a weeknight. I felt insecure being in a new environment and not knowing what to expect. I also thought that the seminar would cost a small fortune, and I knew that I didn't have money. I dreaded being pressured to do the seminar because I simply couldn't afford it. In spite of my concerns and discomfort, I stayed to find out more.

The facilitator introduced himself and gave us some information. He then invited us to choose someone in the room with a different colored name tag than our own. He said not to choose the person that we came with. I chose a man seated to the left of me.

We sat facing each other with our knees about one inch apart. We were asked to tell this person something that we were proud of ourselves for doing. My partner was proud of starting his own landscaping business. I told him that I was proud of myself for being a good mother to Heather and Logan.

The next question was more difficult for me to answer. The time ran out and I had not been able to come up with an answer. The question was: "What do you do in your life that you don't tell anyone about?"

All I could think about was my eating disorder and there was no way I was going to tell this stranger about that. The time ran out and then it was my partner's turn. "I'm a good artist," he said. "I have painted several paintings and I haven't told anyone about them."

Why did my mind immediately go to something about myself that I was ashamed of? I really wanted to find out the answer. I realized that I didn't know myself very well. I wanted to learn the answer to this question and others. I wanted to do the seminar.

The cost of the seminar was three hundred and fifty dollars. There was a guarantee that if I didn't get value out of the seminar then I could get a full refund, but I didn't have that kind of money. The guarantee made me feel more comfortable about committing myself to attend the seminar, so I did. I ended up selling some things and doing some work for a family member to raise enough money.

That might have been the best three hundred and fifty dollars I've ever spent. The experience was transformational for me. I went into the seminar thinking that I was a shy person. After seeing myself over and over, spontaneously participating openly in all the exercises, I no longer thought of myself as shy. Before the seminar, I felt insecure, doubting my abilities in every aspect of my life. During the seminar, I received so many comments about the confidence that people saw in me that I realized that I was much more capable than I thought. I discovered how much value I placed on other people's opinions of me, so much that I gave up doing things that I really wanted to do simply because I wanted to please others.

One of the profound discoveries I made was that I am responsible for myself. No one else is responsible for me. No Prince Charming would come along and take over that responsibility for me. That was a hard realization to discover. It seemed overwhelming, and I wanted to go back to the ease of not knowing. I wanted to believe that someone else was going to come along to take care of me and make me happy, but it was impossible to go back. I had to accept and face it.

As overwhelming and distressing as my newfound knowledge was, it was also empowering. I no longer had to wait for someone else to take responsibility for my life. My life was in my hands. I could create my future through my choices in the same way I created my present. I learned how important it was to be conscious in my everyday life so that I could make choices based on the kind of future I wanted to create for myself and my children. I wanted to teach my children how important their choices are. It was so powerful for me to see that my choices in the past brought into my life everything that I had then and that I have today. It has been the most important thing that I have ever learned.

Early in the seminar the facilitator stood in front of the group of two hundred people and invited us to share. A man in the audience stood and a microphone was brought to him. He talked about a problem that he was having in his life and the facilitator helped guide him through it. The whole time he was talking I was trying to work up the courage to stand up and do the same thing. When the man sat down there was silence in the room. It was obvious that it was an opportunity for someone else to choose to stand. I had paid a lot of money to be here and wanted to get everything I could from the experience. Before I could stop myself, I was on my feet. The microphone was brought over to me and I started talking about Heather and Logan and my divorce. Somewhere in all that I said the words, "My husband left me." The facilitator asked me to say that again. "My husband left me," I said for the second time. Again he said, "Say that again." As I was saying it again, for the third time, the facilitator was running over to me. He picked up my hand, and with his hand on top of mine, he placed my hand over my heart and said, "Say it again." Crying, I said, "He left me, he left me, he left me." I cried harder and harder. I didn't realize how much pain I was living with because my husband, my love and the father of our children, left me. The facilitator helped support me by talking to me until I calmed down. When I was ready, I sat down.

I felt as if I could float. A huge weight had been lifted from my whole being. It felt so strange to go out on break with the people who were in the room when I spoke, because I felt like they knew something very personal about me, and I didn't know them at all. I had many people compliment me on my courage for standing and being willing to share my pain. Some of them told me how much they were helped in their own problems from hearing me work through mine. I went through the rest of that seminar learning more about myself.

One big discovery I made about myself was that I am a very open person. I have always been open with my customers and my friends. I've always been open about discussing Heather and Logan's disabilities. I guess that my openness evoked openness from the people I talked with, so I concluded that everyone was open. In this seminar I learned that there are many closed, very private people who don't discuss personal matters with anyone.

After the seminar I felt very close to some of the people I met, and I felt like hugging them. That was a transformation for me because I didn't hug anyone except my husband and children before that time. This simple act was something I carried with me from the seminar. My older sister, Kathy, nearly fell off her chair with surprise the first time I hugged her as I was leaving her home. I guess I was surprised too, but it felt good to be open and to express the affection I felt.

The same group offered an advanced seminar, but the cost was more than double the original seminar. It would run five full days. I felt so much relief from doing the first seminar, and the second one was so much money, that I decided I wouldn't do it. When I told the facilitator that I wouldn't be continuing, he informed me that someone had anonymously paid for me to do it. I still wasn't going to do it, but after talking to the facilitator, I changed my mind.

One woman surprised me with her openness about how she hated me during the first seminar. I asked her why she hated me. "Because you could speak on the microphone and I couldn't. I wanted to so bad, but I never did," she explained. "I also hated you because you were tall and beautiful. I had always wanted to be tall, but I'm short. Then, I hated you because you were so nice and it made me feel bad about myself for hating you. I realized that I didn't have a good reason to hate you at all. Then I realized it was because of my own shortcomings and self-hate that I turned it on you." We spoke together until we had both gained new insights.

I learned a valuable thing from that conversation: no matter what I do, there will be someone who doesn't like me. It will probably be because of a jealously or a self-criticism that they don't like me and there's nothing that I can do about it. Having come to that realization freed me from trying so hard to please everyone. I learned to do things in life that I really wanted to do, even though someone might not like me. I could enjoy the freedom to be who I am, acting the way I want to, doing what I want to do and not withholding parts of myself out of my fear of rejection.

My new realizations and self-awareness led to specific changes in my life. After Logan was born, I had joined a gym so that I could exercise and lose some weight. Group exercise was just being introduced. Eventually, I worked up enough courage to join them. I made a New Year's resolution that I would exercise no less than four times each week. I stood at the very back of the class because I was more comfortable there. After I'd been going for a few weeks, another girl in class said, "Why do you stay in the back of the room? Why don't you come up front with me?" I joined her and discovered that I worked out harder when I knew people behind me might be watching me.

I liked the girl that taught the class that I attended, but I was jealous because she had the courage to do something that I wanted to do, but was afraid to try. I wanted to teach aerobics. My body wasn't very flexible, and I had weak bladder muscles so high impact aerobics caused me some problems. I always talked myself out of trying to do what I really wanted to do.

After participating in that class for two years, no fewer than four times each week, I decided to attend a workshop on how to teach aerobics. During that workshop I learned how to resuscitate a heart attack victim and got certified in CPR. I also learned some pointers on how to teach. Another year went by and the gym offered the workshop on teaching and CPR training again. I took the workshop a second time. I began to see that I could develop a routine that included moves my body could do while eliminating some of the moves I couldn't do. And there were many good reasons to teach. I could make some extra money and it would be easier to justify taking so much time out of my schedule each week to exercise. Another aspect that I liked about teaching was that I couldn't talk myself out of going to exercise if I wasn't in the mood.

Even though I was scared, I told the aerobics director that I was interested in teaching. She told me that I could audition by getting up in front of one of her classes and teaching for ten minutes or so.

The day came to audition. My stomach fluttered with nerves and I was afraid that I would forget everything I knew, but somehow I managed to get up in front of twenty or thirty people and lead them through the routines that I had been practicing. I was so stimulated that I could barely concentrate, but I managed to do a good job.

The director was impressed. She gave me a class of my own to teach.

I have been teaching aerobics since 1984. I am grateful that I found the courage to try, even though I was afraid of what other people would think and afraid of my own perceived limitations. This important lesson was one I wanted to pass on to Heather and Logan. Even when they were young and didn't fully understand, I tried to impress upon them how important it was to be who they wanted to be and make their own goals in life, no matter what others thought. There is freedom in being true to oneself that can't be found anywhere else.

There was another area of my life that needed work. I wanted to develop my personal boundaries. I learned from the seminar and from Overeaters Anonymous that I was not responsible for someone else's feelings, but I often acted as if I believed just the opposite. I often put the feelings of others before my own. This resulted in feelings of anger towards myself and made me feel like I was a traitor to myself. I believe I was telling myself that I wasn't important, over and over, by making other people's feelings and reactions more important than my own, which hurt my self-esteem over the years.

These discoveries did not come right away, but as I made them, I began to change my behaviors. I still don't like confrontation, but I will confront someone about a situation if it's necessary to be true to myself or to create a change that I want. Setting boundaries meant I had to learn to let people react and feel whatever they were going to feel. I learned that I could not control or stop how anyone else felt. That meant that I had to let people be mad at me sometimes, which was hard for me to do. I like to please people, and it didn't feel good to make a choice that was best for me if someone I cared about was going to be mad at me. It was also hard to see someone feel sad or disappointed because of a decision that I'd made. However, I felt more happiness within myself by taking control of my life and not letting other peoples' feelings manipulate me. I continue to set my boundaries and make choices for myself. The more I do this, the happier I become, and the easier it gets to follow through with my decisions.

I don't know what inspired me to be so interested in personal growth. Perhaps it is just part of my nature or maybe it was somehow the result of having two special needs children and all the experiences that came with them. Regardless of what prompted me to take the journey of self-discovery, one of the best things about it was that I was able to pass on what I learned to my children.

I taught Heather and Logan to make decisions that were best for themselves, and sometimes that has meant that they have to let me be the one that is disappointed, sad or angry. I am proud of them for not letting me control them or manipulate them the way I allowed other people to control me when I was their age. Sometimes they've made wrong choices, and those choices brought them unhappiness in their lives, but that's how we all learn. When Heather became a young adult she read a book by author Byron Katie called, *Loving What Is*. Through applying what she learned she gained acceptance, transforming her perceptions and beliefs that were making her unhappy. By making choices, Heather and Logan get better at finding out what makes them happy, and they make better choices. It's an ongoing process for us all and sometimes brings the unexpected.

Chapter 11

Terry decided to move to Michigan with his girlfriend when the children were eight and five. After our divorce, he had been there to help when Heather or Logan were hospitalized. Now that he was leaving Utah, I would be on my own. I had made peace over our divorce and knew it was for the best, but I had never expected him leave the area and become a stranger to us.

Terry intended to visit, but that didn't happen much. I didn't complain when he didn't show up. At this point, we needed money more than visits. I left it up to him to visit when he could, and when the visits failed to occur, the kids settled for talking with him on the phone. Over time the phone calls came less frequently and the conversations grew shorter. It is difficult to parent and live in another state. Terry had little involvement in our daily lives nor we in his. An awkwardness grew between the children and their father. They became benevolent strangers who exchanged brief and occasional phone calls.

When Terry came to town the awkwardness only intensified. As the children grew older, they felt less comfortable with him. They didn't know him anymore, but were expected to act as if they knew and loved him. Terry and I divorced when they were quite young; his subsequent move to Michigan created a barrier to any relationship that might have developed if he had remained in the area. These dynamics would have been confusing for any kids, but seemed to be even more challenging for Heather and Logan. Finding love and acceptance in the world is difficult for children with physical disabilities, and the loss of a close relationship with their father was a source of pain and disappointment. We would later learn that both Heather and Logan have autism, a condition that undoubtedly made the situation with their father more confusing for them.

I sometimes asked myself if I should have been more demanding of Terry. Maybe I could have insisted that he spend time with our children, but I was more concerned about physical survival. This was my reality: I could not work a full-time job and take care of the physical needs of two children with complex medical needs. We survived on government benefits and the little extra I could make styling hair from home. So we counted on the money and gifts that Terry sent to make our lives just a little easier. I didn't want to rock the boat and cause him to discontinue helping.

Logan's distant relationship with his father was especially difficult, and he started building up resentments as he got older. Watching Logan's pain as he struggled over his relationship with his father was a difficult thing for me, but I have had to learn that I cannot fix everything, nor can I assume responsibility for the relationship or lack of one that exists between my children and their father.

Three years after Terry left for Michigan, I went on a blind date that would change the course of my life.

My sister, Shelli, and her then boyfriend arranged the date. This was six years after my divorce, and I had begun dating, but I wasn't keen on the idea of a blind date. It just seemed so much easier to meet someone and let a connection develop or not. A blind date seemed more high-stakes, so I wasn't all that eager to go in this direction. Eventually, I agreed to meet Lynn for dinner on a Thursday night.

When that Thursday came, I was feeling overwhelmed with my schedule and not excited about meeting someone new. As I discovered later, Lynn was feeling the same way about meeting me.

When Lynn arrived, I was immediately attracted to him. I can still picture him with his blond hair, blue eyes, and wearing a light pink, short-sleeved shirt. Lynn worked in the field of human genetics, so talking about Heather and Logan and their rare disorder seemed natural.

We each continued to date other people for several months, and eventually neither one of us wanted to spend our time with anyone else, so we began dating exclusively. We continued to date for ten years. We may have had one of the longest courtships in history.

Dating was a complicated issue for me. Normally, dating is about finding someone to spend your life with, but I had already decided that I would not be able to remarry until my children were legal adults. Their medical needs came before anything else, and to qualify for Medicaid, I could not remarry and increase our income. I didn't believe I would meet a man who wanted to date indefinitely without any prospect of marriage, so whenever I met someone, I tended to keep him at a distance from my children.

And so, I compartmentalized my life with Heather and Logan and my life with Lynn. I didn't want Heather and Logan getting attached to him should things not work out. I chose Lynn for me. Based on what the doctors told me

I didn't think Heather and Logan would live very long. I didn't want to choose "Mister Dad" and not be in love with him. I honestly didn't believe I could have both. Lynn spent one weekend night doing a family activity with the kids and me and joined us for dinner two additional nights. After dinner Heather and Logan watched their favorite TV programs and played video games while Lynn and I spent time together.

Heather and Logan were my responsibility. I didn't want to impose that responsibility on anyone else. I protected Lynn from the difficulties of raising Heather and Logan because I thought it would scare him away. I didn't request his help with surgeries or much else. I didn't want to depend on him in case it didn't work out. I honestly figured I'd break off our relationship when Logan turned eighteen if Lynn didn't want to marry me, and go find a man who did.

I had also learned about the statistics of second marriages, which weren't encouraging, so Lynn and I chose to date and not consider marriage for a few years. After dating for five years, we decided to take the next step in commitment, which was engagement. We were engaged for five more years before deciding to get married. By that time Heather and Logan were adults. At ages twenty-one and eighteen, they could qualify for Medicaid and other benefits by themselves. My income and marital status didn't matter anymore.

While I was hiking with Lynn in the Wasatch Mountains, I made the decision that I was going to ask him to marry me. Lynn had been the rock in my life, someone stable I could depend upon. I never had anyone I could trust to help me, so I didn't know how to lean on him much in earlier years, but he had been there for me whenever I needed him. Knowing that had meant the world to me. He had been my escape from a difficult life, and now the time had come to take the next step in our life together.

When we arrived at the beautiful and pristine lake, I couldn't wait any longer to ask. "Let's get married," I blurted. "Will you marry me?"

His sunglasses were hanging around his neck and blocking my way to a comfortable hug, so I moved them over his shoulder, to his back. The cord that the glasses hung from wrapped around his neck, choking him. He put his hands to his throat and started gagging, as if I was strangling him into saying yes before I would let him free. Between gags he was saying, "Yes, yes, I'll marry you." We were both laughing.

"Really?"

"Yes, I was thinking that we could get married in St. John when we go there in November."

I was so happy. I had wanted this for so long, and for so many years, I thought it would never happen.

That November, we were married on a beautiful beach on St. John, during a magical sunset. The sky radiated a deep rose and pale lavender, the colors of fairy tales and dreams. It was one of the happiest days of my life. After the ceremony, when we were alone on the beach, I looked at Lynn with tears in my eyes and said, "I can't believe you married me." I had been waiting for that moment for so long, and I was blissfully happy.

Lynn had been living in the mountains about forty-five minutes from the city where I lived. We continued to live in our separate homes for the first year of marriage because I wasn't ready to move to the mountains and Heather wasn't ready to move into her own apartment. That arrangement seemed natural to us because we had already been living that way for ten years. Logan moved into his own apartment when he turned eighteen and Heather lived with me. I began to feel like I wanted to live with Lynn, and felt it was time for Heather to get an apartment of her own and learn to live independently.

After finding a home along the bench of the city that Lynn and I were both excited about and putting earnest money down to hold it, the decision was made. We were excited. Then came the challenge of selling both the homes. Lynn's home in Summit Park wasn't going to be easy to sell. One feature of that home was fifty-three stairs that had to be climbed to get to the front door. My home in Holladay wouldn't be easy to sell either because it was the smallest house on a lane of big homes, and it was an older remodeled home.

To our complete surprise, both the homes were sold in two weeks. We couldn't believe our good luck.

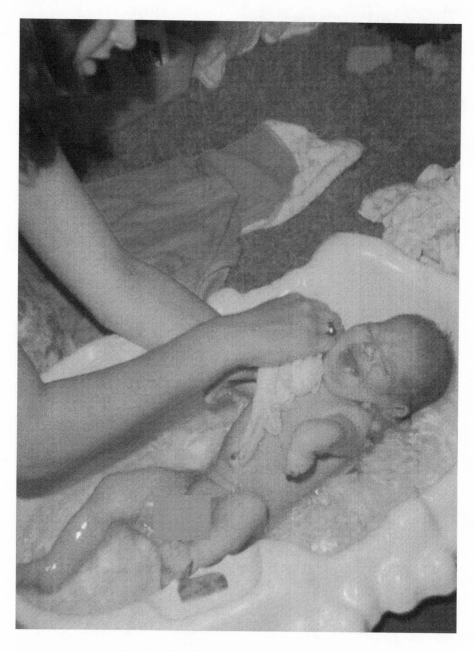

Heather, 2 weeks old, having her first bath at home.

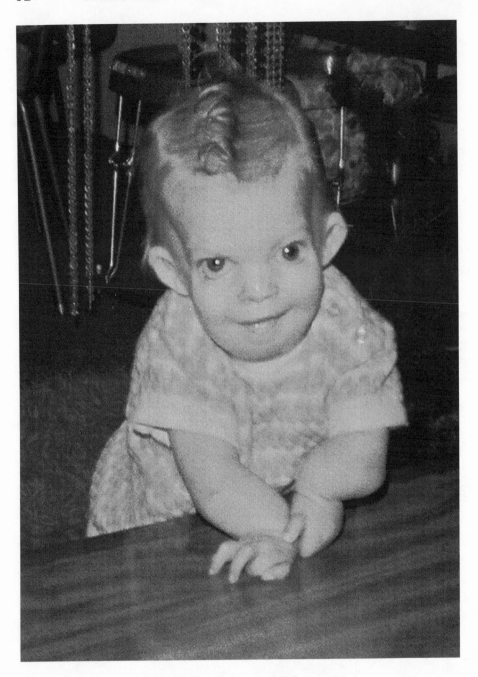

Heather, 9 months old.

Heather, 3 1/2 years old, with her brother Logan, 6 months old.

Heather, 6 years old, with her brother Logan, 3 years old.

Heather, 11 years old, with her brother Logan, 8 years old.

Heather, 13 years old, with her brother Logan, 10 years old.

Logan (left), 14 years old, with mother, Debbie (center),
and sister Heather (right), 17 years old.

Logan, 30 years old, painting self portrait titled "Stuck".
Photo by Logan Madsen

Debbie (mother), with Heather, 33 years old, and Logan, 30 years old.
Photo by Melissa Papaj Photography

Chapter 12

At birth, Heather and Logan's wrists bent ninety degrees, with their hands attached under their wrists, palms facing each other. If they extended their arms straight out in front of their chests and were able to put their palms together in a prayer position, their hands would point to the floor instead of forward.

Surgeries that were done in childhood resulted in Heather and Logan having straight, fused wrists so their hands are at the end of their arms where they are supposed to be. As adults, their forearms are one half to one-third the length of normal forearms. Logan's forearms are a little longer than Heather's. They have no wrist rotation in any direction, a result from having their wrists fused to their arm bones. From Heather's elbow to the tip of her bent knuckle fits in the open palm of my hand. Her complete forearm and full hand are only as long as my hand from wrist to extended fingertip. Logan's are only slightly longer.

Logan's efforts to engage in a high level of activity caused his right wrist to bend towards its original pre-surgery position, resulting in pain. Correction required three surgeries; in childhood, late teens, and mid twenties. During the most recent surgery, the doctor replaced a smaller, broken plate with a larger plate.

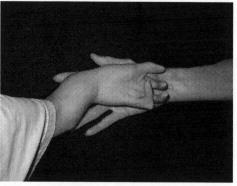

Heather, 33 yrs old, placing her forearm in her mother's palm. 2010

Heather and Logan were born without a pinky finger and their other fingers are permanently bent ninety degrees at the second knuckle, with little to no dexterity. Logan has a little more dexterity than Heather. He has enough dexterity to slightly straighten and spread his fingers enough to touch the top pads of all his fingers and thumbs together, but this position causes pain in his joints. Heather can't do this at all. Because Logan can spread his fingers a little more than Heather, he partially opens his hand and he has a slightly stronger grip. They use pincer movement—pressing their thumb against the side of their index finger—to do all tasks. When a person with normal hands and fingers uses a pincer movement—often referred to as pinchers—they still have an advantage over Heather and Logan because they have long forearms, wrist rotation, full range of elbow bend, and dexterity in the fingers and joints, allowing them to press the pads of their fingers and thumbs together with strong opposing force.

Heather and Logan aren't able to rotate their fingers enough to get any pads together. Logan said he longs to feel his palms together, as in a prayer position. Heather's palms are as soft as a baby's from lack of use.

When Heather is holding a piece of paper with her pincer grip, I can easily pull the paper from her weak grip. I asked Logan to pinch the flesh on my forearm as hard as he could; I couldn't feel the pinch. It felt like he was holding my skin, not pinching it.

Heather can't spread her bent fingers apart much or unbend them, even manually. They are formed in a ninety degree angle. She can manually straighten out her thumbs for demonstration but is unable to bend and straighten them independently. Heather's third fingers, or her "pinky" fingers, are completely useless except when she holds a tall drinking glass in the palm of her right hand; this finger helps grip the bottom of the glass, making it possible for her to drink using one hand. When doing all other tasks this finger just gets in the way because it is so bent and she can't move it.

Although Heather can't open and close her hand or spread her fingers much at all, her left hand can do both movements better than her right hand, because her wrist is still a little bent. Fusing Heather and Logan's wrist bone to their arm bone to straighten their forearms resulted in loss of rotation and less dexterity in the hand and fingers. However, if their wrists remained bent at ninety degrees, we believe the awkward position of their hands would have limited them in other ways.

Because of having short forearms with no wrist rotation, Heather and Logan must raise their arms from their shoulders, straining their shoulders and upper back constantly, and this forces them to exert significant time and energy to do literally everything. The best way for me to imagine what it would be like to have Heather and Logan's arms is to pretend my hand is attached to my elbow.

I wouldn't have normal elbow movement, I would have only my thumb and a bent forefinger; which would have no dexterity or strength, to perform all of life's activities.

Performing daily tasks resulted in Heather and Logan being ambidextrous; using a different hand for each task because of the differing angles of their wrists. Due to the lack of mobility in their wrists and minimum to no finger dexterity, they lack the strength needed to do most tasks without discomfort.

Heather's left elbow only bends ninety degrees and her forearm is too short to reach her mouth, neck or shoulders with her left hand, so she must use her right hand to reach those places. Logan's forearms are a little longer and his elbows both have full range of motion, so he can reach his neck, mouth, head and shoulders.

Most people can raise their arms and extend both their hands high in the air. Heather's arms and hands barely reach to touch the top of her head with one bent fingertip, but she is unable to apply any pressure on the top of her head because there is not enough length in her arm or mobility in her shoulders, elbow and wrist, and none of her fingers extend. Logan can touch all areas of his head, neck, face and ears, but not without discomfort from twisting his joints unnaturally.

Heather can raise her right arm only to shoulder level when lifted to the side. She can raise her left arm out to the side a little higher. She can't arc her arms out to the side and then overhead. She must raise them forward and then up to reach upward. Because of the shortness of her forearms and inability to extend her fingers, her full reach ends slightly above her head. Heather raised her left arm when she asked questions during school because it is little longer than her right arm, her shoulder rotates upward more, and her palm turns toward the front more—but still ends only slightly above her head. When raising her right arm overhead, she isn't able to rotate her hand to face her palm forward to wave to someone. Her palm and bent fingers face her forehead. Heather's only ability to achieve rotation of her hand comes from her shoulder. This puts a lot of stress on her shoulder when she does all daily living tasks.

When Heather holds a pencil to write, she places the pencil between her thumb and forefinger, but instead of putting the pad of her forefinger on the pencil, her finger bends in front of the pencil, which makes the pencil rest on the bony point of the second finger's bent knuckle for leverage. The side of her thumb presses against the side of her first bent knuckle to apply enough opposing pressure to hold the pencil between the first finger and against the side of the second finger knuckle bone. The lead tip of the pencil must extend out from between the knuckles, far enough to reach the paper before her knuckles do, because lack of wrist rotation causes the back of her hand to rub the paper when she's writing. Because her hands and fingers lack fine dexterity, she must slightly squeeze and release her palm and move her arm from her shoulder to move the pencil to write. This fatigues her forearm muscles. Her knuckle guides the pencil as she squeezes and releases the grip of her palm, much like the pincer movement guides the pencil for most people when they write. She must move her shoulder to move her hand, to form the loops of the letters and words. This fatigues her shoulder.

Heather, 33 yrs old, writing. 2010

Heather's thumb faces the direction of a finger more than sideways like a normal thumb position. Her thumb has twisted from using it as an opposing force, much like the thumb of someone with arthritis. Heather is ambidextrous because she has to do things with the hand that performs a particular action the best. She could write with either hand except her left arm has grown more bent through the years and won't rest as well on a table for support when writing. She doesn't feel motivated to have another surgery to straighten the arm again at this point.

When Logan writes with his right hand he must angle the paper to the left at a forty-five degree angle in order to write, and he must have his writing plane level. He isn't able to use a small pad of paper because his arm and wrist would be unable to rest on the same plane due to the thickness of the pad; this is similar to a person with a normal arm and hand writing without resting their hand on the paper.

Logan holds a pencil with his pincer grip as most people do, except he uses the sides of the pads of his finger and thumb. He is able to bend and release his fingers a small amount; using pincer movement, without moving his shoulder like Heather does, however he feels arthritic type pain in his fingers and knuckles when writing because of the awkward twisting of the joints. Logan avoids writing lengthy notes.

Being ambidextrous is helpful when it comes to using scissors. When Heather uses big scissors with her right hand, she puts her first and second fingers through the big hole and her thumb through the small hole, much like normal hands. However, she lacks the dexterity to open and close her hand enough to get the blades apart. She has to reach over with her left hand to open the scissors and then grip with the right hand to close the scissors, open again with her left and close with the right. Even when using this method, she can only open the blades enough to expose about one inch of blades to use for cutting.

When using big scissors with her left hand she is able to open and close the scissors using the same hand, but the blades don't open enough to cut anything. Luckily, she is able to open the blades more with her left hand if she uses smaller scissors—children's scissors—but they aren't as sharp as adult size scissors.

Logan can use scissors like most people except he can only open his grip enough to expose one-third of the cutting blade. He said the act of cutting paper along a straight line can be a stress relieving activity for him.

When Logan opens a large jar the size of a peanut butter jar, he must place it under his left armpit and squeeze it to his chest to hold it high and tight. He has adequate strength and is able to spread his bent fingers just enough to open the jar. Heather can't open a big jar.

Using the computer has given Heather and Logan the opportunities to find support, make friends and learn interesting information that makes their lives richer. The mechanics of their arms and hands has made using a mouse and keyboard very difficult for them.

Logan uses a keyboard and mouse for typing and a computer tablet and pen to do graphic art. His computer sits on an electric table that raises and lowers, allowing him a custom height. Using his creative talents, he found methods to alleviate some of his discomfort. To avoid pressure on his elbow bone, he folds a soft piece of fleece into fours and places it on the table, under his elbow. He uses an average size and shaped mouse but must rotate it to the left; placing it at a forty-five degree angle, lined up with his arm and wrist. Even in this position he feels constant discomfort in all his joints and upper back because of the amount of twisting needed to replace his missing wrist rotation. He imagines the perfect mouse would be one that magnetically sticks to a board, to keep it from falling off when attached to the side of his chair in a vertical position. He could just hang his arm down, and his wrist would be in a comfortable position when placed on the mouse.

When Logan types on the keyboard, he uses the tip of his second fingers—his middle fingers on both hands—and must look at the keys when typing. He uses his left thumb for the space bar. The only shortcut key he can use is control-v, which is paste. To do this he places the front of the nail on his far left finger on control, and his left index fingertip on the v. Logan must raise his arms and hold them in the air, straining his shoulders and upper back, to type. He experiences discomfort every moment.

Because Heather's right arm doesn't rotate enough to face her palm downward, she can't put her palm on the mouse with the right hand. She uses her left hand which rotates enough to place on a larger, well arched mouse with a smooth finish. She can feel the torque in her shoulder, elbow and hand when she is using the mouse, but is able to withstand the discomfort long enough to gain rewards from using the computer.

Typing on the keyboard is challenging. Her hands look much like when she is holding a pencil. The knuckles of her hands are facing the keyboard, with her thumbs hitting the keyboard before her knuckles. She uses her thumbs on the upper row keys and some of the other keys, and her knuckles for home row keys and lower keys. Her third knuckle is used to hit the space bar. She types sixty words a minute, but not without discomfort.

Heather, 33 yrs old, typing on a keyboard. Photo is by her brother Logan. 2010

Heather and Logan don't have the necessary tendons in their knees to hold their knee caps in place. This results in their kneecaps sliding easily out of a normal position, too far to the right or left, causing tears in their meniscus or other knee damage. Logan tore his meniscus when he was eighteen years old while rollerblading. The surgeon informed us that repairing the tear would be useless without a more extensive surgery. This would consist of wrapping a hamstring tendon around the kneecap to keep it in place and avoid tearing the meniscus again. This surgery had not been successfully performed enough at the time we were inquiring about possible surgery, so we lacked confidence to move forward. Heather has been less active through her life and luckily hasn't torn her meniscus.

Logan must be extra careful when doing everything to avoid having his knee pop out of place unexpectedly and to avoid worsening the existing tear or tearing the other meniscus. Sometimes his right knee locks up or hyper-extends causing him immediate pain and fear.

Balance when walking isn't as good with short arms so Heather swings her arms a lot to help. Logan doesn't like the way their short arms look swinging so he refrains, making walking less comfortable. Having to walk carefully and unnaturally creates discomfort for Logan, both physically and emotionally.

Heather and Logan also have abnormalities in their ankles. An ankle tendon that generally attaches behind the ankle bone in normal anatomy attaches in front of the ankle bone in their ankles. Also, their ankles pronate, or turn inward, as if walking on the ankle bone. When they were children, a doctor placed screws in the growth plates of their lower leg bones during surgery to help their leg bones grow more equally, preventing further pronation of their ankles. The results were good but not perfect, so both still have severe pronation in their ankles. Without proper support from orthotics and good shoes they experience pain under the outer ankle bone, knees and hips.

The muscular skeletal malformations caused by Miller syndrome have literally made every daily living task a challenge for Heather and Logan.

Chapter 13

"*In the research lab at the University of Utah where I work volunteer hours, I am meeting new people and experiencing more of my personality and other peoples' personalities. I am also experiencing more people around my age who are interested in academic subjects as a career. This is giving me a lot of social experience and awareness: meeting people, hearing and understanding what they want, seeing if my perspective matches theirs, understanding what I can and can't do around there, and what respective comfort zones are. I am experiencing new situations: meeting people, doing things I haven't done before (using the VCR and video, coding, asking questions), and doing them around people who have never seen me. Because of my shortened forearms and bent fingers with no dexterity, I perform these tasks differently than other people. For instance, I had to have a remote for the VCR and TV switch on the desk so my short arms would not put my face next to the TV screen. I also had my folders put into a higher drawer, so I wouldn't have to bend over so low to reach them because I'm five feet eleven inches tall and having short arms causes me to have to bend my back more often than most people. I have to ask people to repeat themselves more often since I have a hearing impairment, too. After a couple of weeks in the lab, I am now becoming more comfortable doing what I need to do and am able to do all these things with ease and enjoyment.*

At first, I was very scared to do all these things, and doubtful that I would be able to learn how to cope or do things differently than others and still be comfortable about it. One thought that stayed in my mind is that I need to at least try before I make a judgment about the situation. This approach keeps me going, whenever I feel uncertain about my abilities or how to handle a situation. As I let go of any expectations and judgments other people might have, I become more comfortable trying something new. And each time I succeed—both at the task and at feeling comfortable— my confidence grows. My experiences in the research lab has given me more confidence in myself and in others. Growing in this way is exciting.

Along with the experiences from the lab, I am also learning how to tutor adult readers. I really enjoyed the workshop and learned how to be more social with people. I also learned how people can bond so easily and form an understanding about the group as a whole. We all were able to support each other through the workshop, and the experience was more fun than I expected.

There was an activity I needed to do for the workshop, which was similar to what I will be doing for the student. I found the activity discouraging and frustrating, but then I remembered how frustrated the reader will be, and how my being different will show them the courage I have had in facing my own challenges. They will see that I understand how learning to read as an adult is a challenge for them. When I look at it this way, I feel encouraged to keep trying because I know they need me. And in truth, I need them too.

I am more aware of my differences and how they impact the experiences of other people. I am more aware of how my differences teach others about diversity and how my presence in their lives shows them that it is possible to face challenges and still enjoy a happy life. The new feelings and experiences also remind me how I can face challenges, learn how to conquer my fears and doubts, and live in and savor the moment. I am learning to slow down in each moment, love myself as I am, accept and love my differences, and be comfortable with myself."

—Heather Madsen

Heather and Logan are now in their thirties living on their own. The journey towards independence has been long and difficult, but it pleases me to see them discovering who they are and what they want in this world. They have learned that although they are in bodies that have disabilities and look different, they are capable, intelligent people with the power to create a life that reflects their talents and capabilities. This ability to pursue what makes them happy proves to me that on a very basic level that they feel good about themselves. A person must first believe they deserve happiness before they take the steps to create the life they want for themselves. The fact that my children believe in their self-worth is proof to me that I did a few things right.

My awareness of the importance of self-esteem seemed to come naturally. Perhaps that awareness came because of some of my childhood experiences. I sucked my thumb, which gave me an overbite; sometimes kids would tease me about my buck teeth, which only made me self-conscious and ashamed. I was the tallest person in every grade until the tenth grade. The other kids called me "daddy long legs" and poked fun at me for being so tall. I felt embarrassed and just wanted to be normal like the other children. What I wouldn't have given to be an average height and have a mouth full of straight teeth. Later my father paid for braces to correct my overbite, but I was thirty years old before I accepted my height and saw the beauty in being tall.

As a child and teenager, I tried to do everything perfectly. My experiences with my mother's mental illness left me believing that if I was good enough, she would be safe. I transferred some of those beliefs into other situations. The need to be perfect was all tied up with a need for control in situations where I was powerless, such as molestation by my stepfather and my mother's unpredictable behavior. Perfection is an impossible goal. Because I was easily distracted when doing chores; dusting knickknacks or washing dishes, sometimes I accidentally broke things. I felt bad about myself when I felt disapproval from my parents for my clumsiness. When I did my chores, my step father often found fault, and I was told to do them over. This made me think I couldn't do anything right. I was very hard on myself and found little to feel good about. There wasn't much praise in my childhood, and without it, I didn't know how to praise myself.

Remembering these events and how I felt made me determined to do all I could to protect the self-esteem of both my children. No matter what it took, I was going to make sure that my son and daughter knew their worth. I knew that people would react differently to Heather and Logan because of their physical disabilities—it was inevitable that there would be stares, thoughtless comments and even teasing. I couldn't change the way people responded any more than I could change my children's strange appearance. So I focused on building their self-confidence as a tool to handle the reactions from other people. How my children saw themselves mattered to me more than anything. Even though finances were tight, worry about money paled in comparison to how much I worried about Heather and Logan's self-esteem. Sometimes fatigue and impatience got in the way, but I continually worked at the self-discipline and awareness required to accomplish that goal.

When I hear parents tell their kids they're lazy, stupid or slow, it always makes me cringe. I strived to keep from saying those kinds of things to my children. I made mistakes, but I did a better job than if I hadn't noticed those actions by other parents. I believed that Heather and Logan deserved apologies and explanations when I was in the wrong. I did my best to treat them with respect as individual human beings living with me, not as people who were mine to consciously or unconsciously control or mold into whatever I wanted.

I thought it was important not to label my children as handicapped. I tried to treat them like I would have if they had no disabilities.

As Heather and Logan got older, I saw the high expectations they set. Heather was intelligent, stubborn, and always questioning and arguing, but also did as I asked. Analytical and organized, her room was always clean; she did homework diligently. She liked all classes, but especially English, math and science. She did well in school, making top grades in high school. A challenge I had with Heather was that she often questioned what I wanted her to do and asked questions about how to do things that she should have known how to do, or social things she should have known, but didn't because she was autistic, but we didn't know that then. I had to learn to accept gaps in her understanding even though they didn't make sense until years later when she was diagnosed with autism.

Logan pushed himself, too. He saw himself as normal so he expected himself to do everything the same way other people did things. When he went golfing with me, he insisted on teeing off from the men's tee-box. It was a greater distance to the green than from the women's red markers. Because his forearms are shorter, his hands small, and he has no wrist movement, I suggested that he tee off from the red markers with me, which would give him a better chance of getting a lower score. He really disliked it when I pointed out his limitations. His friends and my brother told me that Logan wanted me to stop reminding him of his differences and limitations.

I felt like I was just accepting reality, but I have learned that everyone is different in how they handle reality. I thought it would make life easier if Heather and Logan accepted certain "facts" about their physical abilities and were realistic about goals and expectations. I learned from my own experiences that facing problems head on brings productive results and is better than living in denial and accomplishing nothing. I tried to teach them that having disabilities doesn't make them less important as people. They have disabilities, but they are not their disabilities.

This perception has gotten me into trouble with Logan over the years. I displayed my acceptance of his disabilities by talking about them when we were in a situation where they were obvious. I watched Logan do things the way he knew other people did them, which made the activity more difficult for him, as in golf.

Logan is a great golfer. He can beat me, even though I have more years of experience and I don't have physical limitations. However, he doesn't have the range of motion or strength that most men have, so he doesn't get as much distance on the ball. I accept this as a natural limitation, because of the short length of his arms and his inability to rotate his wrist. I don't judge this as negative or a bad, I just accept it as a fact. It's the same way I accept the fact that I have a compulsion to overeat foods that taste really good to me. Because I accept that fact, I can change my behaviors and make other choices that will bring the outcome that I want to create in my life.

Because Logan keeps trying to swing a club and do other physical movements as much like normal people as possible, he has acute chronic pain.

I didn't understand that Logan resented me for reminding him about his limitations, even though I was being realistic and trying to prevent him from injuries and discouragement. He hated it when I suggested that he tee off at the red tees. However, he didn't communicate those emotions to me at first, and we didn't know he had autism yet. He talked to my brother, Shaun, who then told me about it and suggested that I stop reminding Logan about his limitations.

I had no idea that it bothered Logan so much. I knew that ever since Logan was old enough–around the age of four–to notice that his arms were short and his hands were small and missing fingers, and that his ears looked different from other people, he didn't like it. Logan would wear long sleeves everywhere and during every season, even in the summer. He was embarrassed to show his arms. It was impossible to hide his hands without making himself look obvious, but he could camouflage his short arms by wearing the long sleeves. Later, when he became a teenager, he didn't like his skinny legs. His calves don't have very big muscles. Logan hid his legs by wearing long pants. He was desperate to pretend that he was normal. I didn't realize how strong denial had been for Logan until his mid twenties. I also didn't understand that when I talked about his differences, denial was more difficult for Logan to maintain. He wasn't yet ready to accept his reality.

Later, when Heather and Logan were in their thirties, I asked them if they would show me how they do a few of the basic tasks required for living independently; dressing, eating, vacuuming, grocery shopping, and a few others. I watched Heather and Logan with fresh eyes. For the first time I realized I was clueless about how they do things and how much discomfort they endure while doing them. Seeing what they have to do to complete a task feels very different from just thinking about how difficult things are for them.

I am humbled when I think about all the suggestions I've given them over the years before taking the time to closely watch how they do things or ask how their bodies feel while they're doing them. Words are inadequate when I describe how impressed I am by how much Heather and Logan do every day of their lives!

Sometimes when I'm alone, I think of all their difficulties and cry till there are no more tears. The pain feels unbearable, as if my heart really could break. Afterwards, I feel a huge relief from letting the emotions out and admitting how much pain I carry inside. Sometimes I'm exhausted from crying and sometimes I'm empowered with energy and determination to find more ways to help them make their lives better. I feel joy when I acknowledge how far we've come, the lessons we are learning and the accomplishments we are enjoying because of and in spite of our challenges.

My sister, Shelli, called me from her home in California a few years ago to ask if I liked being a mom. I didn't hesitate when I said, "Immensely!" I meant it then, I mean it now. I love being Heather and Logan's mom. I am the best mom, friend and assistant to my children when I focus on the positive, take actions to create a fulfilling life for myself, exercise regularly, eat healthy and maintain good physical and emotional health. I am committed to creating more happiness in all our lives.

To understand Heather and Logan as completely as possible and to "feel" my empathy and compassion, I use courage to "see" them and the reality of their difficulties. I do not look away to avoid my sadness and my pain. I focus on taking actions to show them I love them by maintaining consistent regular contact, offering them my help in every capacity, and listening to them with an understanding and empathetic heart. I give them encouragement.

I've known that Heather and Logan are intelligent all their lives. I didn't realize that when I suggested "my" possible solutions to "their" problems, I wasn't showing them that I believe they are intelligent enough to come up with their own answers. This resulted in them having less trust in themselves. I lacked insight to this situation because I was subconsciously trying to avoid the sadness I feel when I hear them describe their frustrations. I would hurry and make suggestion after suggestion, hoping to help fix their problems so I wouldn't have to feel my sadness. Now I know that I help them the most when I listen with empathy and love, so they feel understood and validated. This encourages conversations that can lead to their own insights on how to solve their problems, resulting in stronger self confidence and higher self esteem.

Logan is visually oriented where Heather is more language oriented. From a very young age Logan closely studied how people with normal hands and arms did things so he could duplicate their method and look more normal. He practiced doing this with each hand to find the one that works best and has continued doing this all his life. When he drinks a can of soda he crushes the middle of the can, making the can narrower so he can hold it in one hand. The only time Logan picks up a glass like Heather, using the pincer movement on the lip of the glass, is when he stirs chocolate mix into his milk in a tall drinking glass.

Seeing closely how Heather and Logan do things, I fully appreciate their efforts more than ever before.

The first thing Logan showed me was how he takes a pill. Logan's forearms are a little longer and straighter than Heather's so he can reach his mouth with his right hand when holding a plastic drinking glass normally. Logan can hold an average size drinking glass in his hand like most people do as long as the glass is dry. If the glass is wet he holds it like Heather does, balancing in the palm of the hand with bent fingers gripping the base.

The process for taking one pill is complicated. When he takes one small pill that isn't a capsule, he uses his right hand to hold a plastic drinking glass from which he takes a drink filling his mouth with one gulp of water. He holds the pill in his left hand using his pincer movement which is similar to a normal pincer movement except the pill isn't quite on the pads of the finger and thumb. The pill is between the side pad of the thumb and the side pad of the finger by the first joint. His lack of wrist rotation makes it impossible to place the pill in his mouth. He tilts his head back as far as he can, then lifts his arm from his shoulder till his elbow is pointed to the ceiling as high as he can and quickly throws the pill at his open mouth. He is a good shot, so he usually is able to get it to his mouth without dropping the pill. He swallows the pill using the water he held in his mouth as he lowers his head and quickly swallows another gulp of water to be sure the pill is washed down.

He has to get creative when the pill is a capsule. His fingers must be dry and he must have the capsule making as much contact with his skin as possible while he keeps the capsule rolling in his pincer grip, or it will stick to his fingers when he attempts to throw it into his mouth. If that happens, it either stays stuck to his finger or falls on the floor. Bending over to pick up the dropped pill causes additional pain for Logan so he must think carefully about every move he makes to avoid unnecessary movements or awkward movements that can pull muscles and cause himself more pain. Sometimes a pulled muscle can cause him more pain for a week.

When a person extends normal arms straight out in front of their chest their palms can face different directions when they rotate their wrists. Even when Heather and Logan use their shoulders they can't rotate their hand so the palms will face each other so they can pick up a small cup or glass.

When Logan takes more than one pill he uses a small measuring cup that is included with his other medicines. If he places pills in his palm, he isn't able to close his fingers enough to keep them in his hand, so when he lifts his hand to his mouth, his palm tilts and spills the pills onto the floor. He puts all the pills in one cup to act as the palm of a hand. Picking up the small cup is challenging because of his lack of wrist rotation. Logan has an electric table in his kitchen which he has raised to a height two feet taller than the average table height or counter. Even at this height, the angle of his hand when it approaches the small cup isn't quite right to get a good grip. Instead of his hand coming directly in front of the cup at the angle that must be used to pick it up, and to keep it upright, his hand comes down towards the cup, causing him to pick it up like a normal hand would pick up a cup with thumb and finger tips around the rim with the palm facing the contents of the cup. Once in his hand, he must adjust the angle of the cup to be upright with the angle of his grip, so the pills don't spill on the way to his mouth. Then he uses the same method as one pill, except he dumps the cup of pills into his mouth instead of throwing them at his mouth.

When Logan places the small cup on top of his refrigerator, which is five feet ten inches tall, the angle of his left wrist and hand can pick up the cup at the correct angle without adjusting the cup once it's in his hand, so he usually does that instead of trying to pick it up from the table.

Both of Logan's wrists are different angles from one another. The angle of his left hand makes it easier to pick up a cup with no handles, whether on the table or on the fridge. The angle of his right hand makes it possible to pick up a cup only when the cup has a handle.

Heather's method for drinking is different from Logan's. When picking up a drinking glass from the table with one hand, Heather uses her left pincer movement, placing her thumb inside the lip of the glass and the side of her bent knuckle on the outside of the glass to pinch the edge of the glass. Because her pincer grip is weak, she must be careful not to drop the glass before she gets it to her right hand. Then she places the base of the glass in her palm, secured by her fingers in order to drink. She can't use both hands to drink because her left elbow doesn't bend enough. She must use a tall drinking glass because she can't reach her mouth to drink with a short one, and she must use her right arm, as her left arm only bends ninety degrees.

Eating presents another challenge for Heather and Logan. It's hard for Heather to cut meat because she doesn't have the right leverage in her arms to provide the strength needed. Due to the lack of wrist rotation and dexterity in her fingers, the angle of the knife isn't right either. She can only use one half inch of the tip of the knife instead of the full blade. Her right hand is used to hold the meat in place with the fork but made difficult due to the lack of wrist mobility. She has to accept the unnatural angle of her wrist, hand and bent fingers, using all as best she can. She has to constantly readjust her hold on both the meat and the knife. Heather spends more time cutting foods than eating them. To avoid this situation, she chooses to eat foods that don't need cutting. She likes Fettuccini Alfredo with bite size broccoli and chicken pieces and spaghetti made with turkey sausage. She also likes turkey sausage and American cheese on an English muffin. She drinks two Ensure drinks each day to supplement her meals. Eating takes a lot of both time and energy and Heather must eat five times each day to consume enough calories to maintain or gain weight because she is underweight for her height.

When Heather and Logan eat, their elbows raise above their heart in order to reach their mouths. This increases their cardio efforts, making eating a high energy using activity for them. Eating requires both more time and more energy than the average person takes. They both eat several small meals each day rather than three large meals. This works much better for both time and energy conservation and helps them consume more calories. Keeping their calories high enough to maintain their already low weight is challenging. Gaining weight is difficult.

Heather and Logan can't eat a sandwich that is built up with much lettuce, meat and cheese because their hands are too small to hold the sandwich together and their mouths don't open wide enough to take a bite of a large sandwich. Heather must avoid picking up anything that is hot, like a hotdog, because the sides of her finger and thumb have less fat than the pads of her fingers and she will burn herself. She must use a fork or wait until the food cools.

Eating takes a lot of time for Heather and Logan so their hot foods get cold. They don't have much of a natural appetite to begin with and sometimes their medications further reduce their appetites. When their food gets cold they lose interest in eating, so I bought them a warming tray to keep their food warm. I am so happy when we can find an easy, inexpensive solution to help one of their problems.

Logan has difficulty chewing his food because his jaw isn't aligned properly. His lower jaw protrudes approximately one half inch in front of his upper jaw, creating an under bite like Heather's before her surgery. Watching Heather go through her jaw surgery when she was eighteen years old terrified Logan. To make matters worse the cleft palate surgery that had to be redone as a result of the jaw surgery left Heather with nasal speech. Heather must exert extra effort to enunciate her words so people can understand her clearly. Logan fears having jaw surgery will result in having worse challenges than he has now so he chooses not to have the surgery.

Grocery shopping is another challenge. When Logan rotates his hands so his palms are facing mostly towards each other so he can place them on the sides of the handle of the grocery cart, his upper back is strained from the torque it places on his shoulders. His arms are just short enough that when he pushes the cart his feet kick the basket when he walks normally. It works best for him to push the cart to roll ahead by itself and walk behind.

The bending and reaching used to get items off the shelves in the store is tiring and uncomfortable. Logan strains to carry the full bags of groceries and must carry them from his parking stall to his lower level apartment. Exhausted from his efforts, he still has to put the groceries away, and because he eats a lot of frozen meals and his freezer is on the top, another uncomfortable task is necessary. The bags of groceries are usually on the floor and because of his short arms; he must bend lower than normal to reach his items. Then he must lift the items to the freezer. These repetitive uncomfortable tasks cause more back pain. Logan doesn't look forward to grocery shopping. He concludes that most people don't look forward to grocery shopping either so he's not completely alone.

Heather's forearms are shorter than Logan's and she has less finger dexterity so grocery shopping presents even more challenges for her. Because her wrists can't rotate to the correct angle needed, she struggles to hold onto the handle of the cart. Adding the weight of the cart to the unnatural twist being imposed on her wrists, elbows and shoulders, plus adding the bending and reaching needed to use both hands to get items off the selves, Heather suffers discomfort and exhaustion. Upon finishing, she must drive and endure the discomforts of having her knees bent and nearly hitting the dashboard. Safely in her parking stall, she must rest in her car before struggling to carry the bags of groceries up three flights of stairs to her apartment on the third floor. After resting again she wrestles the refrigerator door and low shelves as she puts cold items in the fridge. She stores many non refrigerator items on the cupboard shelves that aren't too high or too low to avoid more reaching, twisting and bending. Finally, she collapses into her glider to catch her breath, too tired to eat, even though she hasn't yet gotten in enough calories for the day.

In Heather's apartment the fridge door opens from right to left and stands six inches shorter than the top of Heather's head. She can get items out of the freezer without too many problems because it's a good height for the angles of her arms, hands and back. Getting items out of the refrigerator in the lower section is extremely difficult and not done without risk of hurting herself. She can get the items that are stored in the door more easily, so she keeps as many items there as she can. When Heather bends her back to make herself low enough to reach into the fridge with her right arm, she isn't able to reach the item because her right arm doesn't have enough range of motion. If she bends her back to get herself lower, then her arm also lowers. She must bend and twist her back, while squatting as best she can with limited bend in her ankles, so she ends up on the balls of her feet, balancing in an awkward position. Then she must grab the item she needs before losing her balance and falling into the fridge herself or backwards, risking dropping the item on herself or onto the floor, breaking the container and hurting herself in the process.

She is unable to use her left arm to reach any better than her right because the door is on her left side, making reaching to her left nearly impossible and her arm is too short after crossing her body for any leverage or length. If she were to reach in with both arms, her head would end up in the fridge before her hands. She is unable to sit on a stool to solve her dilemma because she is so tall her thighs are longer than her arms when reaching.

Logan's fridge opens from left to right. The most uncomfortable step is bending to get items out of his fridge. Because his arms are longer than Heather's, Logan has less difficulty reaching the items in the fridge, but a side by side fridge having higher shelves would provide greater comfort than his traditional style fridge. His left hand is used for reaching and retrieving items and his right arm for balance. He has sufficient strength and mobility in his left hand to use a gallon container of milk. Pouring a glass of milk when the gallon is full is the most difficult step but he is able to accomplish this task.

You would think Heather and Logan could sit and relax comfortably after working so hard to grocery shop and put away the groceries. Unfortunately sitting isn't as comfortable for them as we wish it were. Heather and Logan both have a very large tailbone and they are very thin; their bones put pressure on their skin. They must squirm until they find the most comfortable position. This usually requires pads both to sit on and to support their back in abnormal places. They enjoy padded glider chairs because the motion of gliding or rocking makes sitting more comfortable. They have difficulty finding chairs and couches that are comfortable. The elbow rests on chairs are usually too low for Heather and Logan to use because they are both tall and their arms are short. If they slump to have their elbows reach the rest, their back hurts.

Dressing and undressing is more challenging for Heather than for Logan. Logan can reach his shoulders with both arms so he is able to pull his shirt off over his head like most people do. He puts both his arms through the arm holes at the same time and then stretches the shirt over his head when putting on a T-shirt. He can do buttons but they take more time. Logan loves clothes and enjoys putting stylish outfits together.

Heather has more difficulty dressing and getting clothes to fit her. When Heather puts on a large T-shirt, she puts both arms through the arm holes at the same time and is able to pull it over head much like Logan. Taking the T-shirt off is where she has difficulty. She folds her right arm until her forearm touches her bicep and tucks her hand into the sleeve, pulls that arm inside the shirt, and uses the right arm to lift the right side of the shirt up and over her head. Then she takes it off her left arm. She must have the sleeves reach close to her elbow and the T-shirt must be big enough for the sleeve to be wide enough to do this. She is able to fold her arm into the sleeve because of the shortness of her forearm.

Large shirts are also easier for Heather because her ribcage is larger in the back and on the sides in comparison to her trunk because her lungs are over-inflated due to her lung disease. Her shoulders are rotated forward causing her scapula on the left side to protrude outward further than normal. Usually men's T-shirts work best because the shoulders and back are wider than on a woman's T-shirt. Of course this makes the T-shirt much too big for Heather's small, thin frame, but she is comfortable in big shirts.

Heather's shoulders are very narrow because of the way they are rotated forward. The neck of the T-shirt can't be too big or it will fall off her shoulders. Usually V-neck shirts are too wide for her. When wearing a shirt with a collar and a few buttons, Heather is unable to button the top button as she can't reach.

Heather can't wear clothing with straps, including a bra, because she can't reach either shoulder with either arm to get the straps on or off. If she desires to wear a bra in the future she will need a device of some kind to help her.

Heather doesn't use the pockets in her pants because her arms are too short to reach them comfortably. She prefers to wear a small, lightweight fanny pack around her waist and in the front so she can easily reach her keys, money, glasses and other items.

Logan uses his pockets, but the bending and twisting required causes him discomfort and concerns about inflicting more permanent pain. He gave a talk to medical students and was demonstrating the difficulties he has when digging in his pockets for money to pay the clerk in a coffee shop. He was describing how he gets worried about taking too much time and making a line of people form behind him. As he was speaking, he was bent over with his hand deep in his pocket as he was showing the students how he frantically searches for his money, when he casually looked up at the students and said, "I just hope they don't think I'm doing something else." The room burst into laughter. I laughed so hard tears were streaming down my cheeks. Logan has a great sense of humor.

When Logan was younger he felt like people wouldn't notice his differences if he were dressed stylishly. Also, because Logan is an artist he uses his artistic talent when dressing. He would have been a good fashion designer if he had chosen that career path. There was a time when he would never wear jeans; they weren't nice enough. When Logan felt like he was dressed well, he felt more confident. He also loved changing the color of his hair. Since I was a hairstylist, I could do this for him with little expense. I didn't always agree with his choices of color, but I believed I needed to let him do what he wanted with his hair.

One of the hairstyles Logan chose shocked and upset me: He shaved his head. He used my clippers, which shaved the hair very close, and then he used a Bic shaver, nicking his head in several places. When he walked into my bedroom to show me his bald head, he was shirtless and in shorts. He looked like he was sick. He has very pale skin, his upper rib cage sinks in like a bowl, he is very thin, and together with all his other disabilities, he looked like cancer patients who lost their hair after chemotherapy. And on top of all that he was stooping over using the "cool" cane he bought for himself that was much too short for him. I couldn't believe he had done that to himself. It was hard for me to look at him because the sight of him tapped into my sadness and the reality that he really was sick because of his lung disease, and that someday he could look sicker because his lungs would get worse and he could even die. We talked about it and he admitted that he regretted doing it. I think he shocked himself, too.

As Logan matured, his esteem grew, and he was more accepting of his differences, so he began to feel like he didn't have to depend on being in stylish clothes all the time. This shift in his perception made his life easier because he could dress more casually and comfortably and still feel good about himself. He came to accept his arms and began wearing shirts with short sleeves. As his self-consciousness lessened, he started wearing shorts. In his early twenties, Logan was dressing freely in anything he wanted to wear whether it was casual or dressy. I was happy to see him more at ease with his body.

Heather was too interested in other things to fret about fashion or her appearance. It bothered me that she did not want to dress up for special occasions like weddings, and that she didn't mind looking like a boy. She was committed to comfort. She didn't want to fuss with all the details that women do to make themselves look more stylish: earrings, make-up, hair curling, and so on. Heather decided that it wasn't worth the effort. She knew who she was and didn't need to look a certain way to create an image for the public. Later, we discovered that her attachments to wearing certain clothing were also symptoms of autism.

Heather's lack of interest in her appearance was disappointing for me. I had always fussed over how she looked. When she was a baby, I would comb her dark brown hair into a curl on top of her head and use Karo syrup to glue the bow onto her head, a trick the hospital nurses had taught me. I kept the fine, uneven hairs that grew over her ears trimmed and when the time came, I cut her bangs.

Later I chose a style that framed her face. She had scars on the far sides of her face after eye surgery. The plastic surgeon used skin from the face just in front of her ears for the skin under her eyelids. Unfortunately, the facial hair grew thick on the sides of Heather's face in the sideburn area and to this day she grows hair under her eyes, which to her dismay she has to shave, or have hairy lower eyelids. Wearing her hair as a frame around her face covers some of the scars.

When Heather was a child, her hair had lightened from a dark brown at birth to a very light ash brown, with golden highlights throughout. It was beautiful. I gave Heather her first perm at the age of three, just before she started preschool. She sat patiently while I rolled her hair onto many small perm rollers. Even when I put her under the dryer she remained patient with the process. Heather loved her hair. I believe that keeping her hair beautiful helped Heather feel beautiful, and that helped her self-esteem.

Besides fussing with Heather's hair, I also took extra efforts with her clothes. I spent hours sewing clothes that would fit her long, thin body and her short arms. She had dresses and pants that had ruffles and frills. Her clothes always looked feminine and fancy. Heather imitated those experiences. She spent hours dressing and undressing her dolls; she also styled their hair.

After spending so much time and energy on making Heather look feminine when she was young, it was difficult for me to let Heather take over when she got a little older and wanted to manage by herself. I thought it was important to fuss with her appearance because she looked different, and I thought strangers were more receptive and friendly when she was dressed in cute clothes and had her hair styled.

I knew I had to let her choose her own clothes and dress herself when the time came. I also knew I had to let her choose the length and style of her hair. The hardest thing for me to give up was putting makeup on her scars and blush on her cheeks, to give her pale complexion a little color.

By the time Heather graduated from high-school, she was wearing her favorite clothes of jeans and T-shirts, and no make-up. Heather has a slight bit of natural wave in her hair, so with a good haircut she can just wash her hair and let it dry naturally and it looks great.

When Logan turned sixteen, he got his driver's license. He expressed a strong interest in driving a stick shift. I had my doubts about how much he would like having to shift all the time and I wasn't sure it would be the right choice. I felt like he was physically capable to drive one and I knew it was important for him to see that I believed him to be capable, so we bought a car with a stick-shift. Logan was ecstatic with his new adventure in driving. We found out later that driving a stick all these years has caused him additional knee pain from using his left knee for the clutch and back pain from reaching for the shifting stick and the turn signal lever. Modifications have been made to his car: lengthening the stick, extending the steering wheel, and installing less resistive steering.

When the time came to choose a car for Heather, we found one that had an automatic transmission because it was easier for her to drive and she didn't want to think about shifting. No car would be perfect for Heather or Logan because they are both six feet tall with short arms. Heather has to move her seat close to the steering wheel to accommodate her arm length. This makes her long legs uncomfortable. She has a knob attached to the steering wheel that helps her turn the wheel more quickly and easily. Her physical discomfort and autism make driving stressful for Heather so she limits her driving. Her compromised depth perception makes it unsafe for her to drive at night.

About the time that Heather was learning to drive, she received a letter inviting her to participate in a beauty pageant for teenagers. I wrote about the experience in an article published in "Exceptional Parent" magazine in 1995:

After being the mother of a child with physical differences for 15 years, I am still surprised at the situations that arise to remind me that my experiences as a parent can be very different from other parents. Being a parent to Heather can move along smoothly and life can seem quite "normal." Suddenly, something can happen and I find myself facing a problem I'm not sure how to deal with.

As girls reach junior high, they start receiving mail that would interest teenage girls. One day Heather was excited to receive such a letter addressed to her. When she opened it, she found information about an upcoming Miss Teenage America Pageant. She read all the pages of the letter and approached me with a beaming smile. She proudly told me that she would like to enter the contest.

I felt an incredible pain in my heart. I honestly didn't know how to react or what to say. I have always encouraged Heather to do the things that she wanted to do. I've tried not to discourage her because I don't always know what's possible. I didn't know if I should encourage her to enter a contest such as this because they are usually based on a certain kind of beauty and certain talents. I'd never seen a person with physical disabilities enter this kind of contest. I didn't think it would be good to discourage her either because it might keep her from trying things in the future. Worse than that, I might damage her self-esteem.

I asked Heather if she read the qualifications of a participant. The third rule said that the participant must have good health. Heather said she read it and she felt like she met that requirement because the doctors say that she is healthy. I told her she is healthy for someone with Miller syndrome, but is she healthy in comparison to someone like me. She said that when I put it like that, no, she is not healthy.

I suggested that Heather call the person directing the pageant and tell that person about herself. She thought that was a good idea and she went to the phone to make the call. I told her to wait a minute because the call was long distance and she needed to think about what she was going to say. I suggested that she write down the questions that she would ask, as well as a description of herself.

A few minutes later Heather returned to me and said, "If I describe myself over the phone the person will think I look like a freak." Again my heart ached. I suggested to Heather that she write a letter describing herself and send a picture. That way the person can see what she looks like too. Again, she thought that was a good idea, so off she went to write a letter.

A few days went by and Heather came to me again. She had been doing some more thinking and she had made a decision. She said, "I've decided that I don't want to enter the pageant."

"Why not?" I asked.   She said that if she were watching a pageant like this on TV and she saw someone that looked like her she would think it was weird. After realizing that, she decided not to enter the pageant.

I felt relieved and sad at the same time; relieved that I didn't make that decision for her by discouraging her when she first approached me, but sad at the reality that because Heather looks different, she can't do some of the things that other teenage girls can do.

I admired Heather for her courage and her self-confidence. When I was her age there was no physical reason why I couldn't enter a contest such as that. However, I didn't have the courage or the self-confidence to do so. Along with these feelings that I've described, I also felt relieved for following the direction that my heart took me when the situation came up in the first place and grateful that things turned out for the best.

I was at a complete loss as to handling the situation, but it turned out well. I followed my instincts in what felt like a delicate matter. The "right" words just came out of my mouth, before I had a chance to think them through and make a conscious decision about what to say. I knew I wanted to preserve Heather's self esteem; however, I wanted to be honest and realistic too. Sometimes the balance is hard to find.

Chapter 14

"My fascination with everything gives me a different perception, including an understanding of what it is like for kids and adults to see me for the first time. I feel excited knowing that they are seeing something unusual and that they are extremely curious about what I am or what happened to me or why I am like this.

I always accept that people stare at me or look at me or ask me questions about why I am different. I often enjoy telling people about why I am different because I understand that they are getting a very unique and fascinating experience right then and my attitude about it and what I say about it is going to affect them.

I am very accepting of people's behavior towards me even to the point where I don't understand why it bothers other people with observable differences to be stared at. Since I accept it so well and have other things to focus on like living my life, I am oblivious to people's looking at me unless for some reason I am acutely thinking about people looking at me."

–Heather Madsen

Heather was a baby, sitting in her infant seat in the grocery cart, when I ran into an acquaintance from high school. For a moment, I didn't know what to say about Heather. It was obvious that she looked different, and I didn't know if Ellen had heard anything about Heather's birth or disability. Heather wore a pretty ruffled dress with a matching bow by the curl on top of her head. There was no mistaking that she was a girl. One couldn't miss the strange appearance of her eyes due to the absence of a lower eyelid, the white splints she wore on each of her arms, used for loosening up her bent arms to prepare them for future surgery to straighten them out, and the special shoes that turned her feet outward to correct her turned in feet. I assumed that the news had gotten around, and so I asked, "Have you heard anything about my baby?" She said no, so I introduced her to Heather. I told her a little bit about her. Because of my openness, Ellen and I were both more comfortable.

Even though that was a small event, it was significant because it was the first time I had to handle the situation. Being open made us both more comfortable, so I've always used that approach.

When Heather and Logan were children, their favorite restaurant was McDonalds. It was inexpensive and they loved chicken nugget Happy Meals. Their jaws were developing an underbite that kept their teeth from aligning properly, and the soft nuggets were easy for them to chew. They got to play on all the playground equipment while they were waiting for their food. They loved the bright colors and the chance to squeal and chase each other without restraint. These simple pleasures were often on hold when illness or surgery interrupted regular outings. Heather and Logan were always eager to get back to a more normal life that included clowns, chicken nuggets and playgrounds.

One day we were sitting at a booth eating our lunch when three children approached our table. They had their hamburgers in their hands and were taking bites and chewing, as they stared at Heather and Logan.

Heather and Logan's arms had been straightened out with surgery, but there was still no mistaking the abnormal appearance of their small hands, permanently bent fingers, lack of a little finger, and scars on their faces from the plastic surgery needed to give them lower eyelids.

This was one of the days when I had patience. "Hi, this is Heather and this is Logan. What are your names?" I said.

They didn't tell me their names; they just looked at me. One girl scrunched up her nose. "What happened to them?"

"Nothing." I smiled. "They were just born this way." That was my standard response. Usually that answer satisfied most children.

"Oh," they said, and then they ran away. Sometimes Heather and Logan and I would just look at each other and laugh, and other times we would talk about people's reactions.

Sometimes public reactions can be humorous. When their grandmother took them shopping one afternoon, a woman was staring at Heather and Logan while she was walking through the mall. She couldn't take her eyes off of them. Their tall, thin bodies with their short arms were impossible to miss and when they were together it was a double whammy for an onlooker. They looked like twins. As she passed them she was still looking at them, as if mesmerized, not watching where she was going, and she walked into a pole.

Sometimes the responses from people are not easy to accept or laugh at.

Lagoon is an amusement park in Salt Lake. Typical of most amusement parks, going on a ride means a wait in line. While people are waiting, there really isn't much to do except look at other people.

Once as I stood in line with Heather and Logan, I couldn't help but notice all the people who stared at them. Curiosity is only natural, but most people know it isn't polite to stare. What amazes me is how many people don't seem to care that staring is impolite. Most of the time I don't look around. I know it's natural for people to stare and I accept it as a natural occurrence. Sometimes I can't help but catch a glimpse of someone doing something rude. It's usually teenagers, whispering and pointing, but sometimes it has been more hurtful behavior.

While standing in line at Lagoon, a couple of teenage girls were pointing at Heather and Logan. They giggled among themselves and made distorted faces to mimic the differences in my children's faces. Heather and Logan had scars under their eyes and Miller syndrome causes their bone structure to appear less normal than the average face. I felt so angry I hardly knew what to do. One of the girls was overweight and dressed in dowdy clothes. I wanted to say something hurtful to her like, "They can't do anything about the way they look, what's your problem?" I starred hard at the teenage girls, hoping they would look into my eyes. I wanted them to see that I had noticed their rude behavior. I hoped they would be embarrassed. However, they never did look at me because they were too busy staring at my children.

I didn't say anything to them. I just let it go and went on to have a good time with Heather and Logan.

Every summer we consider going to Lagoon again because we had so much fun when Heather and Logan were younger. Now, it's more difficult because Logan has chronic pain and must take morphine which can cause nausea, and they both have general discomfort. Difficulty walking long distances, finding a comfortable place to rest, needing to eat certain kinds of foods several times a day, and fatigue make going to Lagoon less desirable for all of us.

I arrived home from work one evening, tired from a long day. Heather, who was twenty-one at the time, was sitting at the kitchen table doing homework, an assignment from the previous semester. She had failed to complete coursework for three courses due to depression. I sat down and asked how things were going. She was in the mood to talk, so I listened.

Logan was sitting nearby, drawing in a sketchbook. He seemed to be interested in our conversation and sometimes interjected his own thoughts. I was always aware that sharing a common disability gave Heather and Logan unique insights into each other.

It was getting late, so after a while, I told Heather she could come in my bedroom and talk with me while I got ready for bed.

I was washing my face while Heather and Logan were sitting on my bed talking with me. She was watching me as I washed my face. "I wonder what it would be like to have two big hands and fingers that straighten out instead of these little ones," she said. "I could fill my hands with water and rinse my face, like you are doing. I could do so much more." Logan was listening to Heather's comments and nodding with agreement.

I said, "Hearing you talk makes me realize how much I take small things I can do for granted." Later, when they were living independently in their own apartments, I asked them to show me how they do things.

They both have difficulty washing their hair because of their short arms. Logan can reach all the areas on his head but must stretch and strain his neck, shoulders and joints in the process. He compares the experience to feeling the strain of putting his foot over his head to rest the ankle on the back of his neck. He sits on a stool in the tub, pumps shampoo into his palm and rushes to smash it on the top of his head before it runs out of his hand. He repeats this method until shampoo is distributed in several places allowing easier shampooing. Logan mounted a hand held shower nozzle level with his chest so the spraying water keeps him warm, while he washes his body with a loofa, attached to a slightly curved stick. He puts his fingers through the looped cord on the end of the stick to give him extra length, necessary to wash his back. He stretches and strains to clean all the surfaces of his skin. This is an exhausting chore for Logan.

When Heather is in her shower, she uses a knobby sponge on a stick to reach her armpits and a small area of her back. When drying her body she uses the towel much like most people do, by holding one end of the towel in each hand while the towel is behind her back, pulling from side to side to dry her back.

Shampooing her hair is difficult and exhausting. She pumps the shampoo into her small slanted palm and rushes it to her head before the shampoo drips off her hand. She can only reach the top and sides of her scalp with one bent finger, which she uses to mush the shampoo into her hair. She can't reach the back of her head or lower hair line at all. She must trust that the shampoo cleans her hair simply because it runs through all her hair when mixed with the water from the shower.

This whole process is exhausting for Heather and Logan, especially because they have a lung disease which results in having only half the normal lung capacity of healthy lungs. They refuse my offers to shampoo their hair at my salon five minutes from their apartments because it takes too much time and energy to get dressed, walk to their car, and drive to the salon. Once there, they must unstick their hearing aids to remove them and it's a frustrating process to re-tape and replace the aid when finished. They would both rather shampoo their hair themselves, even though after showering they must sit and rest before continuing to dress.

After dressing and eating breakfast, it's time to brush their teeth. Logan can brush his teeth normally but not without strain. He uses a SoniCare electric toothbrush, which does a better job than manually because of his lack of wrist rotation, which makes it hard to reach all his teeth easily.

Heather has more trouble brushing her teeth because her arms are shorter than Logan's. She must strain to reach all her teeth and is limited in the direction she can brush them. Unfortunately, she doesn't tolerate the vibration of the SoniCare toothbrush so has to brush her teeth manually.

Toilet hygiene is extremely difficult for both Heather and Logan. One of the meanest things ever said to Logan during his school years was, "Your arms are so short you can't even wipe your own ass." I was horrified and terribly sad when Logan told me this. The hardest part is that it's true. They risk hurting their backs and shoulders when they clean themselves. Logan has a bidet toilet seat that replaces the regular toilet to help him. Heather has a hand held device called a "Bottom Buddy" that helps. Someday we will buy Heather a bidet too. Logan received his with the funding he received from the government to help him be a self employed artist.

The simple act of scratching an itch is difficult for Heather and Logan. When Logan's back itches, he reaches for the long metal serving spoon he keeps on the table near his sofa. The curve of the spoon helps him reach the center of his back.

Logan has created an environment in which he can be as comfortable as possible in his apartment. He gets anxious when he thinks of going to other people's homes or out of town for long periods of time because he wouldn't have the items he uses to give him more comfort.

Heather can't scratch her neck when it itches because she can't reach her neck with either hand. She uses a pencil or fork to give her the length and surface needed to scratch the itch. When she gets an itch on the top of her collar bone or along the top of the shoulder or upper back and rest of the back she must rub against the furniture, wall or other stationary piece of furniture to rub the scratch away like a cat. Sometimes she can grab the front and back of her shirt on opposite corners and pull her shirt side to side to rub her itch away.

When I was listening to Heather and Logan while sitting on the bed so many years ago, I was happy that Heather was communicating her thoughts. I believed it was the beginning of her moving toward the necessary place of acceptance. I encouraged her to keep a journal, because I felt that someday she would accept her circumstances and she might want to read about the thoughts, questions and challenges she's had in her past and she would see how far she had come. I told her that she might not remember moments like those, when she was going through the process of discovery, because time can make us forget. I felt like those moments would be valuable to her and to other people with whom she would choose to share her feelings.

Later, while lying on my bed with the covers up to my chin, I continued to listen. Heather was sitting beside me talking. Logan sat on the bed eating a bowl of cereal.

Suddenly, I felt a strong awareness of how close we were and a sense of pride that I had a relationship with my children that encouraged them to communicate with me.

I listened as Heather explained that she didn't know who she was or how she fit in with other people. She was keenly aware of her differences and felt them constantly, especially when she was out in the world doing ordinary daily activities. As she drove down the street in her car, she would ask herself: "Why am I doing this? I'm not like anybody else, so why am I driving a car? I am different and I don't fit in."

Driving isn't easy for Heather. She's driving a 1994 red Mazda Protégé. She has long legs but she must move her seat close to the steering wheel to accommodate her short arms. Her knees touch the dashboard. She has a steering knob—Necker knob, as they were referred in old times—positioned on the wheel to use with her right arm. The back of her hand faces the steering wheel with the knob between her thumb and index finger for grip. She is able to steer, but someday we will buy her a least resistive steering column to make steering much easier. Heather's autism make driving more challenging too. She avoids driving unnecessarily.

She shared how fitting in was hard as a child. "In elementary school, I knew kids would not want to pick me to be on their team because I looked different and they didn't know me. I did not know to even think about why this was a problem for them. I did not know what kids thought of me in elementary school. I just knew everyone had friends but me. I would be nervous to work in group projects with kids in elementary school through college because I knew I did not relate well to my peers. They would either ignore me, tell me what to do, give me crappy things to do, or not do their share and I would have to do both shares. I also did not know how to be part of the group discussion very well and I still don't know. I often will space out during the discussions and think about other things because the topic is uninteresting or I just have nothing else to add. When I was able to provide some input, I might have sounded bossy or rude in 'suggesting' to people what needed to be done and who could do it. Even now, when I understand what needs to be done and want to help, I don't know how to do that without looking strange or rude, I just keep quiet."

When she was sitting in a classroom during college, she asked herself questions about why people wanted to talk to her. On rare occasions, a fellow student would make conversation with her and she would notice that they were treating her like they would anyone else. She wondered how they could talk to her without seeming uncomfortable. After all, she wasn't normal.

Sometimes her professor would call on her to answer a question during class. He seemed to have the same expectations of her that he had of anyone else. She wondered what he thought about when he called on her. She wondered if he expected her to act different since she looked different. She didn't know if she wanted to be there because she didn't feel like she belonged. She also wondered what she wanted to do about it. She said that she always came back to those questions.

At first I was surprised that she had thoughts like those. In the past she didn't seem to pay attention to her differences or question the way other people did certain tasks or how her appearance influenced people's behavior. For years, her autism had caused her to not even think about making such social comparisons. It was only as a young adult and with her experiences talking on the internet that her social development evolved enough to make such comparisons, trying to figure out how she is supposed to see herself in relation to other people. I found her experiences very interesting. I wanted to hear more.

I didn't know what life was like from her perspective. I had already been moving along in my process of acceptance for almost twenty years; it started the day she was born. Now she was going through her own process.

When Heather was a child, I always took her along with me to the shopping mall. I noticed that people would look at her in the stroller, which seems to be something people do instinctively. Whenever someone saw Heather, they immediately looked up at me, as if they wanted to see what the baby's mother looked like. I felt self-conscious, hurt and angry. My defense was to block all the uncomfortable feelings and replace them with pride. I was raising a child with disabilities, something the average person never had to face.

Although my feelings were initially little more than defenses to help me cope, gradually those feelings became more genuine. I accepted the curiosity people expressed about my children and felt proud to be their mother. I held my head high, knowing that I was handling the challenges of parenting two children with disabilities. I was also proud of Heather and Logan, who handled many difficult situations. Our life was not easy, but we were living it to the best of our abilities, and that was reason to be proud.

Even though the stares continue to this day, I have become more oblivious to them. I am comfortable with my children and how they appear. Only a few incidents stand out in my mind, most of them from years ago.

When Heather was a toddler, a little boy in an elevator with us pointed to Heather and asked me what was wrong with her.

"She was just born that way. She is missing a bone in her arms and that is why they are short and different looking," I said.

"No, not her arms. What is wrong with her eyes?"

I responded in the same manner, but I was surprised that he was more curious about her eyes than her arms.

On another occasion, I was at a corner station close to my home getting gas. It was a place I went often and I usually had Heather and Logan with me, but today I was alone. The clerk asked me if I had adopted the two children she had seen with me. I thought that was an interesting question, so I explained the situation about Heather and Logan's rare syndrome to her. She responded with disbelief, as most people do, when they hear the story.

Sometimes I'm not as patient. One summer afternoon, we attended a children's concert at the symphony hall in Salt Lake. The tickets were expensive for me, but I wanted Heather and Logan to experience a live performance. Our seats were close to the stage, as there were only two rows of seats in front of ours. We waited for the performance to begin. Directly in front of us, a little boy around five years old turned around in his seat, hooked his fingers over the back of his chair, and stared at Heather and Logan. Because I wanted Heather and Logan to have a wonderful time at this concert, I wasn't in a very patient mood. I looked into the boy's eyes and said, "Turn around!" I knew it was his parents' responsibility to teach him not to stare, but it was an automatic response from me and it didn't feel as confrontational as the alternative of asking the parents to tell their son to quit staring.

When Logan was in his early teens, he had far less patience with children staring at him. Sometimes Logan would stare back at the child and say, "Boo!" The child would run away as fast as he could go, looking for his mommy. Heather and I laughed along with Logan when he told us about it. It wasn't a very kind thing to do, but we are only human.

Logan understands people's tendency to have judgments about what they don't understand. He struggles with his own judgments of other people. Logan has never been overweight, and because he has been exposed to a mom who is a fanatic about controlling her weight to remain thin and healthy, he has a difficult time understanding how people can let themselves become overweight. He feels like they have taken their healthy, normal body, which he was denied in his life, and caused it to be disabled by getting over weight. He struggles to control anger that wells up inside, which he wants to direct at the person who has become overweight. He tries to accept the situation as one he knows nothing about, and not dwell on it but sometimes it isn't easy for him, especially on days when he is struggling to do tasks that are especially difficult for him. Because he wants people to refrain from judging him when they don't know the whole story, he tries to refrain from judging overweight people.

Heather doesn't notice people staring very often. Having the kind of autism she has protects her from noticing other people automatically. Logan on the other hand feels self conscious and uncomfortable when people stare. Although Logan has autism, it's a different form of autism, so he is very aware of people staring. Because Logan suffers with chronic pain and is always struggling to endure the discomfort he feels when he is walking, driving or doing tasks out in the world, his tolerance for people staring and displaying other annoying behaviors is low. Sometimes he gets angry. Logan doesn't like to feel angry, especially when it makes him frightened that he will lose his temper and say something he could regret later or worse, something that might cause someone to hurt him. Because of this, he tends to stay close to the comforts of home.

After being in public with Heather and Logan for almost thirty years, I seldom pay attention to the stares. I go about my business as usual. However, sometimes I'm surprised by my own reaction.

I've been teaching aerobics for twenty-five years. I go to the gym, teach my class and then leave. Usually no one knows anything about my life and most people don't even know my name. I'm just the aerobics instructor. I never thought about this until a few years ago, when I took Heather to the gym with me.

When I walked into the gym I wasn't expecting to feel the way I felt. I noticed I felt self-conscious, not embarrassed, just self-conscious or shy. I wasn't inconspicuous anymore. I felt like people's attention was drawn right to me and I wasn't used to that at the gym. I felt like they would now imagine me in many different scenarios. Whatever assumptions they had made about me before that moment would then disappear, and they would start making up new stories and forming questions in their minds as a way to deal with their curiosities.

I realized they would make all kinds of new assumptions about us and I had no control over their thoughts. People now knew something personal about my life, but they didn't know the facts, and I wasn't in a position to explain anything. It was a very strange and uncomfortable feeling.

When I'm with Heather and Logan and meet someone new, I often volunteer introductions and include Heather and Logan in the conversation. Sometimes I will ask Heather or Logan a question about something relevant to the conversation, although I am careful to let Heather and Logan speak for themselves now that they are adults. When a person hears Heather and Logan responding, they seem more comfortable and willing to ask questions.

I make an effort to accept people's discomfort at being around someone who looks different. What helps me is that I really like people, and I try to accept them with all their idiosyncrasies and hope they will accept me with mine. I also avoid being around people who are generally pessimistic and negative; those who constantly complain about their life and act like victims. I choose to make friends that want to bring happiness and positive energy into our lives, people who really care about us.

Chapter 15

"The first time I went to the grocery store alone was a turning point in how I viewed people and how they perceived me. Without my mom by my side, I didn't have the distraction of focusing on her or putting groceries into her basket.

I realized that when people saw me now, they would see me alone. They would see me get out of the car and walk into the store. They would watch how I walked and what kind of attitude I carried. They would see me struggle to pull out a basket. They would watch how I pushed it throughout the store and how I got groceries. They would notice that I was alone. I wondered and tried to imagine what kind of thoughts would go through their mind and how my behavior and attitude would affect those thoughts.

I felt a little bit of trepidation and uncertainty. Interestingly, before that moment, I didn't pay much attention to people's perceptions or attitudes when I went to the store. For some reason, that day I was very self conscious about entering the world alone, and I wondered how being physically different was going to affect others' perceptions.

I was also aware of being female and alone, which made me three times as vulnerable to being harassed or attacked by someone out in the parking lot. While I was going through the store, I fluctuated between feelings of curiosity, concern, acceptance, pleasure, and una-wareness about what I was doing."

—Heather Madsen

Sometimes perceptions are all wrong. We see someone and automatically begin to fill in the blanks. We decide based on appearances what a person's life is about, but often those impressions are wrong.

Several years ago, a man approached me while I was on the stair machine at the gym where I taught aerobics. He was older and short with a well-defined, muscular build. His hair, the color of honey and permanently waved, gave him an eccentric appearance. I'll call him Harry.

As Harry approached me, I didn't know what to think. Since I was an instructor there, my natural reaction was to smile and act friendly.

He walked up to me. "You must be so happy with yourself," he said. "I have you all figured out. You are pretty, tall and you have a nice physique. You walk around here with the confidence of a person who has everything going for her. Let me predict, you probably have the perfect life, a handsome man, a beautiful car, a great job and a wonderful home. You have it all."

I was completely taken by surprise by Harry's comments. He was so sure that he knew everything about me because of the way I looked. His arrogance struck me as rude.

I decided I was going to pay him back for being so presumptuous.

Often when people are going to meet Heather and Logan for the first time, I make an effort to prepare them for the fact that my children look different. For example, when I get a new customer in my salon, we talk about our lives. They tell me about their relationships, jobs and children and in return I tell them about mine. When I'm talking about my children, I could stop short of telling the person about the challenges that Heather and Logan face, but usually I tell them the story. I do that because I don't want them to be shocked if they meet the kids, but mainly I don't want to send the message that I am embarrassed about our challenges. They could also hear about Heather and Logan's problems from someone else, and then perhaps think I didn't want to talk about my situation. It has always worked best when I'm open and honest. People seem to be more comfortable about the differences in my life and I'm certainly more comfortable.

Harry was not going to get this courtesy. Because he had been so presumptuous, assuming I had some sort of perfect life simply because I was tall and thin and took care of my appearance, I decided not to spare him the surprise. I felt like he deserved it for acting so high and mighty. He knew nothing about me or my life, and while everyone is entitled to think what they like, he had crossed the line. Harry was going to learn the old adage that looks can be deceiving.

I told Harry that he was right about some of his predictions. I was very happy in my life and I was doing many of the things that I had long wanted to do. I owned my own business as a hairstylist, I taught aerobics, and I was a mother. I had a wonderful man in my life who brought me much happiness, and I felt very lucky about all those things. I went on to tell him that I had two very beautiful children, and that I would love for him to meet them. "In fact, both of my children are here in the nursery," I said, climbing off the stair machine. "Would you like to meet them?" I gave Harry my best smile.

He agreed and followed me downstairs. When we entered the nursery, Heather and Logan ran over to me to give me a big hug. They were chanting "Mommy, Mommy" in that delightful singsong voice children use.

I turned toward Harry. "I would like you to meet my children, Heather and Logan."

Harry's face went blank. He seemed to struggle for words. "Hello, nice to meet you," he said quickly, and then he darted back upstairs.

I felt a twinge of guilt over setting him up like that, but only a twinge. He deserved what he got. I saw him many times afterwards and I always greeted him. We got to know each other a little better, and I invited him to attend a meeting with me to learn about a personal growth seminar that I had attended. We met at the location of the meeting, and twenty minutes after it started, Harry leaned closer. "I can't take this anymore," he whispered. He said that he was going to leave and that I could come with him or stay, he didn't care which. We went to a restaurant nearby to get a bite to eat.

Harry wanted to tell me his new assumptions about me now that he knew me better. He said that I was a martyr. He went on to give me the details of his opinion. I just laughed and continued to eat my chicken sandwich.

After that night, I saw Harry from time to time at the gym, and then again when I went for a walk in a neighborhood close to my salon. As I was rounding a corner, there was Harry, out for an early evening stroll. It happened that he lived in that area. He asked how Heather and Logan were doing. I told him a few things about their recent activities, and we said goodbye. I haven't seen him for a few years now, but I'll never forget him. I don't think Harry will forget me anytime soon either. Sometimes people enter each other's lives for only a brief moment, but the experience can make an impact on the rest of one's life.

Chapter 16

Surgery was ongoing for both of my children from a very early age. They had so many physical problems that required correction, and often times, it seemed that we spent as much time at the hospital as we did at home. Most of the surgeries that were performed on Heather had to also be performed on Logan. Although Terry was present and supportive during the first surgeries, after our divorce and his relocation to Michigan, I was on my own during these procedures. Heather was nine and Logan was six when Terry moved away.

Heather's first surgery was a heart catheter, performed at the young age of one day old. Then Heather and Logan each had their soft palate repaired at the age of six weeks; this procedure prevented their formula from coming out of their noses.

A physical feature of Miller syndrome is the absence of the lower eyelid. Without the lower eyelid, the eyes appear to be very large, as if the lower lid is being pulled down toward the cheek. Tears won't stay in the eyes, so it appears that the person is crying. The eyes dry out and become red and itchy. There was surgery done on one eyelid at a time. Cartilage was used from the back of the ears as a support for the skin used for the lower eyelid. The doctor used some skin from in front of Heather's ear for her eyelid. It has held up very well. The only difficulty is that facial hair grows on the skin, which gives Heather hairy lower eyelids. Sometimes, if the hair gets too long, it scratches her cornea. She uses small electric clippers to keep the hair shaved.

With Logan's eyelid surgeries, the doctor used cartilage from only one of Logan's ears, leaving the cartilage in the other ear for possible needs in the future. This left Logan with one ear that sticks out, which he doesn't like. The doctor used some skin from Logan's upper eyelid as the skin for a lower eyelid. This hasn't held up very well. The cartilage under the skin hasn't stayed flat, so there is a protrusion close to his eye which causes his eyelid to roll in an unnatural way. This causes his eyelashes to scratch his eye. Logan may have another surgery at some point to build his lower eyelids so they will close better when he sleeps and to keep the eyelid from rolling. It's always risky to have surgery because the results may be worse than the problem. Usually it's easier to make the decision to have surgery when it feels like it must be done. When the time came to remove the stitches from the eyelid surgery, Heather and Logan had to be put under anesthesia, so it became another surgery. They had to have their eyes done one at a time because the bandage used after surgery covered their whole head except for one eye, their nose and their mouth.

Between ages one and two, Heather and Logan each had both their arms straightened, one arm at a time. They had worn splints on each arm soon after birth to loosen up their wrist so their hand could be moved into a straighter position. During the surgery the doctor cut a V in the forearm bone (radius), lifted the hand up into a straight position, and then pinned it in place in the V. This fused the hand to the radius, leaving no wrist movement. Heather seems to have done fine with her surgeries on both her arms. Logan, however, has constant pain in his right arm and over time it slowly keeps bending down more. He had a second surgery on his right wrist when he was eighteen and a third when he was twenty-five.

Around the age of two, Heather and Logan both had a second cleft palate surgery, a procedure called a pharyngeal flap. An upside-down door is cut into the back of the throat and then opened up toward the roof of the mouth, creating a flap of skin to cover the hole in the back roof of the mouth. This surgery helped with their speech so they wouldn't sound so nasal. It also helped keep their food and liquids from coming out of their noses. They had to wear elbow restraints for six weeks to prevent bending their elbows; putting something in their mouth may have damaged the surgery site.

As Heather and Logan grew and began to walk, it was obvious that their ankles were rotating severely. If they had continued developing naturally, they would be walking on their ankles. They were both elementary school age when the doctors put screws into the growth plate of the outer bone of the lower leg, stopping growth. This allowed the inner leg bone to continue growing, causing the ankle to straighten as it grew. Heather still has the screws in her ankles. Logan's ankles started to overcorrect when he was a teenager and the screws were removed. They both currently have ankle pain, which limits their activities and may require further surgery.

After years with lung problems, Heather and Logan were tested for reflux, a condition in which the stomach contents (food or liquid) leak backwards from the stomach into the esophagus (the tube from the mouth to the stomach). They were twelve and nine at the time. The test was positive, so they were scheduled for surgery. An incision was made below the ribcage to the lower abdomen. The stomach was wrapped around the esophagus to restrict stomach contents from coming up into the esophagus. Heather and Logan had the surgery done at the same time. It was a very difficult surgery to have them both in pain and needing care. Logan's surgery was so tight he wasn't able to vomit, even when he had the flu. It is still the same today. Heather has problems with reflux and was told the surgery she had was a failure. Currently she has a hiatal hernia and suffers intermittent pain caused by esophageal spasms, making eating challenging. She may need surgery in the future.

All Heather and Logan's dental work was done under anesthesia when they were children because they needed so much work. Their lung disease increases the risks associated with anesthetics. Luckily, there were no problems when they had their dental work performed. As adults having dental work done is uncomfortable. Logan has difficulty breathing when he opens his mouth wide because of his cleft palate repair and his deviated septum. He has extremely sensitive teeth and must be careful to avoid drinks that trigger discomfort. Heather and Logan both have trouble breathing when they are lying flat on their backs. This requires the dentist to keep the chair more upright than normal, making access more difficult.

In their teens, Heather and Logan had their tongues clipped. There was a webbing of flesh underneath their tongues which attached their tongues to their lower jaw, much like the tongue of a bird. When the skin was clipped, they were able to move their tongue more freely, improving their speech and allowing them to lick an ice-cream cone.

Heather needed some inner ear reconstruction. She went into surgery to widen her ear canal and the doctor found a tumor. He removed the tumor and then ended up removing all the small bones of the inner ear; the hammer, stirrup and others. I still remember the helplessness I felt when he showed me the bottle which contained her inner ear bones. He then reconstructed her inner ear. That is the ear requiring a hearing aid today. She had surgery on her other ear, later, to widen the canal, but scar tissue developed which closed off the canal and changed the shape. She isn't able to wear an aid on that ear.

Heather was put under anesthesia to have her lungs cleaned and then again to do cilia brushings to see if the hair-like cilia that line the airway were working. Results were inconclusive about Heather's cilia, which could further explain her lung problems. Finally, when Heather was thirty-three, and after having our genome sequenced, a gene that causes a disease affecting the cilia was found. The disease is called primary ciliary dyskinesia, PCD. Heather is relieved she finally has answers. She has an unusually high-volume of mucus in her lungs, nose and eyes. She was an infant when the eye surgeon inserted tubes into her tear ducts to help with some of those problems. More eye surgery was necessary for both Heather and Logan to correct muscles to bring their eyes into alignment. Logan needs more eye muscle surgery. When he reads, his eyes cross mid-sentence because his right eye stops moving in unison with his left eye.

Heather had her jaw surgery at the age of eighteen. After having the jaw surgery, she had to have her pharyngeal flap done again, leaving her with nasal speech.

Logan had tubes put in his ears when he was a baby because he got ear infections. He also had to have the tendons in his hips and sides of his knees cut because they were too tight and were preventing him from walking. When the surgery was performed and healed, he began walking. He also had surgery to correct a hernia and bring down one undesended testicle. As an adult, Logan's doctors have discovered that he has bones in his hips that aren't fused that should be and bones that are fused that shouldn't be in his tailbone area. This situation contributes to the chronic pain he suffers today, requiring morphine to keep the pain at a tolerable level.

All these surgeries totaled twenty-six for Heather and twenty for Logan.

Chapter 17

A couple of weeks after her second eye surgery, Heather had to go into the hospital to have the stitches removed under general anesthesia. She was about four or five years old, and by then, had undergone numerous surgeries. Terry went to work as usual and I took Heather to the hospital.

Heather was wheeled into the operating room. Afterwards, I opened the book I had brought along to read. I had only finished a few pages when a nurse approached to inform me that the doctor wanted to speak with me. She led me to a private room.

When the doctor entered, I looked up at him with surprise. "Wow, are you finished already?"

"No, I'm afraid there were some complications," he said. "Heather has had a respiratory arrest, one of her lungs collapsed during intubation. The lungs sounded clear in the pre-op examination; however one lung was so full of puss and infection that it was spilling over into the other lung. We believe the infected lung echoed the sound of a clear lung and that is why it was missed during her pre-operation examination."

My heart sank as he spoke. Questions raced through my mind, but I hardly knew where to begin.

"When the pus spilled out of her lung it caused the vocal cords to spasm, making it impossible to put the breathing tube down Heather's throat to administer oxygen," he explained. "Heather was already put to sleep and wasn't able to breathe on her own, so she was without oxygen for several minutes and we don't know what kind of damage, if any, may have been done. We'll just have to wait and see."

I was terrified. I felt breathless. All I wanted to do was see Heather.

"She's in intensive care," he said, and then told me I could see her soon.

I found a phone so I could call Terry and tell him what happened. He was stunned, said he would leave work immediately and come the hospital.

When I entered the critical care area, my eyes found my little girl, lying in a hospital bed with a large tube going into her mouth. Other tubes and equipment hooked up to her small body. Her eyes were filled with terror, and she tried to speak. She mouthed the words, "Can you hear me, Mommy?"

I couldn't hear her voice; the tube made it impossible for her vocal cords to work. "No honey, I can't hear you, but it's because of that tube. I will be able to hear you when the tube comes out." I tried to soothe her fears.

I lost count of how many days Heather was in the intensive care area, but the day finally came when she could be moved to a serious care unit, which meant she wasn't critical anymore. Heather was moved into a small room that she would share with one other young child who was taken off life support while I was in the room. I watched the heart monitor as it went flat. I was non reactive to this because I was focused on Heather and my emotions were off.

After a few more days at the hospital, Heather was released. Surgeries haven't gotten easier over the years just because we have had so many of them; they have gotten harder. We are always aware of possible complications.

What has gotten easier is my ability to speak up and advocate for my children. As a young woman with no experience dealing with doctors or hospitals, I never questioned doctor's opinions or decisions. If they said a surgery was needed, I asked when and scheduled it with their nurse. After years of experience and becoming more mature and assertive myself, I began to question doctors. I have also seen firsthand the results after a failed surgery, so I no longer look at medicine as a perfect science.

As I gained more experience with the pre-operation procedures, I began to recognize some of the same problems. For example, Heather and Logan have very difficult veins to find, sometimes requiring a surgeon to cut into an area to find a vein. After watching my terrified children cry and beg, I began to ask for a flight nurse (a nurse that flies on rescue helicopters and is very good at putting in IV lines quickly) or the doctor to put in the IV line. I knew that if I got a nurse that was inexperienced at putting in IV lines in small, difficult to find veins, it would be close to impossible to accomplish the task. All they seemed to be able to do was insert a needle in the kids' arms and then poke around the area, puncturing the surrounding tissue, looking for a vein, causing Heather and Logan pain and anxiety. Then they would give up and go find someone more experienced.

Because of the scary and painful experiences Heather and Logan had been through, they were always upset before a surgery. After a while we became acquainted with some "purple medicine"—that's what Heather and Logan called it.

That medicine put Heather and Logan in a dreamy state so they wouldn't have to deal with the anxiety of getting the IV. Usually they were asleep by the time the doctor put in the IV line. Another medication was a numbing agent that could be applied topically to the area where the needle was to be inserted. Sometimes that helped with the pain. Being assertive was very difficult for me at first, but after watching my babies suffer, assertiveness was no longer a problem. I knew my children and their needs. Even though the nurses sometimes didn't like it, I was persistent. My children were counting on me.

When Heather and Logan had a surgery called a pharyngeal flap (the closure of the cleft, hard palate in the roof of the mouth), they had to wear elbow restraints. Those were long sleeves that had pockets all the way around the arm, in which tongue depressors were inserted. They had to wear them so they couldn't bend their arms. The doctor didn't want them to be able to put anything into their mouths and risk puncturing their repaired palate.

When Heather had her cleft palate surgeries, I followed the doctor's orders precisely. When Logan had his surgery, I refused to have him wear the elbow restraints when he was sitting on my lap. I was watching him closely and I couldn't see a need to make him more uncomfortable by putting on the restraints.

The nurses kept telling me to put them on and I kept refusing their orders. Finally one of the nurses got so upset she called the doctor and told him I wasn't cooperating. I was called to the phone and the doctor explained again why the restraints were needed. I defended my opinion.

"Is it really worth the risk?" he asked. "If anything happens, by accident, and Logan's palate surgery is punctured or damaged, there is the possibility that it could cause irreversible damage. Are you willing to take that risk?"

Well, I got his point. Even though I couldn't see how anything could happen with Logan in my arms, I put the restraints back on him.

Chapter 18

Heather and Logan were continuously getting pneumonia, and after Heather's respiratory arrest, and discovering they both had reflux, the doctor recommended Nissan surgery. That is a procedure where the stomach is wrapped around the esophagus and secured, forming a tighter opening, which makes it harder for the stomach contents to come back up into the esophagus.

Since Heather and Logan both needed the surgery, I decided to have them go through it together. That was a mistake. Terry had already moved to Michigan, which meant I was left to handle things alone. I had no idea how hard that would be.

After the surgeries, Heather and Logan shared the same room. Each had an incision that ran from chest to belly button. When they gagged from the effects of the anesthesia or from trying to consume fluids, they experienced severe pain. The pain medicine used was administered by giving them a shot. What child would ask for a shot? At one point, Heather was in so much pain she was screaming and hallucinating. After that terrible episode, I asked that it be given every few hours, whenever the proper time had elapsed since the previous dose, and not wait for them to be in any pain or ask for it. That helped tremendously.

Because of the nature of the surgery, Heather and Logan had to be on a clear liquid diet, progressing to a full liquid diet, and then to soft foods before resuming a regular diet. Logan's surgery ended up being tighter than Heather's, so she progressed off the clear liquid diet many days before Logan. While he was still on clear liquids, Heather was in the next bed, eating soft foods and moving on to a regular diet. That was very difficult for Logan. After a week or so in the hospital, both kids were able to eat a normal diet and they were released.

Logan's surgery results still remain tighter than Heather's. If they get the stomach flu, Heather can vomit, but Logan cannot. That inability may sound like a good thing, but it isn't. Logan has no way of feeling better if he has the flu or gets food poisoning until the contents of his stomach go through his intestinal track, causing severe diarrhea. Logan also has abnormalities with his stomach anatomy that causes digestion problems and irritable bowel syndrome (IBS).

When Logan turned eighteen, his right arm began hurting with every activity. It had become bent again over the years, and it soon became obvious that he needed surgery to straighten it out again.

Logan hadn't been through a surgery for a few years. Most of his surgeries were performed before he was in his teens. We weren't prepared for the amount of pain that he would experience during the recovery from that surgery. Because of the intense pain, Logan was yelling and using profanity at the nurses in the recovery room, ordering them to let his mom in. They were very busy and wanted to calm Logan down, so they found me in the waiting area and asked me to come be with Logan. He was crying from the pain. The doctor ordered a morphine pump so that Logan could administer the pain medicine whenever he needed it. It worked well and he began to feel less pain.

Logan was in the hospital for several days and was using the morphine throughout his stay. What the doctors and nurses didn't tell us was that a side effect from the morphine could be an inability to urinate. Logan has a very large bladder, much larger than normal, something we knew from the ultrasound that I had when I was seven months pregnant with him, so he could go a long time without urinating.

When the time came that Logan's bladder was as full as it could get and he couldn't urinate, he was told that he would have to get a catheter. He didn't want any part of that. He was refusing to have the procedure. Finally, he asked the nurse what would happen if he couldn't urinate and if he refused to get a catheter and the nurse said, "Do you know what happens to a balloon when it is filled with water beyond its capacity to hold the water?" Logan had the catheter inserted.

Logan wore a cast for a couple of months during his senior year as part of the recovery from that surgery. I think he liked the attention he got. After the cast was removed, we could see right away that his arm was much straighter.

Logan went on to have another wrist surgery when he was in his mid-twenties. It was so much more painful than before. The doctor discovered the plate had broken, which is why his arm was bent again. The surgeon put in a much stronger, bigger plate, and this time, Logan had the surgery done as an outpatient procedure. The doctor gave him a nerve block, which prevented any pain. When the block wore off two days later, Logan was in excruciating pain. He suffered until the pain pill kicked in, but it wasn't enough to do more than dull the pain. We went back to the outpatient clinic to get another nerve block. Logan's arm was so numb, he was afraid if he bumped it into a wall it would fall off. He feared it would stay that way. Unfortunately, the block only lasted a day and he was again screaming with pain. All we could do was wait for the pain medication to take effect. It's difficult to witness someone in that kind of pain and be helpless to do anything to ease it, especially when that someone is your child.

At this time, Logan lived in his own apartment. He stayed with me the first couple of nights, but wanted to go home. He was there when he had the second nerve block. I stayed as much as he wanted me to stay, and provided some of his favorite foods, including peanut chicken and sweet sticky rice with mangos, but he likes to be independent and was able to care for himself most of the time after the first few days.

Logan is adamant about being independent and doing things as much like people who have normal bodies as possible. He believes that because he is male his ego is stronger than Heather's, which causes him to perform tasks the way he sees normal people do them instead of the way his body would do them naturally, which would make his differences stand out. He fears he may be causing himself more pain from trying to live the way he wants to live, even though it's difficult for him. He wants to remove some of the barriers that block other people from seeing who he really is and not just his disabilities. He wants people to notice his strengths and talents and see him as an equal, not just someone who has Miller syndrome.

We know a lot more about the gene for Miller syndrome than we knew years ago. Recently, scientists found the gene responsible for Miller syndrome and primary ciliary dyskinesia, PCD, (Heather and Logan's lung disease), when my family became the first family in the world to have our entire genome sequenced. The inheritance pattern of both of these diseases is autosomal recessive; both parents must carry the gene for the disease to occur. The risk is one in four, with each pregnancy, of having an affected child. In Heather and Logan's case, because their father and I each carry both the Miller syndrome gene and the PCD gene, against all odds, both Heather and Logan each have both these diseases. Stories about this research appeared on the front pages of the *New York Times* and the *Los Angeles Times* in March of 2010.

Heather and Logan are also carriers of a mutation in a gene that causes cystic fibrosis, which they got from me. It's a good thing their father didn't carry that mutation too. Knowing now that I could have produced a normal baby with another man doesn't make me think I would have chosen to do so if I had known sooner. I knew my future would be full with taking care of Heather and Logan and being a single mother. I had no desire to have more children. This news would not have changed my decision.

It was difficult living for more than thirty-three years without an answer to the biggest question of all, "Why did all this happen to my children?"

Now, I am happy to have answers. More importantly, I feel peace knowing why. We are all pleased to know that our contribution to the family genome sequencing research (scientists sequencing our family's genes) will make a positive difference in many other family's lives. It's wonderful for me to see Heather and Logan able to contribute to something so important to other people, something that "normal" people can't contribute. This experience gives us purpose and meaning. Knowing we have made a positive difference in other people's lives make the challenges we face every day a little bit easier.

Logan was most excited to find out he could produce a normal child. He said, "For once I can do something important that other people can do: I can father a normal child."

Heather was most excited to find out the cause of her lung disease, the biggest threat to her life.

When we received the genome results, Lynn, who has spent most of his adult life in the study of genetics, said that there was only a one in ten billion chance of both my children getting all five of these genes. Considering there are seven billion people on the planet, it's most unlucky.

As more has been discovered about Miller syndrome (postaxial acrofacial dysostosis), we're all happy to have answers to the mystery we've lived with for over thirty three years.

As a result of sequencing our genome, scientists discovered that Heather and Logan's lung disease is caused by another recessive gene called primary ciliary dyskinesia (PCD). We've gained a better understanding of PCD. It's a disease that affects the cilia throughout the body. They are the small hair-like, moving parts that bring mucous out of our lungs. Cilia are also in the nasal passage and affects taste and smell. Now we know why Heather can't smell and why their taste isn't as keen as normal. Cilia moves the egg through the fallopian tubes each month in women, and cause sperm to move in men. Finally, an explanation for the lung disease, loss of smell, less taste, some of the hearing problems, and other things.

Of course the most serious effects of PCD involve the lungs. The treatment is the same as it is for conditions like cystic fibrosis: visits to a pulmonary specialist every three months to do a pulmonary function test and have the doctor listen to their lungs. They are supposed to do airway clearance therapy two to three times each day. Heather does this once daily but they have both decided it compromises their quality of life too much, as it's already compromised, so Logan only does it when he is getting sick. Flu of any type could easily kill Heather and Logan because of their compromised respiratory functions. That is the reality they live with and that I live with, but it makes even the common cold a potentially fatal illness.

Chapter 19

Smell has the powerful ability to bring back memories. Recently, the gym where I teach aerobics got new flooring in the aerobics room. As I was walking up the stairs, I smelled the scent of the new floor. It smelled like a new doll. I was instantly taken back to Christmas morning as a little girl when Santa brought a new doll. That memory returned each time I smelled the new floor.

Smell is a sense that Heather doesn't have. Without the ability to smell, teaching Heather about grooming habits was more difficult. She had a problem with body odor if she didn't bathe every day; because she couldn't smell herself, it was difficult to convince her that she needed to shower daily, especially because showering was so much work for her. She didn't initially understand why she couldn't pass gas in public either. She eventually learned that she would have problems with people around her if she didn't take these matters seriously. Having autism made it even harder to understand other people's reactions to something she has never experienced. Also, since Heather can't smell food when it goes bad, she is concerned about eating contaminated food. She throws food away if the expiration date has passed.

When Heather was twenty-two years old, she had just gotten over a bad case of pneumonia and was doing everything possible to prevent herself from getting sick again. She decided that being on IV antibiotics wasn't much fun, so she was willing to do some of the exercises that the pulmonary specialist had shown her to keep her lungs clear. She also bought a membership to a gym and was walking on a treadmill three times a week even though walking isn't comfortable because of her ankle problems.

The IV antibiotics, along with the breathing exercises and walking had some kind of effect on her nasal passages. One day she called me and exclaimed, "I can smell!"

We couldn't believe it. She was smelling everything in her apartment, and I invited her to come over to watch a movie with me. While she was at my house,

I got out vanilla and almond extract, peanut butter, popcorn, and everything else with an aroma that I liked. Heather smelled the items one by one. We had so much fun. I sprayed my favorite perfume on my neck and had Heather smell it. She loved it. Later on in the evening, during the movie Heather asked me if she could smell my neck again. She put her nose on my neck and snuggled up close, inhaling the perfume. That was the only day in Heather's life that she has been able to smell.

Within the first three years of her life, Heather was diagnosed with a hearing loss. It wasn't easy for the hearing specialist to determine how much of a loss Heather had because she had learned to read lips so well. She seemed to understand all the words that were spoken to her, but her hearing test showed a significant loss. This was a little bit confusing.

The doctor decided to speak to Heather while holding a piece of paper in front of his mouth so she couldn't see his lips. Heather couldn't understand what he was saying. This small test confirmed that Heather was reading his lips and that was why she could understand all his words before when she was tested. It was determined that Heather needed a hearing aid. The next step was to take impressions of Heather's ears so that an ear mold could be made.

Technicians were able to make a mold for her ear and she was fitted with her first hearing aid when she was only three years old. I'll never forget the drive home from the doctor that day. Heather was in her car seat in the car as we were driving along the freeway. "Mommy, I can hear the road under the car," she said and smiled. My eyes filled with tears as I considered all the new sounds that my little girl would experience.

Heather's ears aren't shaped like the average person's ears, so making a mold has always been a challenge. Her ears are cup-shaped, the canals don't run in the usual direction, and she has many bends and folds. When a mold doesn't fit well, it causes the hearing aid to whistle. The average person gets very uncomfortable when they are exposed to the high-pitched whistle that comes from a hearing aid. Because Heather's hearing loss is in the high-frequency range, she can't hear the noise her aid makes when it is whistling.

One day when Heather was sitting in a class during junior high school, she noticed that the teacher was glancing around the room from time to time. As a few minutes passed, the teacher seemed to grow more agitated. Heather also noticed a few of her classmates looking around. They acted as if they were looking for something. Then Heather felt her ear mold slipping inside her ear, as it often does, so she reached up and pushed it into place. The teacher and students sighed. It was only at that moment that Heather figured out that everyone had been looking for the cause of the high-pitched noise. Nobody seemed to know that it was Heather's hearing aid, including Heather. We laughed together when she told me the story, but she was concerned about the possibility of it happening again in the future.

Wearing a hearing aid is made difficult both because of having cup shaped ears with no flat edge to hold the hearing aid, and because of having short forearms, no wrist rotation or full bend in both elbows and no finger dexterity. Heather and Logan must both tape their hearing aids on the hairless skin behind their ears using two sided tape. Logan can tape his hearing aid behind his ear more easily than Heather can because his arms are longer, both his elbows bend and he has more dexterity in his fingers than Heather. He can open the door on the back of his hearing aid to replace the battery while it's taped in place. It's not easy, but he can do it; Heather can't do this.

Heather must cross her right arm over her chest to the left ear where she wears her hearing aid. This overstretches her right shoulder because she must then use her left arm to press her right arm closer to her chest and push it nearer her ear. Even though she holds the aid with her right hand, she isn't able to push the aid into her ear by itself. She must use her left hand to press her right hand and arm to the get aid into her ear. She has to be careful not to catch her hair in the two-sided tape on the aid as she is taping it in place behind her ear. When her ear mold works itself loose during the day, she must perform this awkward, uncomfortable movement again to push it back in place so it won't squeal.

It would be difficult for Heather to wear a hearing aid in her right ear because even though she can bend the right elbow fully, her forearm is too short to reach her ear and she wouldn't have the leverage needed to push the aid into her ear when using her left arm because of the angle of the wrist, hand and fingers.

If the weather is hot and causing Heather and Logan to sweat, their hearing aids won't stick, so they dangle from their ear mold, still attached in their ear. This leads to annoying whistling causing everyone discomfort.

Glasses are also challenging to wear because of the absence of a normal ear and because their hearing aid is taped behind their ear. Logan doesn't seem to have as much trouble wearing his glasses as Heather does. Heather's glasses knock off her hearing aid. With the assistance of the person working in the eye glass store, the glasses can be bent so they don't bump their hearing aids but it's a long frustrating process for both Heather and the worker.

Heather was around thirteen years old when I noticed that I was repeating myself a lot more than usual. She needed to get a hearing test done. I made an appointment with a hearing specialist and while Heather was being tested,

I waited anxiously to hear the results. Then, as I suspected, we were told that Heather had lost more hearing.

Before that final hearing loss occurred, Heather and Logan had been hospitalized for two weeks to get Intravenous (IV) Antibiotics. A possible side effect was hearing loss from nerve damage. I didn't remember hearing about that possibility, but with so many surgeries and medications in the past and my earlier reluctance to question physicians, I'm not sure I would have chosen differently if I had known the potential side effects. The doctor chose the treatment because Heather and Logan had been on antibiotics for approximately nine years to keep from getting pneumonia and he wanted to take a more aggressive approach, as they do with children who have cystic fibrosis. I thought it sounded like a good idea, and since I was too naive to pay close attention to possible side effects, I went along with the idea.

After making the connection, I discussed the matter of Heather's new hearing loss with the pulmonary specialist who recommended putting Heather and Logan in the hospital for the IV antibiotic treatment. He said that he checked the charts that were kept in the hospital where they measured the amount of medicine in their system and none of the numbers recorded registered an amount that was above an acceptable level. I know now that medicine isn't a perfect science and I believe that Heather and Logan lost more hearing from that experience, but nothing can be done, so I don't dwell on it. If I did it could drive me crazy. I have learned a number of lessons on my journey and one of them is that there is very little to be gained by putting one's energy into something that cannot be changed.

Chapter 20

Writing has been a passion for Heather since childhood. She used to create stories and make little books from square pieces of paper. She also wrote plays and acted them out with Logan or sometimes a cast of paper characters she had made. In the fourth grade, she won a writing contest, and later in high school, she began to write poetry. She won the Alexander Graham Bell award scholarship for college and was twice published in books by Art Access called, *Desert Wanderings*.

When Heather writes down her thoughts and I have the privilege of reading them, I feel I understand her better. It's been a wonderful gift for me. That understanding helps me accept and support the decisions that she makes in her life. It also helps me be patient when she resists and questions the suggestions that I make for her. My ideas and suggestions to Heather in the past related to my life, as a healthy, average person and the other lives of healthy, average people that I've known and seen during my lifetime. Now I know that those kinds of suggestions just frustrate Heather. As I gain the perspective that Heather's life isn't like the average person's life, I cannot judge or criticize her decisions. I know that there are some suggestions that just aren't appropriate for Heather. This perspective also has taught me that I cannot judge or criticize the decisions that other people make in their lives, because I don't know the circumstances in their physical, mental, and emotional health that lead them to their decisions.

I believe that as a human being we are more comfortable with the normal, average life because it is what we have experience with. I believe that expectations exist because we don't want to or can't face that a person with a disability has a different reality and set of experiences, and we as able-bodied people, don't always know how to relate to that truth. Heather's writings offer an intimate glimpse into a reality that most of us never experience:

"It is hard to know when I won't be able to do something. Growing up I came across various odd things that I couldn't do or couldn't do well. Some of these include not being

able to open tight jars, open a milk carton, open plastic bottle caps when the plastic seals have to break, retrieve my socks out of the washing machine, carry heavy items or large awkwardly shaped items, write as fast or fluently as other people, play the piano, do martial art punches, and reach items off high places.

Gestures with my body, face, and hands are not the same as people with normal bodies and hands. When someone raises their hand at shoulder level, opens their fingers with palm facing another person, that is a subtle gesture of hello or goodbye or thank you or acknowledgement. I am unable to do that gesture. If someone quickly pats another person on the shoulder or back as a gesture of "I care," I can't do that, because I know it will just draw attention (instead of comfort) to my small hand and the strange feeling of knuckles and bent fingers, instead of a normal hand and palm. I can't wave hello to someone without drawing attention to my hands and the way I move them. I feel very limited not being able to gesture. I feel like some of my subtle emotions are trapped and to never be expressed, so I look like I am more cold and uncaring than another person.

—Heather Madsen

"I have learned that holding onto ideals that don't fit my own preferences or lifestyle makes me unhappy. Some of those ideals include working full time, being financially independent, and having a social life. I kept trying to do everything I could to fulfill those ideals. This led to stress and depression.

Slowly, I began to believe in my own experiences and my feelings about those experiences. I noticed what behaviors and thoughts increased or decreased positive feelings and which behaviors and thoughts increased or decreased stressful feelings inside me. Instead of picking ideals that don't fit and trying to live up to them, I reflected on what my reality was and changed my fantasy to match my reality.

When I thought I wanted to have a social life, I felt unhappy when I didn't talk to people. I began instead to notice my experience, which was that being with people too long or too often increased my stress. Conversely, being alone often increased my pleasure. I understood what behaviors and thoughts made me happy and changed my ideals to reflect those experiences. I understood that I felt more stable when I was alone for long periods and was more ready to be with people for short periods after being alone. After accepting this understanding, it became my new ideal about my personal way to socialize.

The process of this transition will continue all of my life, as my thoughts become closer to reflecting my own reality. This process is revealed as my own way of living. When I live my own path, I am a zipper that connects my ideals with my reality, and I become centered and whole."

—Heather Madsen

"*Talking with new friends on the internet, I noticed something vital missing. There was an empty connection with them and I didn't know why. I felt increasingly lonely the longer we talked. In the end, I was desperate to crawl into my emotional mother's arms and cry. I wanted her to comfort me because only she understands me. I want to be filled with caring and understanding. I want to be filled with love and knowing. I want to be filled with knowing someone is listening to who I am and acknowledging me and my interests. I wanted that intimate connection that the person would wrap their arms around me and hug me for being me.*

I want to have someone where I can talk about all the things I do every day and all the little things I study and research. I want someone who will enjoy listening to me, someone who will share my feelings of curiosity and passion. I want them to be fond of my child-self, a part of me that is strange, but innocent and whole. I want to be seen and accepted for all of me, not just my intellect. I want someone that appreciates my subtle moods and perceptions and knows what would make me feel better.

I want someone that enjoys exploring self-awareness and growth and enjoys those kinds of discussions. I want to share emotions with them, to process our experiences of life together and not always focus on intellectual stuff. I want them to share their internal thoughts and feelings. I want them to also know and acknowledge mine.

I already have the intellectual stimulation, which I provide myself. What I need is a friend that can provide the emotional connection that reminds me I am human and compassionate and shows me that it is enough to just be me."

—Heather Madsen

"*I am only defined by what I think about at any given time. So often, I forget that I look different and don't realize I live a different way. It is funny how often I look into the mirror and am surprised to see that I look different, and that I have a human form at all.*

Sometimes I will just stare at that reflection, wondering what that is I am looking at, since I could change my perception so fast and be just about anything. Sometimes I lean in closely, to stare into my eyes, wondering what is behind them or inside them — what is the energy that moves this body and shapes this form and lives each day? My mind shifts through ideas and concepts with lightning speed, trying to find the answer, but I always end up with a blank. What is that blank? I want to know; yet I know any word I use to fill in that blank is not adequate or expansive enough.

When I shape my mind to think about my syndrome, it becomes Miller syndrome, metaphorically speaking. When I am around people with typical hands and typical arms, that is what my mind sees and that is the shape it becomes. It takes effort to separate myself from my mind. I still don't know what myself is, but it is not what my mind reflects.

I do not see my autism from a social perspective very well. I do not identify with the construct of autism the way other people do, as I am not on the outside looking in to see the separateness and uniqueness that autism causes. My perceptions and perspectives and actions are guided by what resonates within me. When everything inside me and in my environment resonates together to a perfect pitch, I think that is the unity I look for and want. Is that unity a sense of myself or would a sense of myself be apart from that unity? It's a perplexing question. When the food, clothes, sounds, and sights all resonate I feel at peace. Is that peace who I am? Is that peace autism?

Sometimes I have a strong desire to reach out my hand and feel an object, to believe that object is, in a sense, real. My mind gets into a state where I feel separate from everything, including my own body. It is only a thought, though, not an actual feeling; and yet I feel compelled to reach out and slide my fingers along the top of my computer desk, trying to understand just what it is that my brain is interpreting as real. How can my brain really feel this desk underneath my fingers? What is this desk and why is it here?

Other times, I might look at my foot, wondering how I know it is my foot even though it is very far from my face and it is not my face and it is not inside my head. I will reach out and touch my foot with the same fascination as a baby might. I think if my foot were cut off, myself wouldn't recognize that it was once my foot. Is all of this a part of autism or is it just a byproduct of a strange mind?

Unlike the visibility and tangible essence of Miller syndrome, my mind set of autism is chaotic, imperceptible, and always shifting to where it is difficult for me to get a grasp on my own sense of existence at times. It is difficult for me to know how much of my other worldly thinking is due to the separation of me from the social atmosphere of the world, or if it is just a result of an intelligence process. My whole being is autistic and yet I am just me, a collection of energy manifesting itself in magnificent ways."

— Heather Madsen

Chapter 21

"At a young age, I began drawing. The desire to communicate through images extended into high school where I experimented with acrylics and oils, working in non-objective art. After graduating I recognized my fascination for the graphic arts and earned my associate degree in graphic design / multimedia from Utah Career College. The field of graphic design was difficult for me to access. Discouraged and enveloped in depression, I sold all my possessions and moved to Palm Springs to work for my uncle as an assistant landscaper. Exposure to the beautiful nature I was working with renewed my desire to paint. With my hyper focused mind, I decided to paint the side of the palm tree close-up. My vision of becoming an artist was born. I returned to Salt Lake City. A peace lily was my first flower. I painted the background a solid, bright red hue to balance the amplified greens and yellows of the stamen and stalk. POW! Visual ecstasy.

I experienced colors and textures emotionally: the same way I feel love and hate. My art defines my exaggerated senses. Therefore, I call it exaggerated realism. In my compositions, I demand the canvas to explode with dramatic color and precision. These creations are not traditional paintings, but intense portraits of nature, flooding the viewer with enriched passion. Positioning my subject asymmetrically triggers an electrical spark of comfortable recognition inside my brain— inherently creating a contemporary look.

Art has helped me to reach inside myself as well as acting as an equalizer for me in society. Being an artist has allowed me to express my unique perceptions. I've been denying that my disabilities exist for most of my life, because I want people to see the many aspects of who I am. Today I am learning to embrace my inequalities and accept reality. Yes, I am different, and that is becoming one of my strengths."

—Logan Madsen

As children, Heather and Logan loved to swim. It was an affordable form of recreation and good exercise, so we swam often. Once while visiting their paternal grandparents, we enjoyed the use of the condominium swimming pool. That pool had the beautiful view of a golf course through the white wrought iron fence that surrounded it. There was a diving board and we got to relax on soft recliners while we were there.

Heather and Logan were off playing in the pool and I was watching them. There were many other swimmers in the pool that day, but I was just watching Heather and Logan have fun. I was lying on my stomach, facing the pool. I had my sunglasses on as well as a visor.

When Logan spotted me watching him, he got out of the pool and walked over to me and asked me what I was doing.

"I'm watching you and Heather have fun," I said.

"What are you thinking about when you watch us?"

"I'm thinking that it makes me happy when you are happy, and I like watching you swim and do the tricks that you do in the water."

"When you watch us, are you thinking that those are my weird looking children?"

My heart sank. I felt so sad that he would think that, and I knew it reflected in some way, his own sense of himself as weird. "Of course not, honey, I would never think that," I reassured him.

"OK," he said as he shrugged and ran back to the pool.

Logan was around eight years old at the time, but he already had a keen awareness about his differences and what other people thought about him. That awareness made his life very difficult and still does. He experiences rejection every day of his life, and it wears on his feelings of self-worth. As much as we all like to think that we define ourselves, it is impossible to escape the perceptions of other people; those perceptions shape whether we feel good about ourselves or not.

For both Heather and Logan, this has been a struggle. It is not easy to navigate the world and feel good about oneself when people look at you as if you are an oddity and somehow less than human. Being teased and ridiculed damages a child's sense of self-worth. When other children overlook you for games, and the opposite sex repeatedly prefers someone able-bodied, and all the heroes on television are strong and physically capable, the message the disabled child receives is that he or she is inadequate. To some degree, this is even harder for a disabled child who is male, because our culture values physical strength and athletic ability in males. A little boy with a disability may not be good at athletics, and while he may possess the inner strength of a lion, his physical body may remain weak.

These issues, along with perhaps Logan's own personality and sensitive nature, made his adjustment and acceptance of his disabilities much harder than they were for Heather. This is not to say that she did not suffer or struggle, because she most certainly did, and sometimes still does. But the journey to self-acceptance has been darker and more volatile for Logan.

When action figures came into popularity, Logan collected as many as he could get his hands on. One Christmas, he received so many that his corner of the living room looked like a toy store. He was still too young to understand the connection between superheroes and physical prowess and how his disability fit into that whole equation. He was just a little boy enjoying the artistic colorful toys that made him happy.

During her elementary school years, Heather fell in love with books. She had a special needs class with a boy named Adam who always came to class reading a book. She said she was curious why he read so much. Then she discovered book fairs and the school library and learned that books were fun to read. From about fifth and sixth grades on, she was hooked on books, and spending more time in the library looking for books she wanted to read. She had an insatiable appetite for books, spending lunchtime at school, in between classes, and evenings at home reading.

Heather's love of reading has never waned. She devours books and spends many happy hours lost in them. She wrote:

"Reading in the middle of the night captures an absolute peace that permeates my being. Every cell relaxes, knowing there is nothing outside of me asking for my attention and corresponding behavior. With the darkness enveloping the city, there is no sun seeping into my skin, wanting to change my DNA. There are no people calling me on the phone and causing a piercing ring throughout the room, which requires me to dash to the request and utter words into the air, breaking my internal silence. Nothing is calling me to endure the traffic rush when I drive around the city to complete the errands I must do every week. There is only the quieting rhythm of my breath, finding its way deep inside and pushing outward again as it follows the gentle beatings of my heart. My toes uncurl and rest in the softness of the fabric, with my book propped on my legs and my back resting against the couch's embrace. I am experiencing joy created by the rhythm of reading words that fill my mind with ideas and project me into another dimension."

Heather was into anything related to science. She spent hours enjoying her microscopes, magnet sets, electrical circuit set and her chemistry set. How things work has always fascinated her. She also enjoyed chess, playing video games on Nintendo, and watching television. Heather had several favorite TV shows which she looked forward to watching as soon as she got home from school. She had a routine of getting her raisinets, spreading out her homework in front of the TV and used the television as the stimulation she needed to focus on her homework.

Heather and Logan went through a stage where they liked to roller-blade. I was always nervous when they did, because their arms were too short to catch themselves if they fell, and the roller-blades placed them high off the ground. I imagined all kinds of terrible injuries they could suffer from if they had an accident. I bought them the kneepads, elbow pads and helmets and nagged them to wear the gear. Logan eventually fell, tearing the cartilage in his knee.

There was plenty of asphalt around our home, so they had plenty of room to roller-blade. Sometimes I took them to the park where there is a sidewalk that circles the entire park. I would roller-blade with them and we had many good times.

Around the same time, they were also interested in riding bikes. The bikes placed them even higher off the ground and their hands were so small neither Heather nor Logan could work the hand brakes. Thanks to the generosity of a man whose friend owned a bicycle shop, we were able to have special back brakes installed, ones that could be applied with their legs.

Logan turned out to be very athletic and wanted to participate in sports. When he was only six years old, he showed an interest in soccer and asked me if he could play. I knew he had strong legs, and you don't use your arms in soccer, so I thought it would be a good sport for Logan. We went to a sporting goods store to pick out all the soccer gear.

Logan's best friend played soccer too. That made it really fun for Logan. They went to practices together. Logan worked very hard to be a good soccer player, but because of his lung disease, he got very tired running up and down the field, and he ran out of breath easily. After a while Logan wasn't so excited about going to the practices. I think all the activity was just too hard for him and soccer wasn't as much fun as he thought it would be.

I told him that because he made the choice to play, he needed to continue through the season. If he didn't want to play the next year, that would be fine. Logan continued playing and seemed to enjoy it. Heather and I went to the games to cheer for his team.

Logan didn't play soccer for a couple of years. He had ankle surgery that made it impossible to play. When his ankles healed, he signed up to play again. He was nine years old. Logan was a little afraid of getting hurt, so he wasn't very aggressive. He still enjoyed playing, until he got kicked in the ankle. Afterwards he was very nervous, so he decided not to continue. I was so proud of Logan for trying what he really wanted to do.

When he was eight years old, he decided he wanted to play basketball. I didn't know how to react. His hands were small, his arms were short, and his fingers didn't straighten out. How could he play basketball?

I have always encouraged both of my children to do activities they wanted to do, especially because I don't always know what is possible. But Logan's desire to play basketball worried me. If I encouraged his basketball ambitions, he might set his expectations even higher, making his limitations more disappointing. On the other hand, if I discouraged him, he might not try to achieve his goals in the future. I didn't want him to give up without trying.

I called the basketball coach of a recreational team and told him about Logan. He recommended that Logan come to the practice where teams would be chosen. If Logan decided he wanted to play, the coach would work with him. If he decided not to play, at least he would have tried.

Logan went to the practice. He was so excited when the big night finally came. He saw two of his friends there, which made him even happier. Logan lined up with the other boys who were dribbling the ball up and down the floor. When his turn came, he took the ball and began dribbling it down the court. It was difficult for him to control the ball, but he hung in there and completed the exercise. When the teams were assigned, Logan ended up on a team with his friends.

Logan looked forward to the games each week. He always played in spite of his difficulties, but as the weeks went by, he became increasingly discouraged. He realized that the other boys weren't passing the ball to him and he knew it was because they were afraid he couldn't catch it. His teammates were very supportive, but they wanted to win.

Finally, it was the last game, the last quarter and the last minute of play. The ball ended up in Logan's hands. He jumped and shot. The ball went in. The crowd roared. Logan beamed. And so did I.

When the next year came, Logan chose not to join the basketball team. I think he could sense the competitiveness of the boys his age. I didn't detect any regrets on his part, just a calm acceptance of the way things were.

Heather and Logan always enjoyed music. As a toddler Heather would bend her knees when standing and bounce to the beat of any music she heard. She loved her toy pianos, xylophones, guitars and drums. She loved anything that made music. She took piano lessons when she was in high school. That's when she learned to read music. Lacking the physical ability to play the piano will always be a void for Heather. She doesn't focus on that void, she focuses on all the things she can do and the wonder of learning about the world around her.

When she took a music appreciation class in college she taught me when she said, "The symphony is like watching a movie when you understand the music. You listen for the next surprise."

Logan would often sing along with the songs on the radio. When he was in the fourth grade, he expressed a desire to play the clarinet. I didn't think it was possible because of his hands and fingers, but I didn't say so. I knew that ideas came and went for Logan. I decided to wait and see if he remained interested in the clarinet; if he continued to mention the instrument, then I would look into the possibilities for him.

One day I was with a friend in a music store. I saw some little silver flutes. I immediately thought about Logan and Heather because they both loved music, and the flute was just the right size for them. I bought one flute for each one of them.

When they saw the flutes they were enthusiastic about trying them. They picked them up and held them to their mouths. As they tried to place their fingers over the holes, they immediately realized that they couldn't play them. Not only did they have too few fingers, but also their fingers are bent and have little movement, so they couldn't cover the necessary holes to make the different sounds. I was the one who was surprised. I didn't even think about the possibility of them not being able to play the flutes. I thought having bent fingers would work in their favor.

I realized then that Heather and Logan would be limited in what kinds of musical instruments they could play. After this unexpected event, hearing Logan talk about playing the clarinet concerned me because it didn't seem possible. I hoped his desire would pass, but Logan was persistent, so I called the music teacher at his school and told him Logan wanted to play the clarinet. I described Logan's condition to him and expressed my concerns. The music teacher invited us go to his home where he had one of each kind of musical instrument for Logan to try.

Logan tried the clarinet, but it was obvious that he couldn't manipulate his fingers enough to put them where they needed to go. Next he tried the trumpet and then the flute. He kept trying all the different instruments with the same results. Finally he used the drum pad. Yes, this instrument, Logan could play. Logan was disappointed about his inability to play one of the other instruments, but he wanted to play something, so he decided he would learn to play the drums.

We went to the music store and bought a drum pad so Logan could practice at home. At Christmastime, his school had a musical assembly, where Logan played the drums and the bells.

My sister had played the drums when she was in high school. She had a beautiful set of drums that she was no longer using, so she gave it to Logan. He practiced often and showed some interest in being in a band. He never did get into a band, but he enjoyed playing for fun. After a while he lost interest and we gave the drums to someone who couldn't afford to buy their own.

Years later, when Logan was in his early twenties and exhibiting some of the impulsiveness that would continue to be a struggle for him, he bought an expensive set of drums on credit. Because they were electric drums, they could be plugged into a headset, which meant that he could hear them while he was playing, but no one else could. These were drums that he could play in his apartment building. After getting the drums home and getting them all set up, Logan started having symptoms of allergies. He was allergic to the material used for the drum-pads. Back to the store he went, returning the drums.

Logan didn't leave the store empty handed. He exchanged the drums for a six-string guitar, complete with a case. He was so proud. He stroked the beautiful wood as he showed it to me.

He really tried playing that guitar, but after a few weeks, he realized that he just couldn't manipulate his fingers enough to play much of anything. He ignored the guitar for a couple of months, and eventually, I asked him what he was going to do with it. I suggested returning it to the store. I told him I knew the salesperson at the store would understand and empathize with him. I was sure they would credit his account.

Logan didn't want to return the guitar. I believe he was too embarrassed, especially because he had already returned the drums. No matter how much I encouraged him, he refused to return them. I even offered to return them for him, but he said no. Even though I wanted to return them anyway, I kept remembering that I needed to let Logan handle situations in his life. I wanted to respect that he was an adult and had to make his own choices. It was hard for me to let go, but I did.

Eventually Logan put the guitar up for sale on eBay. He sold it for half the price of what he had paid for it. Someone got a really good deal.

Chapter 22

Logan is naturally a very social person who loves to spend time with people. Meeting people and making new friends is difficult because of his differences. Logan spends more time alone than he wants to, and now that he is older and out of school, meeting new people is even more difficult. Because he has chronic pain that requires morphine, he lacks the motivation and energy to do what it takes to go out. Working as an artist also means considerable time alone; there are no coworkers to invite over for dinner or to go out with on weekends.

His best friend, Spencer, has been his friend since kindergarten. When Spencer had a girlfriend, she became Logan's friend. He hung out with them often on the weekends. Spencer's friendship has been so valuable to Logan.

There was a club close by Logan's house where he made some friends, but going to the club was expensive, so he didn't get to see those friends very often.

Logan once decided to place an ad on an online dating service. He and a woman from Germany hit it off when chatting online and on the phone. When it came time to meet in person, she told Logan that even though she saw pictures of him and heard him describe his disabilities to her, she was struggling with her reaction to being with someone who looked different. Although Logan appreciated her honesty, he still had a difficult time hearing this harsh and painful truth. He got discouraged with online dating, and after three months, canceled his membership. I've seen many couples over the years where one person has a disability. I know there are people that will love a person for who they are and accept the disability. I just don't know how to find them. Many single people face these challenges, but when a person has a disability, meeting a potential friend in the park or grocery store isn't as possible as when there's no disability. People are reluctant to approach the disabled.

The real passion in Logan's life is art. He became interested in drawing at a very early age. I still have some of his first drawings. When he was in elementary school, he did some amazing pencil drawings. Some of my customers bought them to hang up in their homes. My basement hair salon soon became a gallery of Logan's artwork. Today, his fine art paintings and giclee prints hang on the walls of my salon. They are breathtaking.

He continued with drawings in pencil for several years. Sometimes, he would sit quietly and draw the person in my chair or a person he saw in public. One Christmas, he decided to draw a portrait of every person in our immediate family. He collected good pictures of everyone that he wanted to draw and used the pictures to draw from.   On Christmas Eve that year, we stopped at a store with a copy machine and made copies of all the drawings for ourselves. Then we drove out to the traditional Christmas Eve party where Logan gave everyone their portrait. Everyone was astonished at the detail and precision of Logan's work. He made that one of the most memorable Christmases for everyone.

When Logan entered junior high, he started taking art classes where he learned many new techniques. His art improved, he became more detailed, and his interest grew. I found out about a good art teacher that lived close to Logan's school and arranged for Logan to take art classes from her for a couple of years; he continued to learn and develop his own personal style and techniques.

Since art has been a passionate interest of Logan's from a young age, it didn't take long for him to discover graphic art when he had his computer during his high school years. He spent many hours designing interesting patterns of art. It was because of that interest, that he pursued a career in graphic art design. After graduating from Utah Career College and having a difficult time finding work in that field, Logan found other jobs to try.

Logan paints with acrylics and oils. He likes to paint very close up, detailed views of his subject. He has a collection of flowers. The flowers are so big that the whole flower isn't included on the canvas. He really likes to paint the details that show dimensions.

Logan loves to drive. Sometimes he will drive around town for hours, just looking around and listening to music. Sometimes when he's doing art, he'll listen to a CD that inspires him, over and over. He says the music helps him leave his problems and responsibilities behind and lose himself into the world of the art piece that he's working on.

While driving around town, Logan likes to find interesting sights to photograph. Photography is another area of art that interests him. He's done some interesting work with black and white photos. One that he did for me was of a lone bird, sitting on a wire, with other wires all around him. The angles of the wires, combined with the black against a light background made the scene very complex.

I enjoy golfing and took Heather and Logan to the golf course where we could putt at no cost. Logan really liked the sport. Heather always enjoys the putting part of golf. Sometimes we went miniature golfing. The putting graduated into buying a bucket of balls and Logan really enjoyed hitting them. He really got excited when the ball went far. His favorite driving range was one that was set on a hill because if he didn't hit the ball very high, it still went airborne. He has continued to enjoy golf. Heather enjoyed the challenge of hitting the ball from the driving range too. She preferred the putting because she was good at it.

I was teaching aerobics at a gym that was within minutes of our home and it happened to be the same gym where Logan's friend bought his membership. I took the leap and bought Logan his first membership. He didn't have his driver's license yet, so he didn't go work out much. I was disappointed, but I realized I should have waited until he could drive before buying him a membership.

Logan became interested in lifting weights when his friend, Spencer, joined a new gym that was also close to our home. Logan was eighteen years old then and he had a job, so he could buy his own membership. He was going to the gym on a regular basis, along with Spencer, for about two months. I was so happy to see him working out. After about two months, Logan started getting out of the habit, usually after some kind of minor injury to his back, knees or shoulder, and eventually he quit going.

Because of Logan's physical differences, it's hard for him to figure out the best way to lift weights. Some machines just don't work out for him because of his disabilities.

I often suggested to Logan that he work with the personal trainer available to him through the gym that he joined. He could receive a few sessions free of charge and I thought a trainer could watch him work out to see if he was doing things in the safest way possible. Logan wouldn't hear of it. I think he felt like getting help would make him look and feel more disabled. He just did things the way they were the most comfortable for his body and that didn't hurt.

When Logan returned from California where he did landscaping with my brother, he expressed an interest in exercising again. He didn't have a job and was struggling with depression and I agreed that he might feel better if he could exercise. I lent him the money to join a local health club and he began working out with a personal trainer. After a couple of months his shoulder and knees began to hurt so much that he felt like he just couldn't continue.

He made an appointment with a doctor that specialized in sports medicine and discovered that one leg was shorter than the other, which makes his hips out of alignment and causes his back to hurt. The doctor recommended physical therapy, which Logan had to wait for a month to get in, and after going a couple of times Logan gave up on exercise. It's sad to see his excitement dampened so quickly for an activity that could be so good for him. He seems to have the natural interest in building his strength and size, but his body makes it hard for him to succeed.

Chapter 23

When Heather was four and Logan was only about a year and a half old, I got them their first kitten. They loved that cat. Unfortunately, the cat was run over. That was Heather's first memory of losing a pet that she loved. A year later we adopted a cat from my mother. We named her Sasha. She wasn't a very exciting cat for Heather and Logan because she was always hiding under the bed or somewhere where they couldn't find her.

Soon after we adopted that cat, Heather decided she wanted a kitten of her very own. She can be persistent and stubborn when she makes up her mind. We went to the Humane Society and found a very tiny, orange tabby. Heather named him Stanley. Stanley grew to be a wonderful pet for Heather for many years. He was a pest sometimes. He liked to chew on plastic and other hard, inviting objects. One night Heather took off her hearing aid, like she always did before she went to bed, and to her dismay, Stanley got hold of it during the night and chewed on it. It wasn't ruined, but she was very upset. She got a special little box to place her hearing aid in after that.

Logan decided that he wanted a cat of his own too. Back to the Humane Society we went. Logan's kitten was just waiting for us. It was the cutest Siamese cat I had ever seen. The face on that cat could just melt your heart. Logan scooped him up and we took him home. Logan named him China. That cat turned out to be a wonderful pet for Logan and our family.

Tropical fish came next. We got the aquarium, rocks, plastic plants, and of course, the fish. It didn't take long for the tank to get cloudy and dirty, so Heather and Logan had to clean it out. They discovered that it wasn't a job they enjoyed and after a while decided it wasn't worth the work. The fish died and we gave the tank and accessories to a second hand store. We also had hamsters, frogs and a rabbit. Logan also had a turtle, a newt and a lizard at separate times.

Logan decided that a rat would make a great pet. He got everything he needed to house a rat and then we went to the pet store. One thing about Logan was that he always seemed to want something new to stimulate him, but it didn't take long for him to lose interest and desire something else. It was no different with the rat. After he lost interest, he gave it to a friend.

That wasn't the end of rodents in our house. Logan saved up his money and bought a ferret. The cage took up a whole corner in Logan's room, and as we discovered, ferrets really stink too. Keeping that cage clean was a huge undertaking. The ferret was fun when we let it out of its cage to run around the house. The ferret liked to play hide and seek. It would run and hide and it would peek around the corner to give us a hint as to where it was hiding and when we came toward it, it would jump and run to another hiding place. Although it was fun to play with, it wasn't much interested in being cuddled. Logan really wanted a pet that would cuddle and he got tired of cleaning out the cage so he placed an ad in the newspaper to sell it.

When Logan turned eighteen and moved into his own apartment, he didn't want to take China with him because he knew China was attached to Heather and me too. He wanted a cat that would be his very own without attachments to anyone else. He went back to the Humane Society and picked out an older black cat. He liked to pick out the older cats and ones that weren't very cute, because he knew they probably wouldn't be picked by anyone else. Logan and his new cat moved into his new apartment to begin a life together.

One year after Logan moved out, Lynn and I decided to buy a home together. Even though we had been married for a year, Lynn still lived in the mountains and I lived in the city. I also thought it would be better for Heather's independence and self-esteem if she had an apartment of her own.

We only had two cats left, because Sasha, our first and oldest cat had died. Now we needed to decide what to do with them because we were all moving. I knew I didn't want any pets. I was tired of all the cat hair and didn't want the responsibility of owning a pet. Logan already had one cat, his apartment was small, and he didn't feel he could afford or handle another cat. Heather was tired of Stanley chewing up everything in sight and she didn't want the responsibility of a pet. She was feeling overwhelmed at the idea of living alone and taking care of herself.

I placed an ad in the local paper and we had two successful adoptions.

Later, when Heather and Logan decided to move in together, Logan was making a little money and decided to buy the dog of his dreams, a Chihuahua. He had always begged for a dog when he lived with me, but I knew dogs were a lot more work than cats. I knew Logan wouldn't do the work, so I always said no. One day Logan said, "If I don't get to have a dog before I die I'm going to

come back as a ghost and haunt you, because you would never let me have one."
Well, now he had one.

He named his new dog Andy, after my brother-in-law's dog. He did discover
that a dog is more work. He decided to give his cat to a friend of Heather's
which left him with only a dog. Logan took Andy to California with him when
he moved, but when he decided to return to Salt Lake, he didn't want Andy to
live in a tiny apartment. There was no snow in Palm Springs, and Andy hated
the snow. Andy had also been living with two other dogs, two cats and a pig and
could run all around in three connected yards, as well as into the house, whenever she wanted to. Logan decided to leave her there.

Logan tried to live without a pet, but he was so lonely for one that he went
back to the Humane Society to adopt another dog. He decided on a bigger dog
that time, an Otter Hound. That dog was out of control. It was a rather scruffy
looking dog, which is why Logan picked it out, and it was hyperactive. Logan
really couldn't keep up with him. After two months, Logan sent an e-mail to
everyone in his office informing them about the dog and that he was looking for
a home for it. A nice family took the dog and all ended well.

What didn't end was Logan's loneliness. When a friend told him about a new
litter of kittens, he just couldn't pass up the opportunity. He adopted one and
named it Rocky.

A few weeks later, Logan adopted another kitten that was born in the same
litter as his good friend Spencer's kitten. He wanted a playmate for Rocky, and
he could take his kittens to Spencer's house for fun. His new kitten had long
gray hair and liked to be cuddled; Logan named her Suede. Having two kittens
added extra expense to Logan's budget, however the companionship was invaluable to him, so it was an expense that he considered important.

Heather avoided the responsibility of owning a pet, but continued wanting
one. She really wanted a ferret, but already knew how much work was involved
with that. One day she called and told me that she had bought a kitten from a
pet store, and after having the kitten for two days, changed her mind. I wasn't
happy, mainly because she paid money that she didn't have, especially when she
was just doing an experiment to see if she really wanted one. I pointed out that
she could have done the experiment by adopting a kitten from the newspaper
ads and arranged to take it back if she changed her mind.

I suggested she take the kitten back to the pet store and see if she could get
her money back. She didn't feel very optimistic about the outcome, but agreed
to try. The pet store gave her back her money. She hasn't gotten anymore pets
since then.

Chapter 24

I assumed there would be some emotional difficulties as a result of Logan's disabilities; there would have to be, given the years of being stared at and ostracized. But I was not prepared for the emotional roller coaster that was to come. The physical difficulties and challenges that Logan has faced pale in comparison to his emotional struggles.

Logan was diagnosed at the age of twenty-two as having attention deficit hyperactive disorder (ADHD). The most difficult times occurred before he was diagnosed. Because the symptoms were missed when he was a child, young adulthood arrived with the full spectrum of difficulties, including a lack of impulse control, boredom, depression, and an inability to focus. Logan was also drawn to marijuana and alcohol, substances that altered his mood and numbed the uncomfortable feelings he had. As I look back on his childhood, I can identify the symptoms that might have led us to the diagnosis of ADHD sooner. With an earlier diagnosis, some of the pits Logan fell in might have been avoided.

When Logan was very small, perhaps as young as three years old, I noticed mood swings. He would get so excited for an upcoming event that he wouldn't know what to do with all his energy. When the anticipated event finally came and was about to end, he would go into a deep depression, even if activities were still in progress. Just thinking about the fun ending made Logan sad. He often commented that Sunday was his worst day because on Monday school started. He would mope around all day on Sunday dreading Monday. Nothing I could say could snap him out of his depressed mood.

Logan responded the same way when it came to doing chores. He would mope around for hours, dreading a task like washing dishes. I would try to reason with him, pointing out that he could have had the job done five times in the amount of time he'd spent complaining about it. He wasted so much energy dreading and avoiding the job that he barely had enough energy left to do the chore. He often said that it was easier to do homework at the very last minute, because the pressure he felt motivated him to get the necessary task done.

Sometimes he did things that annoyed people, like tapping his pencil on the table long after someone asked him to stop. He would start a project only to leave it in the middle and start another one. Logan really got a kick out of annoying Heather. She was often yelling at him and asking me to discipline him so she could have relief.

Completing school assignments would have been impossible for Logan if not for the individual attention he qualified for because of his hearing loss. During elementary, junior high and high school, Logan had a private tutor who specialized in helping educate children with hearing loss. Patti met with Heather and Logan every day for one class period. She made sure they understood their assignments and she helped them develop ideas for papers they were assigned. She also had projects for them in areas where hearing impaired students struggled.

Patti often had to go to Logan's teachers to get the full assignment. He had bits and pieces, but he was usually missing something. Maybe it was the due date, the topic, or exactly what the teacher wanted him to do. I thought the problem had to do with Logan's inability to pay attention while instructions were being given, as I knew children with hearing loss missed important pieces of information too. Because of Patti's help, Logan was able to complete his school years with good grades. When Logan became an adult and tried to do things on his own, he often had struggles. He no longer had someone like Patti to guide him through the steps.

Recess was usually the "class" that was considered a favorite by most children. That wasn't the case with Logan or Heather. They hated recess because they spent it alone. Heather later wrote:

"It is recess again and I am left alone as the kids scatter away from the building to their favorite playtime activity. Looking down at my shoes, I watch my feet step across the rocky asphalt and hear the crunching and popping of tiny rocks slipping out from under my rubber soles. The stiff asphalt supports my weight until I meet a soft spot, where it crumbles around the cracks. Individual pieces break off and scrape beneath my shoes, writing a script of my loneliness as I kick rocks and slide my shoes along the lonely pathway. The sound is comforting, predictable as it greets me each time the bell rings and I dodge my way through the noisy, jumbling kids, out onto the playground into the deafening silence of rejection.

Scouting the area, I wonder if someone just might look in my direction this time and invite me over to join and play. It is a hopeless thought since I know none of the kids and do not understand the unwritten rules of playground schmoozing. I hear them laugh in the distance as they compete at tetherball and race on the monkey bars. They are sharing something special. For whatever reason, I am not privileged to join.

My thoughts are my only friend. A sharp breeze grazes my skin in the cool, fall weather, chilling me as I find my usual spot on the cement stairs to sit and wait, and wonder. I watch the clouds' metamorphosis grow from a brief cheery hello to an extended ominous cover, threatening rain. Glancing at the kids, I notice which had jackets and hats on. One girl lost her hat as she moved about quickly, playing tag with a group. Another girl picked up the hat and gave it back, a gesture of friendship and comfort that I long for.

Feeling an urge from the cold cement siphoning my body heat and an increasing restlessness in my soul, I decide to go swing today. My senses alert me to flying balls and kids running without looking where they are headed, as I make my way over to the swing set. Relief grows when I near the swing set and grab the cold, metal chains. I toss myself into the swing and begin pumping, awakening my muscles to life and sucking my breath as I merge with the wind, flying higher and away.

The snugness of the seat comforts me while I glide through the air in a predictable, rocking rhythm that calms me. I close my eyes and feel the motion penetrate through me. Only after what feels like hours, do I slow the rhythm and stop the swing. In the distance, a bell rings, signaling me to join the others in a scramble for the door. I stand on my feet and say goodbye to my swing. Visualizing my countdown chart, I mark off another recess endured and smile."

Their disabilities prevented them from participating in the physical activities that other children engaged in, and Logan's friend was usually off with the other boys, participating in sports. Logan dreaded recess. He talked about how much he didn't like it and described how he would just wander around the playground wishing the bell would ring so it would be over. Sometimes, he would sit on the step and wait for recess to end. To make matters worse, his eyes got tears in them because his lower eyelids weren't big enough to cover his eyes and they would dry out. The tears would run down his cheeks and he would appear to be crying, which made him feel embarrassed and self-conscious. My heart ached when he described these experiences.

Relief came when Patti suggested that she meet with them during the recess period to have a special education class. They were both very happy that they didn't have to participate in recess anymore. During the cold weather months, Logan and Heather were susceptible to getting pneumonia, so when they didn't meet with Patti, arrangements were made for them to stay inside and read or work on their studies. This was a very acceptable arrangement to both of them.

When Logan was in the fifth grade, he had two teachers instead of just one. He began to get overwhelmed with the amount of schoolwork assigned to him. He got confused about what the assignment was, when it was due, and he had a hard time keeping track of his papers and books. He also had a difficult time sitting down and beginning the assignments. I'm surprised his teachers and I didn't recognize the signs of ADHD; he had all the symptoms.

Another area that Logan struggled in during the fifth and sixth grade was the story problems in math. He just couldn't seem to understand them. If it hadn't been for Patti's help, I don't know what would have happened. She went to the teachers and got the assignments and the due dates. She helped Logan with everything. Logan would show up in class with her, and she would sit him down and help him step by step. She nurtured him and helped build his confidence.

The homework during those two years was too much for Logan and Patti to complete during the school hours, so Heather and I helped Logan at home. I really appreciated Heather's intelligence and knowledge in her studies, especially math, because sometimes I wasn't much help in that area. Often the homework seemed like too much to expect from a young person in the fifth and sixth grade. I felt angry with Logan's teachers because it didn't seem that they worked together to balance the assignments so he wouldn't have too much homework.

Because fifth and sixth grade were so difficult with the excessive homework, seventh grade seemed easier. We were so relieved. The math that Logan did in junior high was a breeze for him compared to the story problems of the previous two years. He still had Patti's help during one class period each day so he did well in his studies.

Junior high, however, was more challenging socially. Logan had difficulty making friends and fitting in with the other students. His differences caused him great pain. Because of his outgoing personality, Logan craved social interactions. The teasing he experienced was very painful and upsetting to him. At one point we had to talk to the vice-principal about a boy who was being mean. The vice-principal talked to the boy and Logan together, and told them that if they spoke to, teased or provoked each other at all, they would be suspended. It worked. That boy didn't give Logan anymore trouble.

Logan's differences often prevented him from making new friends. He hated looking different, especially his short arms. He refused to wear short sleeves or shorts, always trying to hide his arms; he didn't like his skinny legs either.

He had been interested in girls since elementary school. His first crush on a girl in the first grade turned out badly. When she turned around and noticed him looking at her, she stuck her tongue out at him. It crushed him and he never forgot it.

Without a social life, Logan got bored and lonely. He became depressed, self-conscious and angry. He developed mood swings that were hard for all of us to live with. It was when Logan was in the eighth grade that I called Valley Mental Health, the organization that provides counseling to people with Medicaid and to low-income families.

Logan began therapy sessions with a man whom he really liked. Unfortunately, that counselor was busy and allowed phone calls and other interruptions to take priority over his scheduled time with Logan. Sometimes Logan was left in the office while his counselor took a phone call that could last as long as fifteen minutes. Other times his counselor stepped into the hall to talk with someone else. Either way, the message that Logan received was that he wasn't important. He began to dislike his counselor, and I was concerned about his self-esteem. Being treated like he wasn't important wasn't doing him any good, so he decided he didn't want to go anymore. I was disappointed, but I agreed with Logan that ending that relationship was the best choice then. Logan didn't have any interest in finding another counselor.

Because of his boredom and inability to concentrate on one thing, Logan would go from one interest to another. He got interested in a go-cart only to get bored with it a few weeks after he got it because of the necessary rules imposed about where he could drive it. He didn't want to wear a helmet, elbow guards, and knee pads and he wanted to drive it in other places than just on our property. Nothing seemed to keep his interest for long. If something did attract his interest, he would be so focused on it that soon he tired of it and never wanted to go back.

Logan passionately longed to be a grown-up. Perhaps he thought it would be easier to be in this world looking differently if he was an adult. He resented having to do things that children were made to do, and he hated being told what to do. He resisted authority figures and disliked a lot of adults.

As his anger grew, it began to manifest itself in his art. Some of drawings got very dark. I worried about him, but didn't know exactly what to do. There were some good days when he seemed happy, so I wasn't as concerned as I would have been if he had always seemed melancholy.

In high school, Logan kept a journal for a while. He read a little bit to me one day, and I was very impressed at the depth of his thoughts. He was very good at articulating himself and he had a large vocabulary. He liked words.

Logan had some very interesting behaviors and beliefs while in high school. One day he wore a long black skirt to school He also liked blouses that had ruffles on them. Some of them were like the shirts that are worn with tuxedos, and some of them had ruffles on the sleeves. Sometimes he would shop in the women's department because be liked the colors and styles better than in the men's department. He wore a hat all the time, a black beret like artists wear.

Logan later reflected on his wardrobe choices and decided that he was making people stare at his clothes, instead of at him. People's stares felt less intrusive when he knew he was doing something that made them stare. By having some control over people in this way, it made him feel more powerful.

When Logan discovered chat rooms on the internet, he met a young woman named Jessica. They chatted and e-mailed each other and after a while started talking on the phone. For his sixteenth birthday he had a party at our house and invited his best friend, Spencer, a couple of other people and Jessica. They had already met in person and liked each other. They began spending time together. Jessica was still in her last year of junior high school, a little young for dating, but she hung out at our house a lot. She came to feel like a member of our family. I thought of her as an angel from heaven. It was rare for a young woman of Jessica's age to be able to see past physical differences, and I admired her for that.

Jessica went with Logan to all his high school dances. I was so happy that he could finally participate in some of the activities that other young people enjoyed. They dated for three years. During their last year together Logan's mood swings became very prominent. Jessica was very patient, maybe too patient sometimes. Logan's moodiness caused him to be very critical of Jessica, complaining about the way she dressed and did or didn't do her make-up, and judging her personality. He broke up with her one minute and begged her to come back the next minute. Finally, the last time Logan broke off his relationship with Jessica, she found another boyfriend.

Sometimes Logan got very depressed at his loss of Jessica. For years he fantasized about getting back together with her. He believed he would do things a lot differently if they could be together again. He missed their talks and the time they spent together. I'm so happy he had the opportunity to have a girlfriend during his high-school years. It helped Logan fit in and not feel like an outcast.

Graduation from high school was the moment Logan had been waiting for all of his life. He was finally an adult. Getting interested in college was another matter altogether. He attended Westminster College for one semester, but was depressed and had no interest in taking the required courses. One day he had an anxiety attack while sitting in the library. He felt as if he had just awakened from sleep walking and didn't know why he was in college or how to do what was required. His fears and confusion caused him to drop out. After trying a couple of different jobs, Logan applied to Utah Career College and was accepted. Rehabilitation Services would cover the tuition.

He had a very good experience going to Utah Career College, where he studied graphic design. He missed a few days of school because he slept too late, but he did his homework regularly and enjoyed it the most when he was working on his own designs. He would stay at school until late into the day working hard on all his ideas. I was excited to think that we had discovered an occupation that world work so well for him.

Two months before graduating from that college, he met some schoolmates who smoked marijuana. He enjoyed hanging out with them and started experimenting with smoking it too. He felt a relief from the pressures of life when he experienced the effects of the drug. He enjoyed the illusion that everything in life was fine; no problems; no worries. He felt free from loneliness and stress. He continued to use marijuana and keep up with his studies. He graduated from that college with an Associate's Degree in graphic design.

When Logan graduated, he applied for a job that advertised for a graphic designer and was hired. The job paid well and had good benefits. Logan was consumed with happiness. I was happy too. Everything seemed to be working out for Logan.

Logan designed brochures for the business, which was work he enjoyed. Logan continued to smoke marijuana as a reward for a long day's work. It helped him relax and gave him something enjoyable to do in the evenings. On the weekends he enjoyed a few drinks with his friends. He was making money for the first time in his life and he felt confident and secure.

Some of the work wasn't the type of graphic design Logan was trained to do and was difficult for him to do correctly. He began to get frustrated. He enjoyed doing the graphic design, but other aspects of designing the information brochures for the company were just too hard. He began making mistakes in his work and didn't understand why. He also started experiencing negative effects from smoking marijuana; he couldn't wake up in the morning, and he felt depressed and unmotivated throughout the day. He began going downhill fast. Eventually he had a meeting with his supervisor and together they decided the job was a mismatch for him, and they agreed he wouldn't work there anymore.

After leaving the job, Logan wondered if the effects of the marijuana and alcohol were the reasons he made mistakes on the job or if he just couldn't do that particular kind of work. The inability to concentrate on a task that isn't pleasant and the lack of impulse control associated with the condition were some reasons that the job may not have worked out for Logan. I believe his failure to keep that job stemmed from the psychological problems associated with ADHD and autism, and that his attraction to the chemical substances was a form of self-medication. It was as if his body knew that the natural balance of chemicals was off, but of course, self-medication is a sporadic effort at best and never works out. There would be more difficult days ahead as Logan began to figure this out.

Chapter 25

"I do not participate in the social nuances of being female; makeup, dresses, perfume, etc. Most of the time I am not conscious of what people are seeing when they look at me doing things, or what they hear when I talk. I am usually just conscious and concerned with my own perspective.

I don't look at people much when I am out in public; I just focus on what I need to get done so I can go home again. I don't look at new people in the eyes, as much as I do people I know. I don't acknowledge new people that come up to the person I am with very well, if at all. I just space out, go inside myself, become quiet and look everywhere else, but not at them. For the most part, I just observe everything that is going on when I am with people, rather than participate. I can follow the thought tangent in my head, but I don't speak about it. I get lost in the visual stimuli or how my body is feeling.

Showing facial expression is difficult for me, but I can read other people's faces. Conversing with more than one person at once is difficult for me and feeling empathy for another person doesn't come naturally. Hugging, shaking hands or making a social move towards empathetic comfort is difficult for me, as well as, social celebrations and rituals, such as: shaking hands, saying hello, asking how are you, showering or not passing gas around others. I forget to ask about the other person's day and how they might be feeling."
—Heather Madsen

"I enjoy just walking, just sitting, and I want to touch surfaces and feel them. I'm always thinking about how my body relates to my environment—usually to the exclusion of just living the way an average person does—and the exclusion of feeling empathy and connection for the people around me. I can read for hours and days, without interruption."
—Heather Madsen

When Heather was a senior in high school she got a computer for Christmas. She discovered the internet and found chat rooms where people were discussing topics that interested her. Awareness of other people and what socializing could add to her life became her focus. She began to live for the time she spent on the internet talking with friends.

Having friends to interact with was a big eye opener for Heather. While it was a positive activity for her, it made her aware of how little contact she had with people in her everyday life, and she became lonely. She also discovered what people think about when they see other people. She became aware that people would have judgments about her, because she looked different. That new realization caused some depression and seemed to shake her self confidence. For the first time, she realized that looking different was going to affect her life.

Logan had always been sensitive to how people saw him, but Heather had mostly ignored people's reactions, a characteristic that we would later attribute to autism. When Heather was eighteen years old and seated in the high school auditorium for an assembly, she noticed that no one was sitting in the chairs around her. She realized that it was probably because she looked different. When she came home and told me of this experience, my heart ached. I knew this was the beginning of a long journey in reality. A couple of weeks before graduation, senior pictures were taken. Heather looked beautiful in her cap and gown. Because the lifespan of my children is something uncertain and precarious, I did not know if this day would come. Now that it had, I was proud and excited to share this milestone.

When the time came for Heather's graduation, I looked forward to seeing her in the cap and gown, walking down the aisle to pick up her diploma. That wasn't Heather's vision. She wasn't interested in the tradition. She didn't want to go to graduation. "Just mail my diploma to me," she said.

I wasn't sure what to do. Graduation is such a meaningful event for most people in their lives. Mine was for me. I discussed all the angles that I could think of with Heather and she still didn't want to graduate with her class.

Heather seemed sure about what she wanted. When she explained her reasons to me they made complete sense. "I don't even know anyone there. The people don't mean anything to me. The whole thing is long and boring. I don't want to walk in front of all those people." She made so much sense that I realized I really didn't want to spend a free evening like that either. I could think of countless things we could do that would be more meaningful, fun and give us more quality time together than the graduation production. I accepted and respected Heather's choice. We went out to dinner and a movie together. Heather, Logan and I had a great celebration.

Summer had finally arrived. That meant a break from school. Heather continued to get on the internet daily and communicate with her new friends, as well as having a carefree schedule.

Heather had been accepted to the college of her choice and she planned to have the summer off. Unfortunately, things didn't work out as she had hoped: there would be more surgery before Heather started college.

She was having problems chewing because her jaw wasn't lined up properly. Her lower jaw extended approximately one half of an inch beyond her upper jaw. She was told that she would experience severe jaw pain later in her life unless the alignment of her jaw was corrected. It was a very difficult decision to make because we knew that every time Heather was put under anesthesia for surgery it was a great risk. Her lung disease only increased those risks. Problems with her speech and chewing food didn't seem as bad as the idea of having an extensive, risky surgery.

Heather and I discussed the advantages of having the surgery. When Heather spoke, her words were getting harder to understand. We didn't know how much worse that problem would get. The probability of pain in the future was also a concern. Her lung disease and the risk to her life were terrifying. Heather felt that if people couldn't understand her when she spoke, and if she felt pain all the time, especially when she ate, how much pleasure would there be in living?

Financing for the surgery was also an issue. Because she was not yet an adult, she was still covered by her father's insurance. We didn't know if financing would be available in the future. I strongly encouraged Heather to have the surgery done before she started college and life as an adult. She was finished with high school and had the summer to heal before her classes started.

Another factor was that Heather had been wearing braces on her teeth for five years. It was time to decide if she should have them taken off or leave them on, because braces were necessary for the surgery process. We knew that if Heather decided to have the braces taken off then she might not have the financial means to have braces put back on in the future if she decided to have the surgery.

We had been in communication with an excellent plastic surgeon throughout the decision making process. He specialized in cranial facial surgery and would be the perfect doctor. We contacted him and made the necessary arrangements.

Heather was very scared about the surgery. We had talked to the doctor about giving her a sedative before she was to be wheeled into the operating room so she wouldn't be awake during that terrifying moment. Because of all the surgeries, Heather had a strong aversion to the face mask used to administer the anesthesia. Every time she went in for a surgery and the doctor moved the mask toward Heather's face, she would start sneezing and feeling nauseous. Heather wrote:

"The IV or the mask — the choice became critical in my teen years after having been exposed to the mask used for anesthesia so many times in the past. It didn't matter what flavor I chose to inhale as my body fought with the poison that entered my mouth and nostrils and always lost. Though I could not smell the flavors, the hideous onslaught of gas that invaded my face would make me gag. My saliva would imitate the repelling flavor and I'd purposely drool to get it out of my mouth until the drooling took on its own life as I drifted off to unconsciousness. It helped that the doctor would talk soothingly as he pressed the tear shaped mask on to my face, making sure I got it all. I felt vulnerable and helpless to erupting emotions I couldn't dissipate.

Fear rippled inside me while I was lying down on the hard, sterile surface. Mixed with a terrible repulsion of the gas mask, the experience would leave a psychological stain in my memory each time I went under. At home or at school, when I was reminded of the feeling of the gas going into my face, the loud beeping of the machines as it pumped the gas, and the deadening of my body, I would physically shudder and sneeze. The horrible taste would appear in my mouth and I would have to get rid of the saliva by reluctantly swallowing it and quickly get a drink of water to wash out the taste and the memory. Eventually, this experience and the thought of having to go through it again consciously in my teen years were too much for me. I would choose the IV.

Unlike the suffocating mask that played with my brain, the IV was a snake that pinched and bit my flesh as if it was ravenously hungry. The nurse often had to take a long time finding a vein. Each tap of the fingers increased my anxiety and my heartbeat would pound heavier inside my skinny body, but I dared not look away for fear of the snake pouncing without my being ready. As she found a vein to attempt, I gathered my emotions and tried to make them into a shield, but they always fell apart when the needle stung. Sometimes the nurse had to try five to eight times to find a vein. The crusted over holes were evidence of my tears. If she missed, the needle would scrape inside my flesh, biting the nerves and causing bruises, which became colorful rainbows signifying battle wounds that ran much deeper than my skin. Each time that I go back to the hospital for surgery, I must choose — IV or the mask."

Heather was also afraid of dying. During a past surgery she asked me if she could say good-bye to me before they took her into surgery. She didn't want to die without saying good-bye first. I held Heather's hand in both of mine as I looked into her eyes and thought that it may be the last time I saw my daughter alive. I tried to absorb her into my soul through my eyes. Our eyes stayed focused on each other as the doctor wheeled her through the double doors, into surgery. Tears blurred everything around me. I managed to walk to the waiting room, fall into a chair and go to a place deep inside myself to find comfort.

Because of that painful experience, we were grateful that the doctor agreed to give her a sedative right away in the pre-surgery room so she wouldn't be agitated and afraid. During the pre-surgery routine, the nurse had Heather cough up as much phlegm as she could. They were trying to get the airway clear. The nurse couldn't hide his concern about the amount that Heather was coughing up. We were already worried about the risks involved in putting Heather under anesthesia. I was upset that the nurse wasn't more discreet. The nurse gave Heather the sedative that the doctor ordered and I was hoping it would take effect soon. She was worried and scared.

Heather wasn't feeling the effects of the sedative. "I don't feel tired. I'm so scared." She became very agitated. She was terrified. I had never seen her so upset. The doctor kept telling me not to worry because the medicine caused amnesia and Heather wouldn't remember any of what was going on when she awakened. I was upset because Heather was crying and desperate. It didn't help me to think that she wouldn't remember anything when she awoke, because she was aware of her fears at that moment.

The surgery took many hours so it was a long wait. My sister, Shelli, was at the hospital with me; having her near was a huge comfort.

The doctor was going to cut Heather's upper jaw and move it forward and take bone out of her lower jaw to move it back. He was also going to cut her chin-bone in half horizontally and slide it forward to give her a chin and use two pieces of her rib-bone to make cheekbones. It was all so frightening. I was relieved when the doctor came to me to tell me that the surgery went smoothly and Heather was fine. She was on a respirator and would be for a few hours. They were also giving her morphine for the pain.

I wasn't prepared for how she would look. Heather's face was swollen to triple times the size that it was supposed to be. She couldn't talk because of the tube that went down her throat administering the respirator. She was very drugged, which was good because she didn't like the tube. She would fight it once she became fully conscious. It was a difficult few hours.

When the time finally came for Heather to get off the respirator, she could tell the doctors that she hated the morphine. She insisted that she be taken off it. From that time forward the only medication that she took for pain was Tylenol. Heather was in the hospital for several days. The swelling was so bad that she had to have a small funnel placed in her nose to let in enough air for her to breathe.

Her jaws were wired shut, so she couldn't open her mouth to breathe. Nausea was a huge concern. If Heather threw-up, she could aspirate on the vomit. They gave her an anti-nausea drug through her IV to prevent that from happening. I was afraid to leave her at all. I took food and drinks up to the hospital in a cooler and the hospital supplied a cot for me to sleep on. I stayed day and night with Heather. Nurses are very helpful, but they have other patients and they can't be there all the time.

Those first hours and days where the hardest for me. I found it difficult to eat or sleep. The fear of losing Heather permeated every hour. She was so fragile and the surgery had been more of an ordeal than I could have imagined.

Soon after Heather was conscious, she asked for a mirror. I was worried about how she would react and hesitated before giving her the mirror. And then I handed it to her.

Heather looked at her reflection, but didn't seem to know how to react. It's hard to imagine what it must be like to look into a mirror and see a different face from the one you've known all your life. Heather's face was not only swollen, but distorted, as the surgeon deliberately made her cheekbones big for her small face, so she could grow into them. She looked at her image as if trying to absorb it, but she didn't say anything.

I combed Heather's hair and styled it into two braids. She asked for the mirror again, so she could study her face some more. I understood that it would take time for her to accept her new appearance.

The nurse and I cleaned her up and decided that she had improved enough to go in the wheelchair for a walk outside. I wheeled her out of the hospital, crossed the driveway and parked by a pristine fountain. The sun was a gold disk hanging low in the sky. I took a deep breath. The surgery was over and Heather was alive and doing well. She looked so beautiful to me.

After two long weeks, there was so much swelling that it was hard to tell what she would look like in a few more weeks as the healing progressed, but she had recovered enough to go home.

One of the greatest fears I had was that she would get nauseous and vomit. If she threw up when her jaws were wired shut, there was a great risk of choking or asphyxiating. I was terrified of that happening, especially when I was at work. I made a recording that said: "This is an emergency. I need medical help immediately. I cannot speak." I recorded our address as well as my phone number at work. I said the address several times so there would be no misunderstanding. Heather would call 911 and play the recorded message.

The doctor gave me a bottle of paregoric, a medicine to ease nausea and prevent vomiting. Heather was instructed to take some even if she was only a little bit nauseous. She was told not to take any chances. Thankfully, she did not become ill during this time. The fear of losing her was sometimes overwhelming.

Wired jaws required a liquid diet, and as a result, she was losing weight quickly. We were trying to figure out what kind of high calorie drink we could make that she would enjoy. Before her surgery, Heather loved eating the sausage and cheese muffins from McDonalds. We got creative and figured out a way to duplicate the combination of flavors of the muffin and make it into a drink. I added cream of cheddar soup along with some cooked spicy sausage into the blender. Then I heated it up in the microwave oven. Heather loved it.

The other drink that was a hit was a mixture of vanilla ice cream, fresh strawberries, and cream blended into a smooth, sweet milk shake. There, she had it, a main course and dessert. We tried other drinks, but those were the only two that kept her interest enough to drink them.

I was running back and forth from the salon to my house where I could mix up a meal for Heather and check on her. I talked about my challenges to my friends, family members and customers, giving them information about the circumstances, but complaining wasn't my style. The closest I came to complaining was to say, "This surgery has been very hard." I held my emotions inside and remained optimistic.

Sometimes optimism isn't enough, and the only thing that helps is a good old-fashioned cry. One evening after I had finished cutting her hair, a customer asked me how I was doing. She has a son with mental disabilities and we had shared many conversations through the years about the frustrations and hardships that made up much of our lives. That night as we talked, I wasn't able to hold back my tears. I sobbed until I didn't have any tears left. Afterward, she expressed her surprise that I had cried. I had been doing her hair for many years and had never showed my sadness. She told me it made her feel better about her own sorrow that she sometimes felt. Often our greatest strength lies in our ability to be vulnerable, but that is a hard lesson to learn, and maybe even harder for caregivers. When so much of one's life is dedicated to the care of others, it is easy to overlook one's own needs.

Chapter 26

Heather's jaws remained wired for two months. During this time, she was writing all her communication on pieces of paper, which was tiring and frustrating for her. We were disappointed that we couldn't understand what she was saying when she tried to talk. We didn't connect the reason for her speech difficulties until Heather's drinks started leaking out of her nose. Until then, we assumed the problem was the wiring that held her jawbone in place.

When I asked the doctor about this, he admitted that he had to undo Heather's pharyngeal flap. A pharyngeal flap was a repair that was done to close the roof of the mouth so she wouldn't have a cleft palate. She had that surgery done when she was two years old, a procedure which had been quite successful.

We were disheartened to find out that the repaired cleft palate had to be undone to surgically move Heather's upper jaw forward. Not only were we now dealing with increased communication problems, but we were also facing another surgical procedure. I was upset that the doctor didn't tell us this before the jaw surgery was done. I don't think we would have made a different choice, but we would have been prepared. We were worn down from the long ordeal and it was difficult finding out that we had another obstacle when we completed this challenge.

I thought the next surgery, repair of the cleft palate, was going to be our next challenge, but I was wrong. Heather's starting college with a cleft palate was the next difficult bridge to cross. No one could understand anything she said. Her self-esteem plummeted. Starting college is daunting for most freshmen, and even more so for a student with multiple disabilities. To suddenly have a new speech impairment that made it impossible for other people to understand her words was simply more than she could endure.

Heather also struggled with her new face. When she looked in the mirror, she was greeted by a face that was unfamiliar to her. She didn't know what she thought about her new appearance. She was also confused about the reactions of friends and family members. She didn't know how to interpret comments like, "Oh Heather, you look so good" and "Wow, you look so different. Don't you just love the results from the surgery?"

Heather liked the way she looked before the surgery. She liked her face. People were acting as if she didn't look good before the surgery and that was confusing for Heather. Her cheekbones were more prominent as she lost weight, giving her the appearance of suffering with anorexia. Logan was forthcoming and said that he didn't like such big cheekbones. All these opinions made it even more difficult for Heather to adjust to her new appearance. She grew quiet and withdrawn. She spent most of her waking hours on the internet, reading and watching TV.

Heather continued to communicate through writing notes because we could barely understand her words, but this made communication cumbersome and awkward. It was easier not to say anything.

As the weeks and months passed, the time drew nearer for Heather to start college. She was scared about starting a new experience, especially since she wasn't yet over the emotional upheaval from having surgery and all the confusion about her identity. She was also upset to start college without the ability to speak.

I was concerned too, but I didn't want her to delay her education. I encouraged her to begin when the other students did. I assured Heather that everything would be fine, even though I wasn't entirely sure myself that it would be. I only knew that she would be more depressed if she spent the semester home alone. We scheduled the surgery for her cleft palate to be repaired over the Christmas break, so there would only be one tough semester to get through before her speech problem could be corrected.

The day came for Heather go to college. Because she had anxieties about driving, I decided to drive her to college.

Her battles with driving started early. She really didn't want to drive. She communicated feeling overwhelmed because of the multitasking that driving involved. How could she possibly hold so many important things in her mind at the same time? She had to keep the car between the lines, watch the speed limit, look for other cars that could turn into her path, see stop signs and red lights in time to stop as well as drive a car when she was unfamiliar with the mechanics of doing so. She was also constantly aware that she could die in a car accident at any time, or be hurt in some way. These thoughts terrified her.

I hadn't really expected this response. Later when she would be diagnosed with high-functioning autism all this would make sense. I was so excited at the idea of Heather turning sixteen years old so she could get her driver's license and drive Logan and herself to some of their appointments and activities.

She took driver's education in high school along with her classmates. She did very well with the bookwork part of the class. She knew the laws of the roads and was prepared for the driving part of the class.

When Heather had been driving with a learner's permit for the required weeks, and then some, we went to the department of driver's education and licensing for her to take her written and driving examination. She passed. She was relieved and happy, but made it perfectly clear that she still didn't want to drive.

I sold my car and bought a car that Heather felt more comfortable driving. We used that car to practice in and when she got her license, her father paid for the car and I bought myself a different car. I didn't force Heather to drive for a long time. It wasn't really necessary yet because I was still going with Heather and Logan to all their doctor appointments and there wasn't a strong need for her to drive yet. I was disappointed though. I was hoping she could run to the store and run other small errands.

Even though a year had passed since Heather had obtained her driver's license, she was still uncomfortable about driving. During her first semester, I drove Heather to college because I didn't want her to deal with any more challenges than she was already dealing with as a result of surgery.

After a few weeks went by and Heather was into a routine with college, I sat her down and we had a serious talk about her driving. I told her that I was sorry that she had so many anxieties about driving, but she had to make some choices. I had a job of my own along with helping both her and Logan, tending to our home, and running all the errands involved in life. She would either have to learn to drive herself to her desired destinations, or she would have to choose between riding the bus or staying home. I couldn't take on the responsibility of being her full-time chauffeur.

We talked about activities that help make life worth living. We discussed how important transportation to those events is and how difficult participation would be without it. Heather could see that life would be less desirable without those options and even though driving meant many anxious moments and perhaps risking her life, it would be worth it so she could enjoy having the choice to participate when she wanted to.

Heather felt like buses weren't always dependable and she knew that she didn't want to take the bus on a regular basis. She knew walking was impossible for her in most instances, so the only choice left was to drive.

She drove herself to school after that conversation. Heather has continued to experience anxiety whenever she drives, but she drives in spite of it.

Chapter 27

After my first visit to Hawaii with Lynn, it became a new dream of mine to take Heather and Logan there. When Lynn, whom I was dating at the time, offered to send the three of us to Hawaii, I almost burst with happiness. We went after Logan graduated from high school. It was the grand finale of our life together before Heather and Logan started their adult lives. It was fun having such a big trip to look forward to all year. We talked about it all the time.

During one of our trips to Kauai, Lynn had surprised me by arranging a helicopter ride over the island. The pilot made a video with music complementing the scene. The sky was a clear, beautiful blue. We had an unobstructed view of the plush green rain forest below as well as the mountaintops and valleys. I had a wonderful experience. I wanted Heather and Logan to be able to go on a helicopter ride when we were in Maui.

When Christmastime was near, I was sitting on the sofa watching television with Heather and Logan when the phone rang. It was Lynn. "I've been thinking, and I've decided that I would like to pay for you and your kids to take a helicopter ride when you're in Maui." I couldn't believe it. He really knew how to make me happy. Together we decided to keep the flight a secret until Christmas.

It seemed like forever for July to arrive, but it finally came. Heather and Logan were so excited. They enjoyed the airplane flight from Salt Lake to Hawaii, which included a movie and dinner.

We arrived in Honolulu late at night When we reached our hotel, Heather and Logan were so excited that sleep wasn't on their minds. We walked a block from our hotel to a pancake house. We went inside to get breakfast at 2:00 a.m. When we got back to our room, we quickly fell asleep.

The morning came fast, and we were eager to explore the area. We quickly got dressed and walked to the corner where there was a McDonalds restaurant.

After breakfast we continued our excursion. We found the pathway that led between two big buildings and then down to the beach. We walked along the path, feeling a little unsure about our directions, but when we reached the end of the buildings, the beach was there to greet us. We walked along the beach for a while. It didn't take long for Heather and Logan to take off their shoes and socks and roll up their pants so they could walk in the water. I could see the children within them emerging.

When Heather and Logan were young, they were so carefree. They didn't worry about what people might think when they saw them for the first time. They didn't worry about taking care of themselves. Jobs and money were not a concern. As they grew and matured, I had seen the carefree child in them slowly fade away.

As children they would go swimming anywhere. They took off their clothes, put their swimming suits on; the last thing they did before jumping into the pool was hand me their hearing aids to keep safe until they finished swimming. They didn't think about anything except their love of swimming.

Each year as they got older, swimming appealed less and less to them. That was partly because they felt self-conscious about their short arms and thin bodies and their swimming suits left them so exposed, and partly because they didn't like being deaf while they were swimming. It was also hard to get their hearing aids back into place after taking them off.

They had so much fun they couldn't wait to swim in the ocean. We walked back to our hotel room to get our swimsuits, and then back to the beach. I could barely keep up with them on our walk back; they were so excited that they were running.

As we were looking for the perfect spot on the beach, I was surprised that Logan wanted to find a place where there weren't any people. I thought he would want to watch people engaged in various beach activities. But what he didn't want was for people to watch him. We found our perfect place and set out our towels.

Heather and Logan waded into the ocean. I laughed out loud when I saw my happy, carefree children. They walked so far out on the reef that they were just little specks. Soon they were walking back toward the beach. They had forgotten to take off their hearing aids. Just like old times, they rushed back, bringing their aids to me for safekeeping, and off they went. They were laughing and playing just like they had before they became aware of adult responsibilities and all the challenges that came with disabilities. I felt overwhelmed and delighted.

As I watched them enjoying themselves, I was filled with gratitude for Lynn and for my life, for this wonderful opportunity that my children and I were able to enjoy. The intensity of the happiness was equal to the intensity of sadness that

I feel in some of life's experiences. I've learned to soak up the positive energy of good times like these to carry me through the difficult times. There will always be challenges, one after another, so I rest in between to store up my energy for the next one.

I first realized about the repetitiveness of challenges during a conversation with my eighty-year-old grandmother. She was depressed because she had been informed by her doctor that she had to start using oxygen at high altitudes. She was disappointed because she wouldn't be able to travel anymore. No more airplanes. She had been experiencing challenges for years with her heart, so her older years had already been full of problems. Somehow this one came as a surprise and disappointment. When I heard her describe how she felt, I suddenly realized that challenges will never end. That is when I made the conscious decision to enjoy the breathers between the difficulties. I let go of the worries about what may happen and live by the adage, "Cross that bridge when you get to it."

After we left the beach, we headed back to McDonalds for lunch. We were having so much fun in Honolulu that we didn't want to leave, but we were scheduled to fly to Maui in the evening. We returned to the hotel to pack and headed for the airport.

When we arrived in Maui it was dark. We got in our rental car and drove to the condominium we were renting for a few days and went right to bed.

The next morning I was awakened at 5:00 a.m. by a flock of loud birds that had all landed in a tree near my open window. I was still tired but excited to have arrived in Maui. I was looking forward to showing Heather and Logan the beauty of Maui. We had a quick breakfast and headed for the beach that was a little walk around the corner from our condo. We found a perfect spot and decided to walk back to our condo and pack up our beach things, as well as make our lunches. Because we had so much to carry, we drove the car the short distance to the parking lot located next to the beach. It was a windy day, and I was grateful to have such big umbrellas to help block the wind. Once the umbrellas were situated, our day at the beach was perfect. Later that evening, Heather and Logan discovered pina colada drinks and loved them.

We got up early the next morning and got ready for our helicopter adventure. As we lifted off the ground, the music playing on the CD matched the sensation of taking off. It was incredible. The sky was a brilliant blue, and we had a clear view of the rain forest in Hana. The pilot said it was unusual for the sky to be clear of clouds over the rain forest. I felt very lucky to have such ideal weather. The whole experience was magical. I bought a video of the flight, and we still enjoy watching it.

After our flight, we drove around the area by the heliport to see all the beautiful sights in that area, because our condo was on the other side of the island. We saw the lava fields, Big Beach, and the area where surfers ride the big waves. When we had seen the main sights, we drove back to the condo, cleaned up, and then went out on the town. We visited art stores and coffee shops. It was a warm summer evening in Maui. We had a great time.

The next day Logan and I took Heather to a snorkeling spot that had beautiful scenery. The trees grew in an arch over the pathway leading to the ocean. Heather was so happy. Logan and I snorkeled, and we all had lunch. It was wonderful. That evening around 5:00 p.m., I talked Logan into going snorkeling again. Heather decided to stay at the condo and relax. It was later than I like to snorkel because I get cold, but I had a feeling we would see turtles if we went late. We jumped into the cold water and started paddling. It wasn't long before we saw three turtles. One was very large, and the other two were a little smaller. I was so excited I practically burst. Logan was thrilled, too. After taking underwater pictures and enjoying the view, we left the area to go back to the condo. We were excited to tell Heather about the turtles. She was happy we got to see them and was looking forward to viewing the photos we took.

Logan and I enjoyed grilling fresh fish outside our condo every night, while Heather watched from the window of the condo. I enjoyed introducing Heather and Logan to the tastes of the different fish caught around the Hawaiian Islands. Logan and I sat at the grill together and talked while the fish was grilling.

Our last night was rushed when I discovered that our flight back to Salt Lake was earlier than I thought. We quickly packed our bags and dashed to the airport, arriving just in the nick of time to catch our flight. We had a wonderful trip.

Chapter 28

Logan's first job was working at Hogle Zoo during the summer of his sophomore year in high school. He worked at a cash register, which required taking customer's money and giving them back the correct change. At the end of the day when Logan balanced his till, it was consistently short or over. He didn't understand why this kept happening. Perhaps it was because he was distracted with self consciousness because of his small hands. People would put the money in his hand and coins would drop, causing him embarrassment.

Next, Logan went to work at a call center with two of his friends. This was a job he didn't want to do long term. Phone calls are difficult with a hearing loss and a hearing aid.

Logan's next experience job hunting was at the mall near our home. He really wanted to work in a framing store that also sold art. There was a big "Help Wanted" sign in the window and Logan applied. During the interview, he was told that they had already hired someone for the position. The sign remained in the window for weeks. I couldn't help wondering if the owner didn't hire Logan because of his physical differences. That possibility distressed me. I was not only concerned about Logan's future career possibilities; I also worried that the rejection would further damage his self-esteem. So much of a person's identity is based on the work they do, and without this, I feared that Logan's sense of self worth would be harmed. The ability to provide for oneself is a fundamental need, and is especially linked to self-esteem in males. I knew how vital a job was for Logan, and it frightened me to think he would be unable to find work because of people's biases against him.

Rather than torture myself with these worries, I tried to focus on the goodness in people. I chose to believe that there were many wonderful people out there in the business world that would love to give Heather and Logan the opportunity to work and that those people would appreciate them for their abilities.

I had a strong sense that Heather and Logan would go further in the world of work if they had some kind of formal education. I felt that people would automatically think that they had mental disabilities along with their physical disabilities, and a college degree on their resumes would prove that they were mentally competent. I was disappointed that Logan's college experience didn't work out. Later Logan was diagnosed with attention deficit hyperactive disorder, ADHD, and in 2006 PDDNOS (autism), which explained some of the obstacles he faced.

Logan got a temp job with a mortgage company. He was filing, faxing and copying documents. He liked this kind of work and was offered the job full time.

At this time I wondered if he would be better off finding a career where he could use his artistic talents.

Logan had his own computer when he was in high school, and because he often created art on the computer, I could see that a career in graphic design was a real possibility for him. He had often communicated that he didn't like the computer; however he spent hours and hours using it for art. I tried to find out about an education for Logan in graphic design.

I gave Logan some information I gathered about a graphic design course offered by a local technical college and left the rest up to him.

Logan took the ball and ran with it. He not only made the call, he made an appointment as well. He met with the enrollment person and filled out the applications. Logan didn't ask me to go with him to the school. This is something he wanted to do on his own and I knew it was important to let him do it. He went every day, five days a week, for eighteen months. I went to his graduation. It was an exciting accomplishment for Logan, and I was ecstatic and proud.

After graduating in October 2004, Logan answered several ads that were looking for someone in graphic design and was hired by a large company that had a wonderful reputation as a good employer. Logan was so excited about his new job, especially about the hourly rate that he was going to be paid, which gave him more money than he had ever had in his life. He was feeling secure, self-confident and happy. Because he earned his own income he could purchase his own cigarettes, alcohol, and marijuana which enabled him to self-medicate. That made it hard for him to wake up in the morning and impaired his ability to do his job.

When Logan was attending college, his dad promised him that when he finished school, he would buy him a computer. So Logan called him up and asked him to deliver. His dad had never mentioned how much money he was willing to spend on the computer, and Logan had his heart set on a Macintosh. They are more expensive, double what other personal computers cost, so they discussed all the details and Terry agreed to pay half.

Since Logan's credit was good, he charged the computer and worked out an arrangement with his dad, where each would pay one half the monthly payments and have it paid off within the six month period during which interest was charged at a very low rate.

The job didn't last. Logan was having problems focusing and the self-medication he was doing made it worse. He was also experiencing bouts of loneliness along with emotional and physical ups and downs. He was called in for a review and his employer and he agreed it was a job mismatch, as much of the time the job wasn't the type of graphic design Logan was trained to do. Logan made mistakes doing the tasks required of him. To this day, Logan doesn't know if it was the effects of his emotional instabilities that prevented him from being able to do the job or if he really couldn't do that particular job, but he was no longer employed after that meeting.

Logan felt overwhelmed and depressed when he thought about getting another job. He had begun to form negative associations about work and responsibilities. Because of his emotional imbalances and self-medicating, he wasn't able to wake up on a schedule. He could see that patience and persistence throughout an eight-hour day was also a problem for him. Anxiety remained a constant battle for him. The demands of a full-time job in a traditional setting were more than he could handle emotionally and physically. Having smoked marijuana regularly for a year and having autism, but not knowing anything about how autism affects his life, the concentration, self-discipline, and physical stamina required, pushed Logan beyond his limits.

Since he didn't have any money, his dad gave him the remaining money that was going to be used to pay for the computer. Logan used that money to live on, a choice that left him in debt.

Logan wanted to be independent and needed to pay the credit card company. He went back to reading the want ads. He applied at a company that advertised for a graphic designer and was hired. The company was selling seminars, CD's and books in the area of self-enlightenment through listening to subliminal sounds heard through new age music while meditating. They had Logan making signs, brochures, flyers and designing their website. He really liked the work.

The management invited Logan to secret parties called a raves. These parties had the risk of being busted by law enforcement authorities due to the large use of the street drug ecstasy and marijuana. Logan had fun at the raves because of the music, stimulation and socializing he experienced. Part of his job was scouting out the locations where the raves would be held. This is where the company introduced prospective customers to their meditation CD's. Unfortunately, they didn't have enough graphic design to keep Logan busy so they had him painting walls and other chores around the office, just to keep him busy. Logan began having a hard time with the management because the company also required Logan to attend their seminars, listen to their tapes and read their books, without paying him for the time he spent doing it.

After several months of employment, during a company meeting to brainstorm ideas for improving the business, Logan's pent up frustrations affected his perceptions and how he communicated them. (We now know autism affects perceptions and communication.) He felt like there were discrepancies in their definition of how patrons should interpret personal experiences during their meditation. Logan confronted a manager at a meeting and offered suggestions on the ways he felt they could work together to make their business better and make relationships run smoother. Although one would think that a company that encourages open communication and honesty would welcome this approach, they were not at all receptive to Logan's feelings or ideas or the way he was expressing them. After expressing his thoughts, Logan was fired.

Logan's next job was working for a company selling satellite television. He answered the phone when prospective customers called and informed them of all the different packages and prices that the company offered. He made decent money, but he just couldn't do that particular job all day long, day after day.

When Logan needed money between jobs, I paid him to clean my house. That kind of work was very hard on his back and he didn't like it, so that arrangement didn't last long. He also did some work for me at my business. He called my customers each week to remind them of their hair appointments, filed their cards and cleaned the area where I work. I really enjoyed having these tasks done, however, Logan said he felt like a "loser" in the eyes of my customers by working for his mother. I didn't feel that way about our arrangement, but I could relate to how he felt. Children want to be independent when they reach adulthood and working for one's mother doesn't accomplish that feeling. I did not try to talk him out of quitting when he decided he had had enough of working for me. His self-esteem mattered most of all to me.

Logan moved to Palm Springs at one point to work with my brother and his partner in their landscaping business. Logan was very excited about this opportunity to leave home and head out on a new adventure. They expected him to work hard and Logan enjoyed the physical labor, but before long his back, knees and whole body began to hurt. He felt defeated. Eventually, his depression set in and he couldn't even get out of bed.

Even though the experience wasn't long-lasting, some aspects of working in the landscaping business had been positive for Logan. When he moved back to Salt Lake, I could see that he had learned and grown so much. He saw what was needed to be done to do a job and he did it. He cleaned up after himself and kept his apartment orderly.

Logan wanted to be independent, but didn't know what work he would be able to do. Jobs involving physical labor took a toll on his body. Other jobs he had held either bored or frustrated him. One day I asked him the simple question: "What can you see yourself doing on a regular basis that you love to do?"

He didn't need to think about his answer. He summed it up in one word: "Paint." I really didn't know anything about a career as an artist, but I knew Logan had talent and I knew he loved art like nothing else. My goal was to do all I could to support his desire and talent. Money could be an obstacle, but he usually just needed one item at a time so the expenses were spread out over time. I bought him several canvases, along with the paint and supplies that he needed to get a good start.

We found an art gallery called Art Access, a group that promoted artists who had a disability or artists whose art showed a social issue, by displaying their work in the gallery. They required ten completed pieces of art, along with a description of the artist and some comments concerning what inspired them. They accepted new applications on July 1 for the work they would show the next year. Logan made it his goal to meet the necessary requirements and enter.

He completed six acrylic paintings. Five measured 16x20 and one was 24x30. I bought two of his paintings. He wanted to paint a much bigger picture, so I bought him the canvas when it was marked on sale. That canvas was approximately 36x48. He was excited to get started. One thing he didn't realize was that he would get bored from working on the same project for so long. Painting on such a big canvas required so much of his time and focus that he would lose interest for several months at a time. He wouldn't allow himself to start anything else until he finished that painting, so he would go long periods without doing any art at all. The deadline for entering his work with Art Access came and went.

In September 2002, I suggested that Logan look into education again. We met with his counselor at Salt Lake Vocational Rehabilitation Services, (Voc Rehab) and discussed Logan's talent in art and how he wanted to create a business for himself marketing his art. Judy, his counselor, suggested an education in marketing.

Logan studied different aspects of marketing and wrote a proposal for Judy. She was very supportive. As she interviewed Logan, they discussed his lifestyle and habits. Together they decided that Logan needed to stop choosing to self medicate for his emotional problems before he could start an educational program. She suggested that Logan be free from mood altering substances for at least three months and then come back and talk with her. During that three months Logan did work on self-discipline in support groups and counseling. The more Logan thought about the realities of studies, the less he could see himself being motivated and self-disciplined enough to go through the vigorous program.

Logan's interest in graphic art continued and he tried hard to find a job in that field. The market seemed to be saturated with graphic artists and the work was difficult to find. Logan had an associate's degree and employers wanted a bachelor's degree. None of the local universities would recognize the credits that Logan obtained from Utah Career College so he couldn't continue his education using those credits towards a bachelor's degree. He didn't want to start all over from ground zero, so he didn't continue. Logan found a job in data entry. The knowledge that he gained at Utah Career College has helped him in many areas when using the computer, including making him comfortable working on them.

Logan worked for eighteen months doing data entry for a mortgage company. He created an impressive training manual the company used to train new employees when they were hired to do the same job. He also knows many different programs, so he helped me out with the financial programs and accounting for my hairstyling business, designed my business cards and fixed problems with the computer. He had long wanted to build his own computer, an opportunity that finally came to him when Heather got a new computer for Christmas. He used Heather's old computer to successfully build himself a computer. I was amazed.

But his passion for art never waned, and he would soon find himself returning to the canvas and to the life of an artist.

Chapter 29

"I find the seesawing action of my ability to write and the anxiety that comes with it very frustrating. Otherwise, I'd probably be further along in my writings."

—Heather Madsen

"I love to see my writing when it's finished. It's crisp and delicious to me. I am always very surprised at what I created. It's hard to believe it comes from me, knowing how I struggle with expressing language. It is ironic that I can have such talent in expressing ideas in the written form and yet stumble so greatly during the process that it's nearly torturous to write at times. Sometimes writing can flow in the most magical way, providing an addicting tonic to the chaos of the mind. This keeps me writing."

—Heather Madsen

Heather received a partial scholarship to attend Westminster, a small private college near our home. Rehab agreed to pay for the rest of her tuition and books. To keep the scholarship Heather was required to attend full time and maintain a 3.0 grade point average.

The first semester of college was challenging for Heather due to her jaw surgery, however she was able to focus on her studies and pass her classes. Sometimes she would get overwhelmed and ask, "Why am I doing this?"

My answer was always the same. "Because when you apply for a job and they see that you have a college degree they will know that you are intelligent. They will not think that you are intellectually challenged just because you look different and you will be able to get a better job, making more money and having good benefits." When that answer didn't seem sufficient, I would add: "Heather, it has to be college or get a job. Do you want to get a job instead?" That question usually ended the conversation, but only for the moment. We had that discussion at least one time every semester.

Even though she faced many challenges, Heather has always been fascinated by learning. She is a thinker and is introspective. She did so well in her philosophy class that her professor asked her to consider it as a major. She loved math and science, as well as psychology, and choosing a major was difficult. I noticed that psychology seemed to hold Heather's attention the longest so I encouraged her to choose that. I felt it was important for her to choose one and move on. I had heard the term "professional student" and I could see Heather going in that direction. Heather chose psychology.

Opportunities for work experience were available to Heather at Westminster. She volunteered to work in the library where she read letters written to the library and then summarized them for others. She enjoyed that kind of work because it required reading, thinking and writing.

During Heather's fourth year at Westminster she decided to finish her education at the University of Utah. She could attend part time; a slower paced schedule was just what she needed. Even part time got to be stressful when finals rolled around. Heather had difficulty handling stress.

During her last semester, Heather did some work in the psychology department. She was watching videos of mothers interacting with their children and making notes about what she observed. There were certain complications about the mechanics of doing the job, such as where the video monitor was in correlation to the controls, the volume level and clarity of what Heather was listening to and the sunlight that reflected on the monitor screen. Heather felt shy about talking about the problems she was having with her professor. She would discuss them with me first and then I would encourage her to talk to her professor. She finally did and the problems were addressed. These experiences helped her learn how to reduce stress by addressing the source of that stress when and where she could.

Heather worries about repetitive stress syndrome in any job. Because she already has physical limitations and constant discomfort, she doesn't want to suffer more. Most of us don't give this any thought, but in nearly every job there are repetitive physical movements that could cause some kind of side effect after years of doing them.

After graduating, Heather decided to get a job in a county library as a book shelver. That person checks the books in and places them on the shelves. Heather found out very quickly that the job was too physical for her. She couldn't push the heavy carts that were loaded with books and she couldn't reach any shelves that were above her chest. She doesn't have good balance so standing on some kind of ladder wasn't an option for her. Also, she has problems with her knees and back, and putting the books on the lower shelves required bending and kneeling. After doing the job for one day, Heather chose to quit

During her college experience, Heather did volunteer work teaching adults how to read. She worked with one male adult who was illiterate. She had to take some training courses on how to prepare the lessons and in what order to teach the principles of reading to her student. She was diligent about preparing her lessons and taking the time to do it well. When she and her student got together, she was disappointed when he hadn't done his homework and wasn't quite sure what to do about it. Sometimes he would bring a novel with him and tell Heather he wanted to read that. It seemed to Heather like he wanted to skip all the basics of reading and jump into reading automatically. Heather was frustrated with the job and she also got sick just before her six-month commitment was up with the organization. She had to resign.

The man she was working with was so happy with Heather's teaching methods that he offered to pay her for individual lessons; however, he found that he was just too busy to do the lessons and he felt like he would waste Heather's time and his money. That experience taught Heather that she loved teaching when working with one person at a time.

Having had that experience to put on a resume, Heather applied for a job with the Granite School District. Her strengths and education background were matched up with the needs of a teacher and she was called for an interview. She wasn't sure she was ready to work on a regular basis, because her health was inconsistent. She had recently been diagnosed with a sleep disorder and was constantly fatigued. The main reason she filled out the application was because she was feeling pressure from her dad, her counselor at Utah State Voc Rehab and me. She agreed to try, and if she couldn't do it we would know conclusively; she would know as well.

Heather got a phone call from the district about a job as a teacher's aide. The class was special education, taught in a junior high school close to Heather's home. Heather was hired. I was so excited. I kept thinking about how wonderful it would be if Heather liked the work and was able to keep up with the demands of a regular work schedule. I thought about the regular paycheck and benefits and felt excited at the possibility that Heather could accomplish that in her life. Heather was reserved and anxious about all the unknowns and worried about her physical limitations.

Registration for the students was a couple of days before school started and Heather was required to be there to help out. She arrived first thing in the morning. She called me during her lunch break to let me know she was miserable. I wasn't sure what to say. I didn't want to pressure her into doing something that didn't feel right, but I didn't want to make it too easy for her to give up on a job that could work out. New jobs are often overwhelming at first for anyone. I encouraged her to talk to the teacher after school.

After speaking to the teacher, Heather decided to give it more time. She told Heather that she had never taught a special education class and she was a little nervous herself. There wasn't a set curriculum for the class and she didn't know what to expect either.

The day before school was to begin Heather felt convinced that the job definitely wasn't for her. She knew herself well enough by then to know she would not be able to work one on one with another person all day long, day after day. The environment was more suited to someone outgoing and gregarious. Heather was more introspective and introverted. She relished solitude and quiet and knew she would be happier in a position that was behind the scenes, like a research job, an editor, or a writer. She called the district and informed them she wasn't suited for the job.

In the end, the whole experience was an excellent learning opportunity for Heather. She learned what type of environment and situation she would look for in a career in the future and faced her limitations about working closely with people all day. This was all a part of the process of self-discovery for her. Sometimes finding out where a person is happiest means first eliminating those places and situations that make one miserable or uncomfortable.

Now that she understood more of what she wanted and didn't want in a position, Heather worked with a job coach from Voc Rehab. I thought the job coach would arrange for Heather to do some job shadowing in areas where she had interest, but that didn't happen. Her job coach gave her moral support more than anything else. She also taught Heather how to write thank you notes when she was granted an interview for a job. Other than that, her coach simply looked in the newspaper and on the internet for jobs that might interest Heather. These were tasks that Heather could do herself.

Heather applied for a job at the University of Utah doing research in the Psychology Department. She was still working with the job coach, so they went to the interview together. When they arrived Heather noticed a loud noise in the area where they were to meet. Her job coach couldn't hear the noise, however the noise was so loud to Heather that she couldn't hear or concentrate. When the time came for her interview, they had to request going to a different area to conduct their business. Her hearing aid picks up silent alarms or signals that are emitted by certain types of alarms, including ones at airports and the devices plugged into electrical sockets to keep away bugs and rodents.

The person interviewing Heather said that another person who wore a hearing aid also heard the noise; that person learned to tune it out and work anyway. Heather said she didn't think she could do that and said that she would have to work in a different area. It was discouraging, because Heather was very attracted to that particular job and felt like she could do it and enjoy it. It was the only promising position she had found in her search for employment. She didn't hear anything back from them. When she called to inquire, she was told the department was still trying to decide if they could afford to hire anyone at all.

At one time, Heather thought she would work with small children. During her last year of college, she had the opportunity to do classroom observations in a program serving children with autism. She enjoyed working with the children, but children with autism can be a handful physically, and Heather was concerned about her ability to do the physical tasks involved with working with special needs children. It was also very apparent to her that small children get sick more regularly than adults, and when Heather gets a cold it often develops into pneumonia. Those risks keep her from pursuing a career involving young children.

Job hunting is stressful for most people. The anxiety Heather experienced was magnified because there were so many variables for her to consider. She had real concerns about her physical limitations; many jobs require physical abilities that Heather does not have. She experiences pain simply performing routine physical activities; at home she can vary her routines to accommodate her pain, but in a job situation, tasks are expected to be performed according to the work schedule. Because of her unstable health and sleeping patterns, she just doesn't know from one day to the next how she will feel and how much energy she will have. She was getting worn out from reading the want ads every day and worrying and obsessing over what kind of job she could do. She wasn't enjoying her life at all and was miserable. She felt like she needed a break from all the anxiety and worry that she was experiencing, so she stopped looking for a job.

After a while, she felt pressured by all the people around her that didn't accept her limitations and had expectations and hidden agendas for her. She applied for a job that involved going into homes of people with different kinds of disabilities to help them in some way. She was hired immediately and was scheduled for a series of training sessions.

One of the sessions was CPR training. She was required to be certified to work with people. Heather discovered that she was physically unable to perform CPR. The organization couldn't afford to send Heather on a job with another employee every time, and since Heather felt like she didn't have the physical and emotional ability to do the job anyway, she resigned. Her employer agreed with her decision and seemed relieved that she didn't have to deal with the touchy situation anymore. Heather admitted that she had doubts she could do that kind of work when she applied, that she had made the effort because she just felt pressured to show people in her life that she was willing to try. She felt she needed to prove to them, and to me, that she really couldn't do the job.

I began to accept Heather's limitations more than ever before and developed a new respect for her. She knows herself better than I, or anyone else, could possibly know her. I began to trust her to know what is best for herself. I decided to accept the possibility that she may never hold a traditional job. The truth is that Heather expends more effort and energy taking care of her own health, personal responsibilities and doctor appointments than many people devote at a full-time job. Accepting this reality has brought us both peace.

Chapter 30

Heather has always been introspective and is able to make more sense of the world through written words. In an essay about writing, Heather addresses her relationship with words this way:

"I am interested in writing about my different perspectives dealing with my life experiences. I would like to write about my experiences with a hearing impairment, physical differences, a lung disease, my passion for learning and knowledge, and my seemingly "unique" way of thinking. I'm also interested in writing about my philosophical conclusions drawn from those perspectives.

My objective is to present my unique perspectives and enlighten other people about different ways of experiencing and perceiving life.

I also like exploring words, sentences, and the ideas resulting from various combinations of them. I enjoy reading and writing poetry, to taste words and experience humor. However I'm not very good at humor yet.

There is one major obstacle I have to contend with. I am afraid of writing, or rather, I have trouble getting my thoughts organized on paper and this causes me anxiety. I failed three upper college classes—two philosophy classes and a history class—because of this anxiety and difficulty of putting together ideas.

I had to write a paper on Nietzsche and one on Heidegger, coming to a conclusion about one of their main points and finding supportive evidence of my conclusion in their writings. I really wanted to write these papers, but I couldn't figure out how to start, despite my ability to understand them in class.

I'm not quite sure what the difficulty is. I think it's hard for me to get the whole of a concept and the details of the concept together in a coherent piece of writing. It seems my grasp for calling up language has only two switches: painfully slow and disorganized or very flowing. It feels like the language "faucet" in my brain will either be set on drip or full blast. The chasm in-between is even greater when I have to talk, hence my silence in and after class where it's on drip."

—Heather Madsen

Heather and I decided to take a writing course together. Since I was in the process of writing this book, I knew I could also benefit from any class about editing or writing, and Heather was interested in developing her skills as a writer.

I signed us up for an editing class at the University of Utah. We attended class one evening each week for six weeks. After completing this course, we were hungry for more.

We signed up next for a creative writing class. Our instructor had so much excitement about life and writing, and his energy was infectious. He offered to be available to mentor anyone in the class who was interested in developing further. Heather and I took him up on his offer right away, bringing a collection of our work to the second class. Heather is writing more now and I'm excited to include some of what she has written in this book.

Because of Heather's love of reading, she volunteered again for The Literacy Center. They didn't have a student for her to teach then, but they did need help writing their newsletter. Heather was excited at the possibility of writing for them and offered her assistance. Her supervisor gave Heather a pile of papers, along with a deadline of when she needed the entire job done. Heather took the pile home where it sat. She felt like it was screaming at her every day to get started.

Heather was just recovering from several months of pneumonia, with a fever every day during those months. She realized she wasn't prepared for such a big job and her anxiety increased at the whole idea of letting the woman down by not doing the work. Finally, Heather had to call the center and tell the woman that she had overestimated her abilities and wouldn't be able to complete the task after all. The woman was very understanding and the experience ended on a positive note. Heather continues to think about writing for groups where she has direct interest in the topic and feels she could positively influence other people, but she also faces obstacles and stress:

"I have struggles around the act of writing. These include poor recall ability; a small expressive vocabulary; poor creativity access; limited experiences and not knowing what to write about. While I can improve these areas and already have started, my success at dealing with these issues and becoming a writer (paid or not) is uncertain and that makes me want to reject the whole idea. I don't know how to embrace an uncertainty like this."

—Heather Madsen

Two years after writing about her experiences in looking for employment, Heather was diagnosed with high functioning autism. The diagnosis was an explanation for so many of the struggles that she had faced and still faces today.

She continues to write and has hopes of finding work someday as a writer. Until then, she works hard every day taking care of the demands her body places on her. She has a regimen of different kinds of physical therapy and going to doctor appointments that consume much of her time, and is probably something few people think about unless they themselves contend with multiple disabilities or illnesses. Maintaining a healthy body takes the average person a minimum amount of time each day, but for the person with health issues and disabilities, keeping the physical self going becomes a persistent and continual task. Heather also continues writing and meditating to keep down her chronic stress levels. She makes an effort to have regular sleep and dietary habits, and spends spare time exploring hobbies and other interests to help bring positive experiences and pleasure into her life.

Chapter 31

Terry and I worked out an agreement to help pay the expenses that Heather and Logan incur that are legally acceptable for us to pay. We are not allowed to pay rent, utilities, food or clothing or it will be considered income to them and they would not be able to get Medicaid or other help from the government.

I have a continuous challenge of making the decisions of what to help them with, what to do for them, and what to let them do for themselves. Sometimes when the tunnel seems very dark to them, I like to do something for them to give them a light and remove some of the burden. Before Logan's diagnosis and subsequent medical help, he had some personality behaviors and mood swings which he could not control that caused him to get into charge card debt. He was employed with his first good job and he decided to charge a new computer. The plan was to pay it off in six months before the interest rate moved to twenty-one percent. Three months later he got laid off. He was broke. As a result, Logan still had a large balance on his charge card. He was being charged late fees and over the limit fees as well as paying the highest interest rate. He had another card that was at its limit as well. He found himself in a mess, financially and emotionally.

Logan's uncle offered him an opportunity to start over in Palm Springs, California. Before he left he spent what money he had unwisely. If he really needed something then I would buy the item, but I tried to make my choices carefully. I felt stressed and worried about everything that was happening. I finally decided I had to ignore what would happen to his credit rating if he couldn't pay his bills. I had to let that be his problem. He lived in California for two months, but because he hadn't been diagnosed and didn't have the necessary medication and counseling, his problems got worse.

When Logan moved back to Salt Lake he seemed to have learned some lessons. He showed more appreciation for Heather and me by treating us with respect and seemed to enjoy being with us. He got counseling to help manage his mood swings. He was trying to paint while he looked for a job. I was so happy to have him back. I was thrilled that he was trying to get his life in order. I could see his potential. The trouble with seeing his potential is that sometimes I made decisions based on potential instead of actions.

Logan had been irresponsible with money. If I lent him money by paying his charge card and allowing him to pay me back with the lower interest rate that my card company charged and without the late fees that his cards charged, would I be enabling him? Sometimes I couldn't see the line. My charge card company had informed me that I could get money at an extremely low interest rate for the life of the loan. I made the decision to get money from charging it to that card and paying off Logan's debts; he would pay me back.

When the check arrived I had second thoughts about my decision. I didn't want to tell Lynn about my decision because I was afraid he wouldn't agree, but it went against my nature not to share this with my husband. I struggled with my decision. When the check came I was perplexed. I decided to talk with Lynn. I really needed his perspective on the matter.

Lynn had a great idea. He suggested that I use the promise of the loan as an incentive to encourage Logan to show responsible behavior. He suggested that Logan and I talk after three months to see how his progress had been. Then we would decide what to do about the loan based on his progress. I realized that Lynn had the best perspective on the matter. This approach would be the right way to teach Logan how to be responsible.

I learned from that experience that giving certain help or rewards while the behavior is not acceptable is probably what it means to enable. By continuing to give Logan what I thought would make him happy in the moment, even though he was still making poor decisions, I was unintentionally encouraging him to keep making the same undesired choices.

Logan was committed to making his life better, and with the proper medication and an understanding of the behavior characteristics of ADHD, he knew he could do it. Changes take time, and when Logan found himself struggling to keep his finances and spending habits in order, I offered my help to act as his accountant and advisor. Logan took me up on the offer. Together we planned his budget. He gave his money to me. I paid his bills and gave him the spending money that was allowed in his budget. We continued in this arrangement for several months.

When Logan got a job, he received his paycheck every Friday and as agreed he gave it to me. After a month of working hard and not having the responsibility of paying his own bills, he realized that he wasn't feeling the rewards of working. He told me that he needed to take over his own affairs because it was hurting his self-esteem to have his mother handling them.

I had no idea how attached I had become to rescuing Logan. I felt some anxiety and worry about allowing him to handle his money. It felt so good to me to know that all his bills were paid on time and he wasn't getting any late fees or over the limit fees. It was one less thing for me to worry about. But I knew Logan was right, and my ultimate goal was helping him be independent.

I started analyzing my behaviors and reactions to letting go. I needed to allow Logan to be in charge of his life working smoothly or not. I realized that it was time to let him make his own decisions and learn the lessons and natural consequences that were a result of his choices.

I called the leader of a local support group for adults with ADHD and asked her if she knew of a counselor who specialized in ADHD. She gave me the name of someone that not only specialized in ADHD, but who also specialized in substance abuse treatment. I was amazed that he also saw his clients in the evening hours. I felt so hopeful, even excited, about the possibility of Logan getting help and support from someone who knew what they were doing.

After telling Logan about the counselor and even going as far as to make an appointment, my excitement faded. Logan said he wasn't going to go. After giving the matter much thought, I decided that I would go. I felt like I needed help letting go.

After I saw the counselor, my mind was getting clearer about what I needed to do. That first weekend, after my appointment, I made the conscious effort not to call Heather or Logan. I couldn't believe how difficult it was. It felt like being on a diet and struggling not to eat the forbidden foods. I felt like an addict. Seriously. Now I really knew how important it was that I become less involved with their lives, especially if I want to achieve my goal of helping them become independent from me. I wanted to know that if I died today, Heather and Logan would be able to take care of themselves in every way. I also wanted them to have greater self-esteem, and I knew from my own experiences that being independent strengthens self-confidence. I knew it wasn't going to be easy to let go. It still isn't easy, but little by little, I'm getting there. I think this will be a lifelong journey.

Chapter 32

I was on the phone with Heather when the conversation turned to Logan. I sensed uneasiness in Heather's voice. At some point in the conversation, Heather decided that she needed to confide in me about something Logan had told her. She felt conflicted because she had promised him that she wouldn't share this information, but in the end, she decided it was something she should share with me. Logan had told her that he intended to buy a new car.

Logan was not in the position to handle a car loan. When Heather told me that Logan was going to buy a car the next day, my heart sank. I knew he couldn't afford it.

After Heather told me the news, I realized that while I was disappointed, I wasn't shocked. The previous day I had gone to lunch with Logan and he had mentioned cars that he liked. I didn't think anything about his comments because he had talked about cars that he liked during past conversations. It just seemed like a natural part of our conversations every now and then.

In hindsight, his comments seemed more like a decision that had been made for a particular car than just random thoughts. But I hadn't made the connection during our lunchtime conversation. I wasn't sure what to do with the information Heather had given me. Should I call Logan? Should I let him make his own decisions without giving him my opinion? I asked Heather what she wanted me to do; she said that she was going to call Logan and tell him that she told me, and then I could do anything I felt I needed to do.

I waited for several minutes for Heather to call him while I mulled over what to do. I decided to call him. I wasn't surprised when he didn't answer my call. He didn't want my opinion, but I wanted him to have it anyway. I left him a message: "Hi Logan, Heather told me you are going to buy a car. I want you to know that I think that buying a car is a wonderful goal for you, something to work towards when your finances and emotions are more stable. I'm asking you not to buy that car tomorrow. I really think you should wait. You and I have an agreement that you won't buy anything else on credit until you have paid me back for the money I lent you. You have already broken that agreement when you bought a guitar on credit. If you buy a car right now, I am going to keep the money you have been saving to pay other debts, and you will then owe them instead of me. Please wait to buy a car. I love you." I hung up the phone and felt better. I made the right decision for myself in that moment. I knew that was all I could do.

A couple of days went by and Logan was in the process of changing his mind about a new car. He had just about made up his mind to follow my advice when his cousin offered him a really great deal on her Maxima. She sold it to him with some built in equity; it was an offer he felt he just couldn't resist. Logan applied for a loan and was delighted when he qualified without a cosigner. I wanted to share his excitement with him, and I did to a certain degree, but I also felt it was important that he understood the bigger picture. I reminded him that the reason he had good standing with his credit was because I had been helping him with his budget. I had made his payments on time each month for the past several months.

He bought the Nissan and drove it with pride for a few days, but his enthusiasm began to wane. I called him after a couple of days and asked him how he liked his new car and he said it was all right.

"All right?" I asked. "Why just all right?"

"The car is fun to drive and everything, but it's no big deal especially when you are in debt and don't have any money to spend ever. I don't think it's worth it. Now that I know I qualify for a loan on my own credit I think I will sell the car and get a loan for a less expensive car so my payments won't be so high."

He listed the car on a free website to try to sell it. After a couple of weeks, he and his friend analyzed the market and figured out that they couldn't sell it for what it was worth. Logan decided he would do a voluntary repossession. His cousin heard about his decision and found a couple of friends that were thinking about buying the car, but a few more weeks passed and there were no takers for the car.

Logan's payoff to the bank was more than the price that he felt he could get for the car. He couldn't get the title to give the buyer, because he didn't have any money to pay off the bank.

Logan and I went golfing during all this car drama. That is when he finally asked me for my help with managing his money and figuring out a budget. I felt like he was in too deep for me to know what was in his best interest financially, so I called a credit counseling service.

I collected all the paperwork from the credit counseling service and made an appointment with Logan to fill out the papers and get all the required records that were needed. I then arranged for a phone appointment with one of the company's counselors so we could get started right away.

Sometimes I wondered if I was doing too much of the legwork by getting the ball rolling in this situation. Logan was an adult, so he should have been handling these matters himself. Was it possible that I was enabling Logan again? Sometimes that line is so grey. I had been doing the running around and phone calls because Logan was at work and had no car and very little time. I did not want him to jeopardize his job because that would only make his financial problems worse. I wondered if I was just telling myself these things to give myself permission to go ahead and do things for him, or was it really important that I help him? I honestly didn't know.

The phone conference with the credit counseling service was informative. A woman helped us look at Logan's budget and set realistic amounts for the necessary living expenses. Living on the proposed budget allowed enough money to pay the creditors an amount that would get Logan out of debt in five years. The amount of money set aside for the kind of lifestyle Logan would have to live would be so tight that it was overwhelming for him. Living that way for five years seemed harsh and impossible to Logan.

The financial counselor also suggested bankruptcy. She shared with us that she had gone bankrupt two years previously, and it was a great relief for her. Going bankrupt allowed her to get a new start on her life. She gave us the name of a lawyer that worked for her company. Logan and I scheduled a phone conference with him.

The next item on the agenda was what to do with Logan's car. After talking with the counselor, it seemed like Logan's best choice was doing a voluntary repossession. Even though he was disappointed, there was also a sense of relief. He was doing the best thing for himself. After realizing the extent of Logan's psychological problems and the realities of the harsh years ahead, Logan filed bankruptcy. He felt it was the best decision for him and he was backed by the credit counseling service, because they felt it would be best in Logan's situation too. It was a new start for Logan. He learned many lessons and hoped to create a better future for himself.

Chapter 33

Just about the time Heather was going to start attending the University, Lynn and I had been married one year. We had maintained our separate homes during this time. Lynn lived in his mountain home while Heather and I lived in a suburb of Salt Lake. Lynn and I decided the time had come to sell both our homes and buy one house where we could live together.

Logan had already been living by himself for the past year and I thought it would be best for Heather to move into her own apartment. She wasn't excited about the prospect of living in her own apartment and handling the responsibilities that came with that degree of independence, but she reluctantly agreed with the idea.

I wanted Heather to have more opportunity to grow in her personal life; living on her own would be an important part of that process. Heather and I were having lunch in a restaurant one afternoon discussing the practice of children growing up and then leaving their childhood home. Heather expressed feelings of loss at the whole idea and talked about how it didn't make sense. "We leave the people we love, to live alone or apart from them. Why don't we live with each other as a family, the way people do in other cultures? That makes so much more sense to me," she said.

Her comment made me feel sad. I had to agree with her that living with people who support and love you and give you companionship seemed like the most desirable situation, but I didn't think that staying at home and remaining dependent on one's parents would provide the environment for the personal growth, self-esteem and possible happiness that living independently would bring. Moving into a place of one's own would allow for experiences to grow and learn. The ability to make decisions and choices and handle the unforeseen was a part of growing up, and this level of independence would be hindered by living with one's mother indefinitely.

Logan had been eager to strike out on his own, so I hadn't faced these particular feelings. Sometimes my heart ached during the conversation with Heather,
because I didn't know what the best thing to do was. I felt guilty for wanting her
to leave the nest when she didn't want to go, but my job as a mother was to think
about the bigger picture and try to decide what was best in the long run. What I
felt in my heart was that I would be inhibiting Heather's growth if I allowed her
to remain with me. I also felt like our relationship would blossom and develop
in new and healthier ways if we had some time apart.

I asked Heather if she wanted to live in the apartment that was in the basement of my new home. I thought that might give her a transition period from
living with me to living on her own. "No, I need light," she said.

We talked about the difference between sharing spaces and having a space
of her own. Gradually she began to see some of the advantages of living on her
own. "I like to do my own thing and not have someone aware of what I am doing
and how much time I spend doing it," she said.

The conversation went on like that for a little while, and in the end, Heather
realized that she wanted privacy and would enjoy living by herself. It was just
hard for her to imagine doing it because she had never done it before. I tried to
reassure her that most people felt anxiety in new experiences and transitions in
life. Most of us have some fear of the unknown.

Paying rent wasn't going to be easy for Heather because her financial
resources were limited. After some hunting, we found an apartment where
the owner was responsible for finding a roommate to share the rent and utilities. Heather was quite anxious at the idea of living with someone that she
didn't know, but she realized that it was the only way she could afford to live
on her own.

The apartment was close to a hospital where Heather's referring physician's
office was located. It was also close to the hair salon where I worked, so I
wouldn't be far away. The apartment was in a white brick building that had been
turned into condominiums. Heather's unit was located in the back of the building on the ground level. There were two levels above hers. A covered parking
stall was located just in front of her unit which would make carrying groceries
from the car easier, as well as making the walk to her apartment shorter so she
wouldn't get so tired. She also felt safer. When she looked out her window,
she saw grass with a low bush hedge growing around it. She had a bathroom in
her bedroom and her future roommate had her own bathroom in her bedroom,
with the living room and kitchen between the bedrooms. This arrangement gave
Heather the privacy she wanted. The landlord wasn't able to get a roommate for

several months so Heather had time to adjust to her new home without a new roommate to get used to at the same time.

Heather's first weeks were harder than we expected. She developed pneumonia, and for the first time, oral antibiotics proved useless. The doctor wanted Heather to be hospitalized where she could be administered intravenous (IV) antibiotics. Heather had small veins that were next to impossible to find, so the decision wasn't an easy one for us, but with oral antibiotics failing to eliminate her infection, IV antibiotics were the best choice, the only choice.

After inspection of Heather's veins, the doctors decided the best procedure for Heather was to put the IV in the carotid artery. I was horrified. "In her neck?" I repeated, thinking to myself that this just couldn't be any worse. I couldn't believe it. Why couldn't anything be easy for us? The doctors assured us that they were going to use an ultrasound to find the vein and they would be watching a screen that allowed them to see what they were doing when they inserted the IV, so the procedure should go smoothly.

Heather was so scared. I felt helpless as I stood there watching the terror in her eyes as the doctor was inserting a big needle into the artery in her neck. My eyes were brimming with tears as I tried to remain calm. I was her mother. I was supposed to protect her from the pains of this world. But all I could do was stand by and watch. The sense of helplessness and despair were sometimes overwhelming, but somehow I made it through and those awful moments passed.

After spending a couple of days in the hospital, the doctor informed us that Heather didn't need to stay in the hospital. She could go home with the IV in her neck and wait out the rest of the two weeks of treatment. Heather was doubtful about the situation. Having an IV in her neck was scary and uncomfortable; furthermore, she was terrified that there would be some kind of problem that she could not handle. The doctor assured us that he would arrange for a nurse to visit every other day. The nurse would change Heather's bandage and make sure her IV was clear. With some persuasion, Heather agreed to go home.

Heather stayed at my house for the first few days, and after she was more comfortable with the whole idea, decided to go to her new apartment. The nurse came regularly as promised. The whole ordeal was very rough for Heather. She worried constantly about the possibility of a problem. My salon was only five minutes from Heather's apartment, so I visited her often and she came home with me at night to sleep. Finally the two weeks passed and Heather's lungs were the clearest they had ever been.

Heather had gotten used to her first roommate, but when the roommate decided to leave, Heather asked her cousin Desiree if she would like to live with her. They didn't live together very long, but she was Heather's favorite room-mate.

When Desi moved out, Heather didn't like the idea of having a stranger move in again, so she invited a friend of hers that she had met on the internet to move in. They could relate to each other because they both suffered with chronic depression. They were also both deep thinkers and stimulated each other mentally. However, her friend liked to smoke marijuana, and since Logan was also smoking marijuana to self-medicate during this time, he came over regularly and hung out with Heather's roommate. This arrangement became unbearable for Heather. She is an introspective person who enjoys quiet time to think and read, to work on her writing. Logan is far more social and enjoys interaction and activity going on around him.

One night at midnight I received a call from her. She said, "I can't stand it anymore. Will you come pick me up?" She said she really needed to talk to me.

When I arrived, Heather was outside her apartment, in the dark, waiting for me. She was more upset than I had ever seen her over the matters of relationships and her living arrangements. "I have to get out. I don't know what to do. I can't live this way anymore."

We discussed the situation and decided that she would give her notice to the landlord and to her friend. The hunt for another apartment would begin again.

Chapter 34

Logan had been living in a one-bedroom apartment in someone's home for the past two years, but they informed him that they were going to move. Logan wanted to help Heather out by offering to move in with her, in a new apartment, so she wouldn't have to have a stranger live with her. Despite the problems they had experienced during Logan's visits to her apartment, neither one of them could afford to live alone, so they decided to find an apartment and share the expenses.

Heather and Logan found a pleasant two-bedroom apartment on the third floor of a complex. They were very excited about their new home. I also helped them apply for government, or Section Eight housing, which is a program that assists low-income individuals, including those with disabilities. The government gives the landlord at the apartment of their choice a voucher toward payment of the rent. There was a wait of two years to get on the program. I was sorry I hadn't thought of applying before then. Now that Heather and Logan wanted to live on their own, the additional financial assistance would help.

Living with Logan turned out to be a challenge for Heather. He was emotionally unstable and self-medicating, which made him unpredictable and erratic; his moods, whether they were high or low, affected Heather. He was very critical of her inability to get a job, as well as her inability to develop a normal sleep pattern. She was staying up all-night and sleeping most of the day.

At that time Logan was managing a sleep schedule that was close to normal because he had a job that he intended on keeping. Later, Logan had to face his own difficulties that prevented him from maintaining any kind of normal sleep pattern, and he developed empathy for Heather's struggles with abnormal sleeping patterns.

Sleeping is extremely difficult for Logan. He has sleep apnea but because of his cleft palate repair he isn't able to use a medical device called a CPAP machine, used to treat apnea. It would dry his mouth and palate too much to maintain comfort.

Logan's eyes dry out significantly when he sleeps because his eyes can't close and his tears fall out of his eyes. We need our tears to lubricate our eyes. He resists getting surgery on his eyelids because he knows surgery is painful. He has finally established a comfortable balance with his pain medication and doesn't want to upset that balance. He also knows surgery has risks. Because eye surgery will change his appearance, he's afraid he won't like how he looks. He knows it wasn't easy learning to accept his appearance and he doesn't want to go through it again. Logan said he understands why people want to have plastic surgery when they get old. They got used to the way they looked most of their lives and don't like changes. They want their original appearance back; so they have surgery.

Logan's pain level escalates when he lies down to sleep. He places a fluctuating air mattress on top of his memory foam mattress but still isn't able to sleep comfortably. He often falls asleep in chairs, on the floor and sometimes even on the toilet, where his tailbone feels most comfortable. He leans over and rests his upper body on his thighs and lets his arms dangle down. Sleeping in different places helps him get sleep, but not the kind of sleep that brings the most rested state.

Logan's natural sleep pattern is to sleep during the day and be awake at night. Every day he struggles to awaken at 11:30 a.m. so he has time to go to his doctor appointments, grocery shop, walk his dog and get sunlight. He uses sleep aids but the side effects of his medications and his chronic pain override the abilities of the sleep aids to work effectively. Logan remains hopeful that his sleep problem will get more manageable like Heather's eventually did.

Heather discovered that her normal sleep pattern was to go to bed at 4:00 a.m. and wake around noon. Since she didn't have a job, she followed this sleeping pattern and scheduled her doctor appointments and other commitments around 2:00 p.m. Later, after seeking a medical opinion about her insomnia, Heather discovered that she had a sleep disorder. With proper medication and a commitment to go to bed at the same time every night and rise at the same time every morning, Heather maintains a normal sleep pattern today.

At that time, having Logan criticize her because of her sleeping habits and her personality hurt her self-esteem, but she decided she would rather live with Logan than with a stranger, so she stuck it out until her Section Eight housing became available a year and a half later. When Logan finally moved out, eleven months later, Heather felt sad and lonely. She wrote:

"I remember the first night that I moved out of the house. It was scary and lonely, but I got used to it.

Yesterday, my brother moved to California. It is strange to live in this apartment all alone. Everywhere I look, there are memories and emotions waiting for me. Although there were many conflicts during the time I lived with Logan, there were joyful moments of sharing feelings and intelligent understandings as well. I learned about choosing happier moments when they are available. Sometimes choosing joy is better than choosing to learn. Sharing thoughts builds a connection between two people. Even if the thoughts are small or appear insignificant, they are still one more step for that bridge. I also learned that sometimes having more objects that represent the individual in the house displays potential and personality. It punctuates the personality and brings color into life.

Last night I felt like I had lost someone I loved. Having him leave showed me what grief over the loss of someone might be like for people. Remembering things that were around the house, which represented him, gave me a sense of having known, having experienced and understood him as well as a sense of loss. Recognizing his feelings about different ideas and objects is like realizing that he existed and got into my own soul."

—Heather Madsen

Chapter 35

Heather researched jobs that were available, but usually reached the conclusion that there wasn't a lot out there that suited her abilities and her unique emotional and physical challenges. Continuing to look in spite of the bleak odds created anxiety for her. She didn't want to displease me or other people by not looking for a job, but eventually she had to stop for her own sanity.

Heather knew that her personality wasn't like the personalities of other people that she observed, but she didn't know exactly what was different. She spent her days on the internet, chatting in different support groups. Through some of those conversations, as well as her own independent research, she started gaining an understanding of herself and her differences. She began to put pieces of information together. Everything she learned and discovered brought her to a condition that seemed to describe most of her traits and symptoms. That condition is called autism.

When Heather introduced her suspicions to me, I resisted the idea. I didn't want to accept that she was really different in another area beyond the physical disabilities she already faced. It was like finding out that she had a new disability. I didn't want that to be true. How many conditions can one person be expected to handle? As much as I resisted this new possibility, I had to admit that the information that I was reading about autism really did talk about characteristics that described Heather's personality. I couldn't deny that there could be a connection. The more I read about it, the more I believed that Heather had a form of that condition. The traits were there in black and white and there was no denying that they fit my daughter.

Heather met a doctor through the internet that specialized in Asperger syndrome (a condition similar to high functioning autism) in female adults. She read the description about Heather and agreed that it sounded like she had the condition. She offered to send a book to Heather. The information in the book confirmed our belief that Heather had some form of the condition. The trip to see that particular specialist would have been quite costly, so we decided to postpone further exploration of the diagnosis. Heather believed that it was true and I supported her, because I saw the characteristics myself and believed she was right.

For instance, Heather is especially stubborn when she wants to avoid mistakes. She knows when a person reads the manual and instructions of any new device, they will be less likely to break it. She can get very frustrated when they don't follow her advice. She once bought Logan a remote control helicopter as a gift. He was excited to start flying it and didn't want to take the time to read the instructions. Heather was persistent and frustrated when she could see he wasn't going to follow her sound advice. He chose not to fly it rather than read the instructions to keep Heather from getting mad at him.

She gets so confused when there are rules and obvious reasons to do something or not to do something and some person chooses to break the rules. This is shocking to Heather. As she has matured and learned more about people's individuality, she had learned to make good choices for herself, give her advice when she can see it can help someone, and accept that people will make their own choices in the end, and sometimes that means they won't think about what they are doing and what kinds of results can occur if not done correctly.

Heather does best with very clear directions of what is expected of her. She doesn't always know how to ask for what she needs because she doesn't know what she didn't learn automatically like other people. Because she has learned so much about autism, she has a better idea of what to ask for when she needs clarification from someone about a subject or task.

When she was younger, she would ask me questions where the answer seemed obvious to most people. I couldn't believe she was asking me the question. I wondered if she was trying to save herself the efforts of thinking of the answer herself by having me answer for her. Later I learned how people affected with autism don't learn the everyday cues and body language of communication like the average person does. She genuinely didn't know the answers to her questions. I know Heather well enough now to know that she won't ask me any questions to which she knows the answers. Sometimes I had to explain over and over for her to understand the concept I was teaching her.

Heather gained insights into herself and learned where her difficulties were. She was constantly working to overcome her limitations in those areas; she continues to work on them now.

Months later Heather was reading a draft of this chapter. She said, "If you're going to mention that we think I have autism, I think we should get a professional diagnosis."

I agreed. We found a specialist in Salt Lake, but that doctor wasn't taking new patients. I asked to be put on a waiting list, and two months later, received a telephone call. After Heather went through the interviews and testing, the specialist confirmed that she has high functioning autism.

A lack of social awareness is one characteristic of autism that Heather exhibits. When Heather was twenty-five years old, she and I visited my sister, Kathy, in Orlando, Florida. From there, we drove with Kathy to Stuart, Florida to visit our father and his wife. We stayed at their home for a couple of days. Heather had decided that she wanted to learn about social etiquette by participating more in the conversations and by asking questions, rather than reading her book all the time. She decided to put effort into making conversation.

One evening while my stepmother and I were clearing the dinner table, Heather remained close by, listening to our conversation. "I really like these placemats," I commented. My stepmother told me that she had found them at a flea market, along with the matching basket that held them.

The conversation was going along in that fashion when Heather spoke up. "Do you guys really find what you're talking about interesting?"

I didn't find this question offensive because I knew Heather was trying to learn. I understood that most people would take offense to this comment, and I sensed that my mother-in-law was offended. I explained what Heather had meant by her question. Then we spent the next sixty minutes discussing why small talk is necessary, how deep conversation takes more effort and sometimes people don't want to work that hard. We also explained the importance of listening to other people, even when you don't think what they're saying is interesting, because you want to show them that they matter to you.

The next morning we women were sitting around a glass table on the patio. We were enjoying the beautiful, sunny weather and relaxing. "Can we talk about something that I would be interested in?" Heather asked.

We all agreed and asked what she would like to talk about.

"Let's discuss what our goals in our lives are and the things we are working on to improve ourselves." Heather loves deep conversation, so we asked her to start the conversation by telling us what she was doing to improve herself; then we followed her lead. We managed to get a good conversation going, but it took some effort. Deep topics require that you dig deep into yourself to think about your answers.

The conversation was moving along well when my dad came out of the house, onto the patio. He was talking as he entered the area, interrupting our conversation by telling us about something he had just discovered on the internet about a topic he was researching. He was very excited and continued talking for several minutes. When he paused, Heather asked, "Is what he just did considered socially acceptable?"

Of course he took offense to that question. Anyone would. He said that he would just go back into the house and stay away. I could tell he felt rejected. I followed him and explained that Heather was trying to learn and didn't mean to offend him.

When I returned, we spent the next hour teaching Heather about the dynamics that occur within groups. We explained that people come in and out of the area, sometimes interrupting the conversations that are in progress. Perfect manners would be to say, "Excuse me," before sharing your thoughts, or you might ask if you could interrupt to share something. You also could just wait until the person talking is finished with their comment. Most people are used to the interruptions of others in a situation like this and they don't even notice. After a week of Heather's questions and deep conversation, we were all worn out, including Heather.

Without having an understanding of autism, extended family members have a difficult time relating to Heather. Since they don't see her very often, they don't get used to her inability to socialize in expected ways. Sometimes her lack of interest in people and lack of social awareness causes her to say or do something that results in misunderstanding from the people who love her. When this happens, I remember how difficult it was for me to learn about Heather's differences and understand the way she says and does certain things. This helps me be patient with my loved ones to create understanding and closeness. I don't want to be overprotective and angry about what might seem like a lack of empathy. I recognize that they need my understanding and patience just as much and we need theirs.

When Heather was twenty-three, she didn't want to celebrate a traditional Christmas by giving and receiving gifts. Her uncle loves to give gifts for Christmas and feels a void without that tradition.

Christmas Eve came and we were excited about our loved ones visiting. There was a knock at the front door. When I answered it my brother and his partner were standing at the door with big smiles on their faces and their arms loaded with gifts. Heather didn't know what to think when they pointed out which gifts were for her. She drew into herself while she processed this new information. She was confused at the gift giving because she told her uncle she didn't want to receive any gifts. The gifts were just small, fun items.

After taking some time to process her feelings, Heather said, "I feel very ignored and disrespected concerning my beliefs I communicated about not wanting to celebrate Christmas in this way." She pointed out how unpractical the gifts were for her.

I explained to Heather that the reason Shaun and Matthew bought gifts was because Matthew knows Shaun cares deeply for his loved ones and he enjoys tradition. Shaun loves watching the family open the gifts and enjoys everyone's reactions.

"I did not understand why Matthew and Shaun did this until my mom told me later that day, and then I felt very sad that I had been so rude and disrespectful in front of everyone. After the reasons were explained, the emotional connections that prompted their actions make sense to me," Heather said. "Mom also explained to me that Shaun and Matthew did not believe I really did not want to celebrate Christmas the traditional way anymore, especially because I enjoyed gifts so much when I was younger."

Christmas of 2009 was very different. I felt a void because I don't buy gifts for Heather and Logan at Christmastime. I give them gifts all year round and it doesn't make sense to me to make them wait until Christmas when they need something.

Lynn traveled to Billings, Montana to see his mother for Christmas because she has delicate health issues. That left Heather, Logan, Rubin (Heather's companion) and me to celebrate Christmas together. We each decided to buy a family gift that would give us some entertainment on Christmas Day and throughout the year. I also asked Heather to shop for a new Wii game to add to our collection.

Heather was overcome with the spirit of giving. Logan and I told her she could shop for the gifts we were to give because we were both busy and tired. She had so much fun shopping that she used some of her own money to buy Logan and Rubin remote control helicopters. She bought me some books on CD, a book and a meditation board where I can paint with water and watch it disappear. She was more excited about Christmas than I had seen her in years.

Now she really understands how happy it makes people to give gifts, even if the gifts aren't really needed by the receiver. It's the fact that the giver thought about you and loves you.

Outside of her environment, Heather sometimes tries to control others so that she can maintain the feeling of control that she had in her home. Heather feels less anxious when her surroundings are predictable. She feels most at ease when she is home. She knows that she won't learn and grow as much if she doesn't spend time with people, so she forces herself to do so even though she would prefer to stay at home.

I have learned a lot from Heather, especially because of her tendency to speak her mind. Where she is blunt, I am sometimes evasive or unclear while expecting people to understand what I mean. I avoid conflicts, and in the process, sometimes lose my ability to communicate effectively. When Heather confronts me, I discuss the situation with her, and the conversations serve as learning experiences for me. I am able to take what I learn in my communication with Heather and apply the same principles to other conversations.

For example, when Lynn is out of town, I will often invite Heather to my house for dinner and a movie. She is excited about the evening and waits in anticipation for me to pick her up when I finish work. I am always eager to leave the salon, so I make phone calls from my cell phone as I am driving to Heather's home.

Once when I arrived, Heather got in the car and acted annoyed that I was on the phone. When I finished my phone call Heather said, "I really don't like it when you are on your phone when you pick me up."

"I have calls I am going to make. Would you rather I stay at the salon to make those calls and take some of our time from the evening by picking you up later or make those calls while I am driving to get you and while we are driving to get the movie?"

Heather explained that she has things to say to me when she sees me. She needed that time to adjust to a new environment and to reconnect, but after discussing the topic for a while she decided that she would rather I come right away, even if it meant my being on the phone.

These types of conflicts would arise often before Heather learned more about social interactions. Sometimes I would wonder why I was excited to be with her, because I felt like I was being criticized, scrutinized and controlled. I knew I did want to be with Heather and it was a great opportunity for me to learn communication skills. I have grown because of them.

When Heather doesn't understand why a disagreement occurs, she can't stop talking about it or thinking about it until she understands what happened and until she feels understood. She will ask a lot of questions and remain focused on looking for clarity before she can let the topic go. As she has matured, she has learned that sometimes a person must give a topic a rest before any resolution can come. She has learned to trust herself to bring up her questions about the topic another time, after emotions have calmed. She learned that when a person gets saturated in their emotions they aren't able to continue effectively in a discussion and she must walk away and stop asking questions.

Heather has learned to accept my idiosyncrasies and mistakes and even finds some of them endearing. I have learned to change some things that I was able to change. Heather now knows that she can't control other people, and she has learned that what she says will affect people one way or another. She works hard to be positive and accepting. Along with this, she has learned to respect herself and not allow herself to be a doormat by compromising her values. She expresses what she wants and has learned to compromise with others. She has her boundaries and respects other's boundaries. Mostly, she just needed to learn and gain experience.

We have come to recognize that our conflicts arise because of the expectations of what we think is going to happen during our time together. Heather's expectations are automatic because of her need to control her environment, and from lack of experience around other people. Mine are out of habit and sometimes a lack of consideration. We have both learned to be more considerate of each other, communicate more completely and talk about our expectations. We are gaining a comfort level with each other that allows us to bond and teaches us how to connect with other people.

Even though Heather enjoys the comfort of her safe controlled environment at home, she gets lonely for people. She has her friends on the internet, but sometimes she feels a void. Even a person who enjoys her time alone sometimes gets lonely, too.

Heather understands that people are very busy in their lives and don't have much time to call, email or socialize regularly with her. However, she can't help but feel like she is skipped over by the people who say they love her and care about her. She understands that relationships are two sided and would require her to make regular contact. Because she has chronic fatigue from doing the necessary tasks of life, and because she has autism, she doesn't have the energy or skills needed to initiate contact. The lack of attention from family and friends causes her confusion. They say they love and miss her but they don't call, email, visit or send cards. She is left feeling isolated.

She believes she isn't an interesting person to other people. She feels she doesn't have enough activities and exciting information to draw people to her. Even though she researches topics that interest her the information is hard to access due to her autism and they may not be topics that interest the other person. Autism keeps Heather from knowing how to make small talk; she doesn't know what to talk about.

Heather believes she has to "do" something interesting and different all the time for people to want to talk with her regularly. Because of her disabilities she can't "do" much so she concludes she is not interesting to people. She enjoys listening to people in her family and people she knows when they tell her what's happening in their active lives because then she feels included. Because everyone is so busy, they may think about her but she doesn't know it, because they don't make any effort to communicate with her. She doesn't fault people for how they behave and she doesn't take the lack of attention personally, she just feels isolated. She notices how the words people say don't match with what they do. She notices people are out of integrity much of the time. She values integrity and admires people who live their lives with integrity. She hears people say they want to be honest, kind, generous, trustworthy, caring, attentive and have values like these but notices their actions don't match their words. She has learned most people's words and actions don't match.

Heather enjoys following politics. She notices how people criticize the government for saying one thing and doing another, and yet they seem to be blind to the reality that this is the way they live their lives too. These observations can be confusing and upsetting to Heather. However, she notices that when she is deeply focused on a project that interests her, she too can fall out of integrity with some of her values; eating enough healthy food calories, responding to received emails, following through on goals. Then she understands this as a characteristic of being a human being; something that needs constant attention.

Recently, Heather gave the following talk to the Society for the Advancement of Genetic Research (SAGE), at the University of Utah. She sobbed as she spoke these words.

"I am glad to be here to talk about my experiences regarding the genome research. But first let me tell you a little about myself. I have Miller syndrome, a lung disease called bronchiectasis, autism and I am hearing impaired.

I have a BS degree in psychology from the U of U. My activities include reading books, writing and speaking about my life experiences, and researching topics. I am fascinated by the world and its myriad topics to explore. I especially enjoy researching about autism and diabetes, other medical conditions, pharmacology, nutrition, and learning about technological advances. As a natural inquisitive researcher, I like to find the causes to problems and figure out how things work.

As humans, we look to each other to find similarities so that we feel like we belong. Because of having Miller syndrome, I look different and I am forced to do things differently. This makes me separated from others in ways that we can't relate. Consequently, I have always felt a sense of isolation that was indescribable. I felt like I did not belong.

Along with Miller syndrome, I grew up with the lung disease, bronchiectasis. I thought that I might find a sense of belonging to the group of people having bronchiectasis. However, it seemed that I didn't belong to this group either because I had other symptoms doctors attributed to bronchiectasis that these people did not have. Things just didn't add up, leaving me with more questions and more isolation.

When the opportunity for whole genome sequencing arose for my family, I was very excited. Being the inquisitive person that I am, I was extremely interested in helping researchers look for answers. I was hopeful that they would find a gene responsible for causing Miller syndrome. If they didn't find anything about the Miller gene, at least I will have been helpful to genetic research. If they did find something, the new information might help others with genetic abnormalities find the peace that they seek. While researchers were looking for a Miller gene, they discovered the cause for my lung disease.

I was informed that I had genetic mutations for primary ciliary dyskinesia which is the cause of my bronchiectasis. I felt a sense of deep satisfaction in finally knowing what has caused me so much pain and grief. Several months later researchers discovered the gene for Miller syndrome. I was elated. This was exactly the find for which I was hoping.

Throughout my whole life I struggled for a sense of belonging. The field of genetic research and whole genome sequencing has given me the answers to many of my struggles. Even though the results do not change the fact that I have multiple disabilities, I now feel resolved and validated for all the challenges that I have been through and my sense of isolation that I have had with others.

Knowing that Miller syndrome and PCD are part of Mother Nature's working things out, I feel like I belong to a community larger than just that of mankind. Genetic research gave me my community, my sense of belonging and peace of mind."

—Heather Madsen

Chapter 36

Like many young men, Logan struggled to prove himself. Our culture expects males to behave in certain ways and demonstrate physical strength. Physical disabilities work against these characteristics and create social and personal turmoil for Logan. Once we had scheduled movers to meet with us and help Logan move into a new apartment. The move was planned for a Saturday, but when the apartment became available on Thursday night, Logan decided to start taking his boxes and other belongings over to his new apartment each evening after work. He used a dolly and furniture sliders to help but with his short arms and small hands that don't have normal strength this kind of work hurts Logan's back and joints. By the time Saturday arrived, Logan had moved everything he owned except a dining room table and a small freezer. He called me on Friday night around 10:30 p.m. to tell me he was going to sleep in his new home and that he had moved everything himself.

I asked him how his body felt, and he said that his back hurt and he knew he would be sore all over.

"Logan, you really didn't have to move anything. That's what I hired the movers for," I said.

"Mom, I had to do it for myself. Sometimes I don't feel like a man because I can't do as much as other men. Nobody would ever ask me for my help like they would another man, because they don't think I can do anything. I had to do it for myself."

I understood.

During difficult times, Logan has wondered about his reasons for living. When he is in the mood to talk, he can be very open concerning everything, including his thoughts about suicide.

He once admitted that he's thought about all kinds of methods a person could use to commit suicide. He knew he wouldn't shoot himself if he decided to end his life because he couldn't hold a gun steady with his small weak hands and short arms. Without much finger dexterity he could just barely pull the trigger on certain guns. He told me about an experience he had in a gun shop one day. He was with his friend, and the sales clerk in the store let them shoot a gun. Because he couldn't shoot it with much accuracy, he concluded that using a gun for suicide wasn't an option for him.

It disturbs me that his thoughts about suicide have gone that far, but I'm glad I know what's been on his mind. Hearing him express his thoughts and feelings gives me insight into what causes him and other people to want to die. It helps me to understand. I believe that when a person is given the opportunity to talk about what's going on, even when the topic is painful, it helps bring emotional relief and a more healthy perspective. I encourage him to talk to me, and I work hard to be a good listener and respect his separateness from me. I work hard to appreciate him as his own person.

I heard a saying once that has influenced my approach to motherhood: "My children came to this earth through me, but they are not mine." I work hard to respect their separateness as human beings with minds of their own. They have their own ideas about what they want to do, what they value and how they feel. I try not to control them by pushing my beliefs and ideas on them. This isn't an easy task and emotions sometimes get in the way. If I'm feeling my own fear and discomfort or if I'm thinking about myself, it's hard to hear what is being said.

I know what works for me, but I really can't say what works for Heather and Logan's lives or anybody else's life, and if I think I do, I believe it's a terrible display of self-righteousness. Because I've learned many lessons through my life's experiences, I often feel like I want to share my opinion and try to teach Heather, Logan, and others what to do, what not to do, and how to think. I want to "save" them from making some of the mistakes that I've made. I try to be careful not to think I know what's best for them and remember that their life is their own to live and to learn their own lessons. I can share my experiences, and if something I say helps another person, great, but I work hard to refrain from judging their choices, beliefs and ideas about their lives.

Logan doesn't feel safe in this world. He knows from his experiences with a few mean children in school, some rude adult behaviors and from watching TV, that there are people in this world who like to hurt other people. He fears that a person like that will want to hurt him and he doesn't have the ability to protect himself like a man with a normal body. He fears he will hurt himself by insisting on doing things without asking for help when needed or from having an accident of some kind, resulting in becoming more disabled. He fears people will judge him for not achieving more, painting more, or being more involved in the community. These fears make it more difficult for Logan to accept his disabilities and validate his accomplishments. The anxiety and OCD Logan struggles with are fueled by all these fears and from facing the constant limitations caused by Miller syndrome and autism.

In the middle of 2002, Heather took Logan to a support group for depression. He had been going to a mental health facility for depression and rehabilitation from substance abuse; his counselor had suggested going to group therapy. He went to the group for the first time that morning and wasn't very impressed with the dynamics. He told Heather about his experience, and it gave her the idea to invite him to a support group that met that night, one that she had been going to for a year or so. He agreed to go, but wasn't very optimistic.

I was cleaning up a few things at work when I received a phone call from Logan. He was at the University of Utah emergency room. The doctors wanted to keep him there to talk with him, until they were convinced that he would be safe enough to leave the hospital. If they decided he wasn't safe, they would admit him to a hospital.

He seemed quite agitated. He said that when he went to the support group, he shared his feelings about suicide, and he discussed the method that he would use to accomplish that end. He told the group that he intended to drive his car into a garage, close the door and leave his car running until he was asphyxiated. Hearing this, the leader of the group became alarmed and felt like Logan should go into the Valley Mental Health's three-day hospital for evaluation. She called the hospital; the nurse told her that Logan had to go to the emergency room to be evaluated before they could consider admitting him into their facility.

When I arrived at the hospital I waited with Heather for a couple of hours. Finally the social worker came out to talk with me. She said, "Logan has classic symptoms of attention deficit hyperactive disorder." She felt that he should be medicated for that condition and suggested the drug Adderall. She emailed his caseworker at the mental health facility to inform her of the diagnosis. She requested a crisis appointment with a psychiatrist to prescribe medication for Logan immediately. I was so grateful for the time she spent with Logan and I felt so optimistic about the possibility of finally getting some help for him. I had suspected attention deficit hyper-active disorder (ADHD) in the past.

When Logan came into the waiting area he was feeling calm from the tranquilizer the doctor had given him. Finally, Logan would get some real help.

Heather drove Logan home as I followed in my car, and the next day Logan made an appointment with a new psychiatrist. The psychiatrist disagreed with the emergency room social worker's diagnosis but expressed strong concerns about the way she suggested the drug Adderall, which is addictive, to someone with a family and personal history of substance abuse. She wanted him to go get his kidneys tested to see if he would be able to take a drug called Lithium, or another drug in the same category. Logan and I were disappointed. We hoped things would go more smoothly, but he had his kidneys tested.

In the meantime, I was looking in the phone book for someone who might specialize in ADHD. I saw an ad for "The Mood Disorder Clinic." It was located at the University of Utah. I called and talked to the secretary. She told me about a study they were running on ADHD. She said it might not be a good idea for Logan to participate in the study because some of the participants would be receiving a placebo. I asked if the doctor who specialized in ADHD sees patients outside the study, and she said yes. Logan had to fill out a questionnaire before he could have an appointment; she agreed to send the paperwork in the mail.

A few days later the questionnaire came. I helped Logan fill it out, and we drove up to the doctor's office to deliver it and get an appointment. The doctor didn't have an opening for four weeks. That seemed like an eternity to wait.

The day finally came. It was an expensive appointment, and I thought we would have a long time with the doctor. After forty minutes, he said, "Well, we will have to stop here. I'm sorry the scheduling was done like this, but I have another appointment now. I would like to see Logan again in two weeks." It is an understatement to say that we were disappointed. We didn't know how we were going to survive the wait without some help.

Logan was prescribed a mood stabilizer to help him through the two week wait. Logan was so happy the morning of his appointment because he knew he was about to get help.

Later that day, Logan went back to the pharmacy to get his medicine and took his first dose. He had the best day that he had experienced in a very long time. He was able to focus, had motivation and a general excitement about his life. He went out to a coffee shop to celebrate with his friends. He was drinking tea, Pepsi and smoking cigarettes, all stimulants. This ended up not being a good combination with the new medication and Logan called me at midnight telling me that he felt like he was going to have a heart attack. I suggested that he call the doctor on call for the Mood Disorder Clinic. At one a.m. Logan called me back to say that the doctor wanted him to go to emergency. Logan wanted me to go with him, so I got dressed and off to the hospital we went.

After examining Logan, the doctor informed us that the medicine some-times caused heart palpitations. The added stimulants just made the symptoms worse. She suggested a lower dose of the medication or a different medication in the same category. The doctor also informed Logan of the condition of his lungs. "You had better quit smoking. Your lungs are already expanded. You are on your way to emphysema," she warned him. Logan was scared. Maybe now, he would have a strong enough reason to quit smoking.

Chapter 37

One day in March of 2003, I was describing to one of my customers how good I was feeling. "I feel like I'm floating. I feel light and unburdened from worries at the moment. It feels similar to enjoying a ray of sunshine. I know the warmth and brightness from the ray that is momentarily coming through the clouds will not last, so I am soaking it up while it is here, enjoying it, relishing how it feels."

I didn't know how short-lived my bliss would be.

The next morning, I was finishing up with another customer's hair when the phone rang. It was Logan. He started the conversation in his usual greeting: "Hi, what's up?"

"I'm just finishing up a haircut, and then I'm going to lunch with my friend, Jan. What's up with you? Are you at work?"

"No, I'm at home," he said.

"At home? How come?" I thought perhaps he might be ill.

"I got a DUI last night."

My heart sank. Logan had been abstinent from alcohol for nearly five months. I asked him to tell me how this happened.

Logan explained how he liked to go to a club located close to his home. Some of the employees there, mostly women, treated him well and he had gotten into the habit of going there when he was feeling lonely. That night he stayed until the place closed at 1:00 a.m. As he was driving through the parking lot, he could see that there was no traffic on the main street where he was about to enter, so he didn't come to a complete stop. A policeman was watching and pulled him over.

Logan admitted that he had two beers in the club and the officer could smell alcohol on him. He noticed Logan's hearing aid, so he told Logan that he didn't want to seem insensitive but he needed to know if his balance was affected by his hearing loss. Logan said he didn't think so, but he didn't really know. The police officer asked Logan to walk the line and do the other tests that determine if a person is under the effects of alcohol. He had Logan blow into a breath analyzer, which showed Logan's blood alcohol level was just barely over the legal limit allowed in Utah. The police officer told Logan that he was going to take him to the police station.

He explained to Logan about the necessary steps of impounding his car and handcuffing him. The officer tried to cuff Logan's arms behind his body, but because Logan's arms are shorter than average, one set of handcuffs wasn't enough. He had to use two sets hooked together. Logan said he felt humiliated. When they arrived at the station, an officer had to fingerprint Logan. His small, bent fingers made the task difficult and embarrassing. Logan hated the whole awkward and humiliating experience.

Even though he hated being arrested, he described a feeling of satisfaction from knowing what the experience is like. He had always wondered if a police officer would treat him the way he would treat anyone else who broke the law. Logan found out the hard way that the officer treated him no differently.

After hearing Logan's story my immediate concern was getting him to work so he wouldn't lose his job. He was working at a mortgage company as a temporary employee and had just been offered a full-time position with the company. I was terrified that this DUI could cost him the job.

Usually I keep my cell phone next to my bed in case Heather or Logan needs me during the night. That night I forgot. When I awakened in the morning, I saw that I had eight missed calls. That was very unusual. I was immediately frightened. "What if something happened to one of the kids during the night?" There were no messages, only missed calls, so I checked the call log and saw that Logan had called. I didn't think of checking the time of the calls. If I had, I would have seen that the calls started coming in at 4:00 a.m.

At first I was disappointed that I wasn't available for Logan during his time of need, but after thinking about it, I realized that it was for the best. Logan had to experience the consequences of his actions by himself.

I wasn't sure I wanted to tell anyone about what had happened. Usually I was open about events that occurred because talking with friends and family had been very therapeutic for me. Sometimes I wanted to be able to handle my problems without talking to anyone, especially when the problems included my adult children. I didn't think it was fair for me to be as open about their lives as adults as I had been about my own and about theirs when they were children. I struggled all day. I felt so burdened and overwhelmed, but I was determined to stay quiet.

Logan called me after he had gotten his car and finally arrived at work. He told me that everything would be fine at work; he was going to stay and work late to make up for his lost time that morning.

Dinner that night with my husband was not comfortable. I was trying to act normal. Half way through the meal, I lost my appetite and could hold back no more. I put my hands over my face and started crying. "Something really awful happened last night and I need your support."

He was so concerned when he asked me what happened. I related the whole story to him and felt much better. I realized that it wasn't Logan's getting a DUI that worried me as much as his state of mind when I talked with him on the phone that night just before dinner.

Logan told me that he didn't know what to do. He hated going home alone after work. He had been going to the club each night after work to feel validated and to feel like he existed. "When I'm alone I feel invisible, like I don't exist and I don't know what to do about it," he had said. "Nothing means anything to me."

I was worried about these feelings and where they would take Logan. He had been doing so well. He hadn't smoked pot for almost ten months and was sober for more than four. The feelings that he described were the same ones that led him to chemical substances. They were just too hard for him to handle.

I called Logan and invited him to come to dinner. He declined my invitation. He was at the grocery store at the time and seemed a little bit better. I knew that was all I could do, and I also knew that Logan didn't like me being in his face all the time.

How much is a parent supposed to do for their adult children? When is it too much? I just don't know the answer to those questions.

Chapter 38

Inside me is an inner voice. It is my voice that I hear, and I could describe it as the verbalization of my true intentions, my deepest desires. It is the voice that directs me. Sometimes it feels as if I have two selves. One self is strong and has definite goals and strong intentions to achieve those goals. There is another self that gets fatigued and overwhelmed from all the emotions and challenges of life. There are moments when I don't care about the long term goals, but I have listened to the guidance of my stronger self for so many years now that I don't think about it much. I hear it telling me what I need to do, and it seems to override my weaker self. I heard that inner voice telling me it was time to let go.

I found a new counselor that specialized in ADHD and substance abuse. I hoped that Logan would go to him on a regular basis if he liked him, but Logan didn't want to go. He didn't want his dad and me to spend any of our money on him anymore. I was disappointed, but then the light went on and I thought, "I will go to the counselor. I will get help separating myself from Logan in a healthy way." I needed help.

I told Logan that I was going to get help to learn to do what he had wanted me to do for years, which was to let go and be less involved in his life. He seemed pleased. He even called me that night just to talk. I wanted to be there to listen when he wanted to talk, without taking over with my advice and judgments. I was looking forward to our new relationship.

When I talked to the counselor, I received the validation I needed. I was confident that my goal of separating from Logan, and letting him make his own choices and experience the consequences that came naturally, was the right direction.

As Logan made choices that brought positive results for him, his self-esteem would grow. He would become more confident in future choices and in himself. As he experienced consequences that were unpleasant, he would think more carefully about his choices in the future. He would feel his own power to create his life the way he wanted it. I was finally realizing that by imposing my will on him to make certain choices, I was denying Logan the rewards of learning for himself.

A strong sense of relief and peace came over me when I thought of letting go of the responsibility that I imposed on myself concerning Logan's affairs. I had previously dealt with this issue in my relationship with my mother. I eventually learned to accept that I was not responsible for my mother's happiness. Until then, I had a strong sense that her life depended on my doing everything and anything that she asked of me or she would break. Because of her emotional challenges and instabilities, I saw her as fragile. I took the responsibility to protect her, even at the expense of myself sometimes. What a great relief I felt when I had the new perception that she was responsible for her own life. Now was the time to do the same in my relationship with Logan.

I went to that counselor only two times. He helped me see that I was on the right track and that I was handling my relationship with Logan well. Logan decided to see the same counselor to see what he had to say to him. He went for a couple of months on a weekly basis. The counselor validated Logan's ability to evaluate himself and told him he had good insight, especially for a young man. When Logan no longer had a car, and riding the bus to see that counselor was too difficult, he quit going, but arranged later to see another counselor.

Logan was paying the $850 fine for his DUI in installments of $85.00 a month. He also had to do forty-eight hours worth of community service over the span of four months. He decided to do some yard work for a nonprofit organization called, "The Sharing Place." They counsel children who have had a loved one die suddenly. He struggled completing the community service because of his back problems.

Logan's back pain is caused by several different problems with his anatomy. He has scoliosis, which is abnormal curvature of the spine; his neck is malformed, and his back is too flat, lacking the natural S-curve of a normal back. He has bones that are fused that normally aren't fused in his hips, and bones that aren't fused that should be fused in his tailbone area. Miller syndrome affects the muscular-skeletal development and each person with the syndrome experiences variations.

Heather, to our knowledge, doesn't have the same differences in her spine as Logan. She has scoliosis, but so far she doesn't experience pain. She has intentionally stayed less active during her life to avoid future complications.

It's fair to assume that Logan has more problems and pain because he followed his natural desires and abilities to be active throughout his life. Now, he is forced to be less active to avoid pain or additional future complications.

Logan suffers severe chronic pain and requires morphine three times each day, along with muscle relaxants and anti-inflammatory medicines to keep the pain at a manageable level to make life worth living. His medications cause unpleasant side effects but the pain would make life without them unbearable.

He managed to complete his community service and pay his fine. It was a hard way for him to learn to avoid drinking and driving, but he learned it well.

Logan was working for a mortgage company, doing data entry, at this time. He worked hard, sometimes putting in overtime on Saturdays or Sundays. He liked the work he did and enjoyed his coworkers. The opportunity to put in overtime and earn extra money was an added benefit. He worked there until the company had financial difficulties and had to lay off over two-hundred employees. Logan was one of them.

Chapter 39

For a couple of years in Heather's early adult life, before she received the diagnosis of high-functioning autism, she struggled with the question of whether she wanted to live or die.

Heather's first expressed her thoughts of suicide when she was in her early twenties. We had several open discussions about the topic. I wasn't surprised when the topic came up because I had always been concerned that my children might have thoughts of suicide at some point in their life because of the difficult challenges they face. Expecting the topic of suicide to come up helped to alleviate the shock, but there is nothing that reduces the heartbreak of knowing that your children have lives so difficult and painful that they sometimes long to escape, even if that means taking their own lives. It is only natural for a mother to want happiness for her children and to be deeply saddened to think that her children feel despair.

Heather once told me she had been reading a book about suicide and thinking about it a lot. The book discussed methods of suicide. Heather told me she had decided that she would use pills if she ever made the decision to end her life. She said her physical limitations eliminated her ability to use other methods that were discussed in the book.

Heather described having strong feelings of fatigue from living life. She could see the endlessness of her efforts, just to take care of minimal responsibilities. She had spent many hours trying to find some kind of hobby that she could participate in that would bring her some happiness and make the efforts of living worthwhile.

For many years, Heather found happiness watching television. She was able to get involved with the characters in the programs, and she could imagine that she was participating in life because she watched certain shows regularly. Seeing the people in the program do daily tasks—grocery shopping, going to the doctor, getting gasoline and other common chores—made it easier for Heather to do her own chores. She felt like she learned some of life's lessons through the characters' experiences.

After a while, Heather felt that television prevented her from participating in real life. She wasn't out trying to make friends or have new experiences. She was watching other people have experiences rather than having them herself. There is a limit to how much satisfaction a person can receive by merely watching others. There is a desire inside most of us to experience things directly and to engage with other people. Heather made plans to find activities and make new friends.

She joined a star party club where people were interested in astronomy. They met regularly in locations where they could view the stars and planets through telescopes. She became fascinated with the stars and planets and all the other wonders of space. She discovered a group of people with the common interest of space. Many of them had very large telescopes and they met at regular intervals. Heather wanted to attend a star party, but was anxious about driving to an unknown location. I offered to drive her to one that was being held by the Great Salt Lake, which was about a forty-five minute drive.

The weather wasn't very warm, and unfortunately, the sky was full of clouds that night so we couldn't see as much as we would have liked. We did get a look at Jupiter and Saturn, which were fascinating, as well as some clusters of stars. Heather recognized some of the people by their names, because she had chatted with them online. It was a wonderful to see Heather exploring an interest that she could share with others. We walked around the area and looked into all the different telescopes, which had been focused on different points of interest.

Heather was motivated to go to another star party that summer. She was anxious about driving in an unknown area. She wanted to go badly enough that she overcame her resistance to driving and set out with map in hand. Along the way she became lost. She pulled over and asked someone for assistance and was directed in the right direction. I'll never forget the phone call I received from her that day. She was so proud of herself for getting outside of her comfort zone and having a successful experience. She found the party and discovered that getting lost wasn't as bad as she thought it would be. She realized that with a map and someone kind enough to offer directions, there wasn't much to worry about. She has continued her interest in astronomy, but hasn't attended any more Star Parties. That interest kept her occupied for a while, but it lost its glamour and was too much effort for the experience.

Heather desperately wanted to play the piano. She wanted to buy one. She bought a keyboard instead, which was smaller and cheaper. She learned to read music by taking lessons. She practiced the keys as best she could. A music teacher wrote her a couple of songs that she could play with her limited abilities. After a while she lost interest because of her limitations.

Heather read many books on many subjects. She loves to learn. She got discouraged because she found that she couldn't remember much about what she was learning. She had a hard time interjecting the interesting information she could remember into a conversation. She had a hard time thinking of a topic that she had learned about to start a conversation. Again disappointment and frustration set in.

Heather was having a hard time seeing any good reasons for going on with her life. She lived with chronic discomfort, fatigue, lack of motivation and physical and emotional limitations. The simple tasks we all complete each day were ongoing challenges for her. Many of us experience short-term pain from an accident, illness, or injury, but unless one has lived with chronic pain, it is hard to imagine waking each morning to know that you will experience yet another day of discomfort. It is difficult to find joy when a person is fatigued most of the time. There is no sense of satisfaction in a job well done for the person who is unable to hold a job because of disabilities. All the benefits of work are absent in Heather's life, including the opportunity to interact with coworkers and to work together on projects or common goals. Most of us form a large part of our identities around our work.

When Heather talked about the lack of reasons to go on, I could understand why she felt the way she did. She felt miserable most of the time and there were no easy solutions to the myriad difficulties she faced. I tried to focus on my realization that she is a separate entity from me and that she has her own circumstances in this life that she has to make decisions about, but no mother can listen to her child express thoughts of suicide without feeling a deep and gut wrenching sorrow.

I'm sure I must have blocked off my emotions so I could be an understanding listener, because the sadness, despair and fear would have otherwise paralyzed me. I wouldn't be much help to Heather if I couldn't listen to her with an open mind. I tried to see things from her point of view, even though my own is quite different: I love Heather and I want her alive. I don't want her to end her life. I want to hope for a better future for her. Circumstances in life change and so do perceptions.

Heather seemed to feel relieved after talking about her thoughts and feelings. I felt some relief knowing what she was thinking.

I believe that one of the terrible things about having one of my children commit suicide would be to not know what they were thinking beforehand. After our conversation, I knew what was on Heather's mind.

Ongoing therapy and antidepressant medications helped lift her out of her depression; she continues on medication for depression today.

Chapter 40

In May, 2005 Logan and I met with Judy, his government benefits specialist.

"I would love to have my own business as a self employed artist," Logan said as he dug in his pocket for his portfolio. He handed it to her.

Judy smiled as she looked through the portfolio at the 4 x 6 prints of the flowers Logan paints with acrylics.

"I've sold all the originals and many prints," Logan continued. "I'm painting a collection to show in an exhibit at Art Access Gallery here in Salt Lake."

Judy explained about benefits for which Logan could apply that would fund his dream of self-employment. She wrote the details on a big white board.

I was amazed. "It's hard to believe what you're telling us," I said. "It seems too good to be true." I had no idea such opportunities really existed.

I looked over at Logan, who sat quietly. He has been struggling for so long. I think he was afraid to believe all this could really happen.

"Judy, I'm ready to do whatever it takes to make this happen." I desperately wanted to help Logan find a reason to get up in the morning, an avenue to use his talents and gain self confidence, a career to give him the opportunity to make his own living, and a reason to live.

Logan didn't have the experience, motivation and will to do the necessary tasks this project required. We didn't know about his autism yet; that alone would make it hard to do this kind of work. He was also battling depression.

I didn't know where to start, but I was ready to do whatever it took to give Logan a reason to live.

The following morning I opened the phone book to check for small business support. I found many avenues to pursue. I worked my new goal into my regular schedule wherever I could. As I walked on the treadmill, I read books about the art business and about writing a business plan.

We applied for the government benefits that would give Logan the funding he needed. Experience working with the government for medical benefits gave me a glimpse of what I would be expected to do. There are always hoops to jump through. Applying for this assistance and enduring the long waits for answers tested my patience like no other time.

We were working with both the federal and state governments. Piles of paperwork and many appointments were necessary.

A welcomed break came when Heather, Logan and I went to Washington, DC for a vacation. We stayed with Lynn's brother and his family. We enjoyed seeing the sights during the day and eating a home cooked meal and having conversations around the dinner table at night. Heather and Logan enjoyed the drive around the city at night the most.

Even though Logan was struggling with depression and anxiety, he engaged in conversations about the meaning of life, spirituality, religion and other heavy topics. Heather, excited about her new relationship with Rubin, a man she met two weeks before we left, was eager to share her experiences and views. We were getting to know Lynn's family and having a wonderful time.

We returned home to piles of mail. Among the mail was a letter from the federal government informing us that Logan qualified for the benefits for which we applied.

"Logan, Social Security approved you for benefits," I said, smiling into the receiver.

"Wow, cool." Logan still seemed a little worried about believing in something so good after so many disappointments. We had waited five months for this moment. Logan qualified for this benefit because of all the years he had worked, gained income and paid into the social security system. His hard work was paying off. It was time for the next step: Another application to the federal government for additional benefits.

After a month long wait, we got approval on November 7, 2005. My eyes filled with tears as I read the email, "Logan Madsen has been approved." We were overjoyed with this news, and it came at a perfect time, as Logan just had surgery on his right arm five days earlier. Screaming with excruciating pain just the day before the good news, Logan experienced again the contrasts in his life.

Heather and Logan have both remarked how much unexpected joy they can feel on a day following a previous day of wondering if life was worth living. This experience keeps them appreciating the good in life and sustaining the decision to live each day. They both say, "Life is worth living and I am glad I'm alive."

Logan dreams of having a time when he has one commissioned piece of art in progress with another person waiting for him to finish so he can paint theirs. He loves the idea of "having to paint" giving him security and structure in his life. He fears he may not be able to physically or emotionally paint enough to support himself, but he dreams of having enough work to feel like a full-time artist. His biggest dream is being recognized as an artist who inspires people. He dreams of making enough money to support himself.

We worked long hard hours every day preparing for Logan's first art exhibit and supplying the government with satisfactory results for biannual reviews so the benefits would continue. The work seemed overwhelming.

When I get tired and worn down, I remind myself why I'm working so hard: I am giving Logan a reason to live. He can visit art and gift stores to market his art and paint original art to make a living, but my biggest motivation is to give him a reason to wake up in the morning and have a choice: Do I want to paint or not? Do I feel well enough to paint today or not? His disabilities limit his choices in many areas. Giving him an opportunity to choose in this matter is so important. It gives him the chance to find meaning and purpose in his life using his artistic talents. Having an answer to the commonly asked question, "What do you do for a living?" is important to Logan. He has his answer: "I am an artist."

The work involved in gaining the benefits drained our energy and stressed our relationship. He reacted to my phone calls as if I was a bill collector. Sometimes I felt hurt, but I focused on why I was doing this. Commonly, the work felt much too hard for Logan and he lacked the motivation to continue.

"I don't even know why I'm doing this. I'm not even sure this is what I want," he said.

"We don't have to do this. We can stop anytime. Do you want to stop?" I asked.

"I don't have anything else."

So we continued with our pursuit for self-employment as an artist. We had this conversation every couple of months through the two years of funding.

Many of my friends helped mat, bag and label Logan's art prints; count and separate the greeting cards and envelopes into five different groups; place them into clear sleeves, and label them with name and price.

After many months of hard work, November 2006 was finally here: time for the public exhibit of Logan's art. This was a dream come true.

Logan completed seventeen acrylic paintings of flowers and one large painting of a close-up view of a frond from a palm tree. He decided to paint a series of flowers, knowing they would sell easily in the Salt Lake culture.

Logan's artist statement reads: *"I was born in Salt Lake City on April 1, 1980. I am a self-taught, representational artist who magnifies the overlooked details of everyday objects using acrylic paint. My choice of using vibrant colors arouses emotions. Bold shadows* and highlights create texture and depth. I offset my subject to produce a contemporary look. My dramatic art allows a glimpse into my vivid mind. Through introspection I have gained an awareness which embraces the present moment.

Experiencing a life with disabilities has given me the insight to appreciate the ordinary. I was born with a rare condition called Miller syndrome. This condition primarily affects the face, forearms, hands and hearing. Looking different gives me unique perceptions on life, such as having a natural attraction to the unnoticed details of objects and people. Those details are accentuated in my art. The art of graphic design caught my attention. I gained an associate's degree in graphic design/multimedia, but then decided a fine art career is more fulfilling.

My interest in the details of nature began when I lived in California for three months and worked in landscape design. After moving back to Salt Lake, I began painting flowers and commissioned subject matter. Receiving positive feedback on my paintings, I sold them and decided to continue on this path. I am now a full-time artist and look forward to a lifetime career in fine art."

As we entered the art gallery, our eyes locked on Logan's art covering all the walls of the gallery. Spotlights made the colors in his flowers pop. His prints were displayed in black racks and his cards in baskets. Even though we spent many hours transporting the art to the gallery before the exhibit, seeing it in all its beauty was magical.

The exhibit was a huge success. All Logan's original art pieces sold except one, which I managed to keep for myself. Having two kinds of prints—giclee and Kodak—and having various sizes to choose from made the art affordable for fans of various income levels. At the end of his three week exhibit, the gallery director had an announcement for Logan. "We made more money during your exhibit than we have ever made before," she said.

Logan stood tall and smiled.

Working for two years to meet the requirements set by the government to gain accommodations and funding for Logan's art business was a lot of work. The rewards were worth the effort.

Logan purchased many items to make his business a success. He has two ergonomic electric tables that adjust to the height needed whether he stands or sits to do his art or work on his computer. He has a new laptop computer. He owns a Subaru Forrester to transport his art and supplies. He has ergonomic solutions to some problems created by his disabilities, invented by an electrical engineer and Logan. With these tools, tasks won't cause him so much pain. He has a custom steering column installed in his car that requires less effort steering. His gear shift stick is extended to accommodate his shorter arms so he doesn't have to hunch forward to shift. His kitchen sink and faucets are raised a full two feet so he can stand straight when doing dishes and preparing food. Lying in bed to sleep causes Logan pain. He has a memory foam mattress to help. Everything one could think of to help Logan be successful as a self employed artist was supplied.

Logan has prints and greeting cards printed from his art. This gives him an inventory of products to sell besides the originals he paints. Having prints wasn't in Logan's original plans. It feels too commercial to him. He prefers to sell his originals. It was necessary to have prints to show the government he would have enough to sell to be able to make a living. Because of his challenges, painting originals fast enough to make a living is difficult.

With the exhibit over and the funding complete, I stopped hounding Logan to work so hard all the time, as I promised I would. It was a little strange to go days without calling Logan, after calling multiple times each day. He welcomed the break, but also felt a little ungrounded without the structure that the project brought into his life. Even though he felt resistance to talking with me, he also got dependent on having me push him past his pain and challenges to accomplish our goal. He dealt with many feelings of resenting me, because he needed me. He didn't want to need me.

Exhausted from a long, hard two years of pushing harder than his health would allow comfortably, and realizing how painful it is to do the thing he loves the most, create art, Logan went into a cocoon. He was suffering from acute chronic pain along with all the other the challenges he faces.

When Logan paints or does computer graphic design, he feels constant acute pain, even with his pain medications. He must use his mind to block his discomfort to do these tasks long enough to accomplish anything worth doing. Blocking the pain allows him to work for longer blocks of time, but he pays a high price the following day. Knowing he will suffer more when he paints or uses the computer, he has difficulty motivating himself to start lengthy projects. He is inspired when he thinks about creating art, both by painting and with computer graphics, but because he knows what it takes to achieve the results he wants, his inspiration is crushed. Logan fights this battle constantly every day of his life.

Following the completion of his collection of art pieces and work with the government, Logan wanted to manage his life by himself as much as possible. He encouraged me to let him handle his doctor appointments and his schedule without my help. He was ready for some independence.

One year before his art exhibit, Logan went to a pain management clinic, but found little help to manage his chronic pain. He hit bottom on December 23, 2005. I received an early morning phone call and heard Logan say, "Mom, I am a danger to myself." I drove to his apartment and brought him with me as I drove Lynn to the airport to spend Christmas with his mother in North Dakota. Logan came home with me and slept through Christmas Eve and Christmas Day.

He was trying a medication for OCD. It was the six week mark and obviously it wasn't working; it was making him feel worse. When he was emotionally able, he dragged himself out of his dark hole and worked on his magnolia painting.

During those years, I was desperate to find help for Logan. His dad and I paid for him to get EEG neuro-feedback therapy to treat his ADHD. It was during that time he was diagnosed with autism, pervasive developmental disorder not otherwise specified, PDDNOS. The date was February, 2006.

We paid for a second opinion from a doctor specializing in autism at the University of Utah. The diagnosis of autism was confirmed, along with the diagnosis of obsessive compulsive disorder, OCD, and depression, along with his ADHD.

When I heard about a new clinic at the University of Utah—The Neurobehavioral Home Program—I was optimistic. There was a family doctor, physician's assistant, nurse, psychiatrist, and therapist, all in one clinic. Our efforts paid off. For the past three years the staff at the clinic have been happy to care for both Logan and Heather and have always gone the extra mile to see they receive the help they need. The staff meets regularly to discuss each patient's treatment. Logan sees his psychologist each week and I go with him to meet with his psychiatrist and family doctor once each month. His medications are being monitored closely. He is doing the best he has done in years and we are hopeful he will continue to keep getting better. He is learning acceptance. I am relieved and happy to have the support and help from this fine clinic.

The past five years, while I was working with the government to get funding for his art business and pushing him to paint enough paintings to have an exhibit, he struggled because he wasn't able to live his life in denial about his disabilities anymore. He couldn't use marijuana and alcohol to dull his difficult reality because he knew that self medicating only made his life worse. I likened his experience to what a person might go through after an automobile accident leaving them disfigured and disabled; accepting a new reality is difficult and involves real turmoil.

Chapter 41

Once while visiting New Orleans, I went sightseeing while Lynn was busy in conferences. I was a little nervous about being on my own in a large and unfamiliar city. As I was walking past the exciting shops, restaurants and new sights, I felt fortunate and awed to be in this magical city. After walking for a couple of hours, I sat by a beautiful fountain, appreciating the experience of having a wonderful man in my life and being able to travel to an interesting city. I was overjoyed.

Suddenly, my happiness turned into intense sadness. I got a lump in my throat and my eyes started to tear up. I felt as if my heart would break from this ache. This sudden change confused me, but I soon realized the sadness was because my two beautiful children have such difficult lives. I felt with full force the impossibility of changing certain circumstances in their lives. I couldn't give them normal arms and hands; I couldn't make their faces look normal. I couldn't make friends for them or stop people from staring at them. There was no way I could make their lives more like the lives others enjoyed. I felt so helpless, a helplessness that was heavy and pervasive, like claustrophobia. I cried for my children and for myself. After a few minutes of feeling the sadness, it began to fade and soon I had buried it away again, deep inside of me. Acceptance was the only answer for me. I had to make the most of my life and theirs. That is what I've always tried to do.

I experienced the same type of episode on a backpacking trip with Lynn. We were in the Uinta mountains, a few hours from our homes in Salt Lake. We'd been hiking for a couple of hours through tall, thick pine trees, enjoying the wonderful sounds, smells and sights of nature. We stopped to rest and to observe a beautiful waterfall. The intensity of my joy made me feel as if I wanted to cry. Again, almost immediately, the happiness turned to a deep sorrow. This time I recognized what was happening. I let myself feel the sadness. I accepted it as part of my life and then it began to subside.

The third time it happened in response to a wedding. A customer of mine was getting married and invited me to come. He was twenty-three years old at the time, the same age as Heather. I had cut his hair since he was in elementary school. I had watched him and his brothers grow up and had heard about many of the happenings in their lives.

The wedding reception was on a Friday night. I was tired from a long week of work and I just wanted to go home, eat dinner with my husband and then relax while watching a movie, but I also wanted to go to the reception. This family had been a part of my life for so many years and I wanted to show my support.

I had two movie tickets in my wallet, and I liked the idea of giving them the tickets to go to their first movie as husband and wife. I bought a wedding card and put the tickets inside.

I drove to the reception center after work. It was dark, cold and raining. I managed to find a parking place.

I walked through the entrance door and signed the guestbook. I saw the wedding line standing to my left. There were only a few people in front of me, so I quickly got into the line. The groom and his bride looked beautiful. My gaze continued down the line, taking in those five handsome young men in their tuxedos. I got a lump in my throat as I thought about all the years that had gone by. I thought about how small and young they once were and now they were men. I felt so proud. I noticed their mother and father greeting their guests. They were smiling and talking with everyone who came through the line. I thought of how happy and proud they must be. I thought of all the experiences that they went through with their five boys to get to that moment. I was overcome with joy for them.

As I left the wedding reception center, I was still feeling elated only to be hit with a bout of intense sadness. When I was safely in my car, sitting in the dark, I sobbed. I felt so much sorrow. I told myself that I didn't understand, but I knew, that deep inside of me there has been an intense sadness ever since Heather was born.

As I drove away from the reception center, I thought about the source of my sorrow. I knew that my life wasn't "normal." My children's lives weren't "normal." Children grow up and get married; they have careers; they have children; they buy homes where they create new memories. I knew that I probably wouldn't have many of the "normal" occurrences of ordinary lives. I hoped my children would find a companion to share their lives with them, but I knew it would be difficult to find a person who could see past the physical differences and allow themselves to get to know Heather and Logan. I also knew that it would take a brave person to "choose" to face the unknowns of the physical challenges with them. I will always believe it is possible, but I know it won't be easy.

I started thinking about the events in my life that had occurred that had brought me great joy. Events like when Logan could finally walk, when a surgery was successful, when Logan made a winning basket in a basketball game, when Heather went on a date in high school and when Logan had a girlfriend all through high school to take to the dances and enjoy other activities with. I thought about many other experiences and realized that I have many happy moments that occur along my journey of life, just like other people do, mine just look different.

Not long ago, Logan questioned my acceptance of Heather's and his health. "I don't believe you're dealing with it in a healthy way. If you were you wouldn't talk about it and you certainly wouldn't write a book about it." Logan liked to live life as if he was just like everyone else. Sometimes I wondered if he was living in denial and maybe that was causing his depression and impulsive behavior. When I talked about challenges, Logan was forced out of his denial and he didn't like it.

I respected Logan's opinion and wanted to be open to the possibility that he could be right, I asked him if he wanted to see a counselor with me. He agreed to go.

Logan and I went to the counselor's office together. I knew that sometimes I talked too much so I wore a bracelet that would remind me not to monopolize the conversation. Logan told the counselor about his opinion that I didn't handle life in a healthy way; I briefly shared my thoughts.

The counselor told us that he thought we were both handling the situation in a healthy way, but each of us had a different way. "Debbie handles the situation by talking about it and Logan handles it by keeping things to himself and just living his life."

He went on to help us choose a code word or action that lets the other one know when his toes are being stepped on, so the offensive words can stop. Logan and I benefited from this time spent together and I believe it instilled more confidence in each of us.

To this day, I believe that the sadness of Heather and Logan's condition will always live with me. I don't let it control or dominate my life. It just lives within me and will forever. Sometimes events or emotions trigger it and bring it out. After I feel it for a few moments, it just fades back into its place, where it stays until next time.

At this time, I had never experienced an early death in my immediate family. My grandparents passed away when they became old, a natural part of life. It was sad, but not shocking like an unexpected death of a mother, father, brother, sister or child. I imagined that someone who experiences that kind of sadness doesn't just "get over it." I imagined they might handle it much the same the way I handle my pain about Heather and Logan.

In July 2008, my precious nephew Brandon died from cystic fibrosis at the early age of thirty-one. The pain I felt seemed unbearable. My memories of the quality time I spent with Brandon and his family, and thoughts of his accomplishments in his short life—married to a loving wife, Drena, having a healthy son, Xander, success as a fine chef, and designing his own restaurant which was scheduled to open soon—and seeing Brandon laugh, helped me through these painful feelings. As I imagined, I haven't "gotten over it." I cry when I feel the pain and then I place the experience in a safe place in my heart, and go on.

My mother once made a comment about pain that made sense to me. She said, "Pain is like a fragile piece of china. Sometimes you take it off the shelf and examine it. When you finish, you place it back on the shelf. Until the next time."

Chapter 42

Going to Africa was an adventure Lynn and I often talked about. One of my customers owns Nakker International. Dennis arranges trips to Africa. He brought me literature containing descriptions and photos of places we could go and possible excursions. He interviewed me by asking what kinds of things Lynn and I like to do when we go on vacation.

Because I had traveled so much with Lynn, I knew that along with the adventure, traveling brought some stress too. In my fantasies about traveling, I didn't get tired, stressed, uncomfortable, frustrated, hungry, and thirsty or have any uncomfortable feelings. My fantasies brought only visions of adventure and excitement.

As I've gotten older and after experiencing three years of intensive focus and efforts to work with Logan, Voc Rehab, and the federal government to assist Logan in gaining self employment as an artist, I was feeling tired. I was also thinking that we were not getting any younger so going to Africa wouldn't get any easier. When I arrived home one evening I asked Lynn, "Would you like to go to Africa?" He said he would love to go to Africa. I suggested that we have my customer put together the trip of our dreams, and Lynn agreed. We got everything arranged: We were going to South Africa on May 5, 2008.

On Monday, March 31, 2008, Heather went to her see her lung doctor. She hadn't been feeling well and she had a vague pain in her chest that she hadn't felt before. Respiratory problems weren't new for Heather, so she and the doctor weren't alarmed. The doctor suggested antibiotics as a precaution. Usually he would send her home with a prescription. Medicaid was requiring a special unalterable paper for prescriptions, beginning April first, the next day. The doctor wasn't thinking very clearly, as he was feeling ill that day, so he told her his office would mail the new prescription. Heather went home and waited. By Thursday, the pain in Heather's chest increased to the point of going to the emergency room. They sent her home with a muscle relaxant. By Friday night, Heather's pain was unbearable. She was hospitalized. Breathing became difficult. The hospital physician put her on the antibiotics that her doctor had prescribed Monday, four days earlier, which finally arrived in her mailbox that Friday, the same day she was hospitalized. That weekend was a nightmare. Heather struggled for breath and was on oxygen. The oxygen was being increased as her difficulty breathing increased.

Knowing that Heather and Logan had a lung disease, and watching my nephew, Brandon, die from cystic fibrosis only a year earlier, I wondered if this is the pneumonia that would take Heather's life. I have lived with the reality that the day may come when I would lose both Heather and Logan to their lung disease. I did my best to accept this possibility by developing who I was along with being Heather and Logan's mom. I was terrified of losing my identity and purpose if they were to die. I was a better mom because I created a life with personal interests and activities to fill my needs. Knowing I might not have them in my life very long has made me appreciate every moment I spend with them. I am always as conscious as humanly possible. I don't want to miss any part of our time together.

On Saturday night, I pulled Heather's nurse aside. "I've known the time could come that Heather's lung disease could take her life. I know this may be that time. What can I expect?"

The nurse got emotional and seemed unsure what to say. "Heather is doing very well. She's breathing well with the oxygen. She will be okay," she said.

"I need to know what to expect. What will happen if her infection gets worse and she doesn't respond to the antibiotics she's given?"

The nurse could see that I really wanted to know and the best way she could help me was to tell me everything. "Well, I don't think this will happen, but… as her struggle for breath increases, the oxygen will be increased. Right now she has an oxygen tube in her nose, but as the oxygen is increased she will wear a mask over her nose and mouth and will eventually be on 100% oxygen assistance. When she still can't breathe, her brain won't have enough oxygen, so she will lose consciousness and her heart will be stressed from lack of oxygen. This will take her life."

My eyes filled with tears and my chest tightened. My whole body tensed from restraining myself from bursting into fitful sobbing. My "switch" flipped and my composed self remained calm. I thanked the nurse for her honesty.

The hands on the clock seemed to stand still. Heather's struggling increased. I looked at the dial on the oxygen. I had seen the nurse turn it up when I informed her of Heather's increased struggles. With uncertainty, I turned the dial a little, increasing the oxygen. Heather liked the result. Finally, I could control something that could make Heather struggle less, even if only a little. I continued to make sure Heather was comfortable. I tickled her forehead, wiped her face with a cool washcloth, rubbed her back, rubbed her legs, moved her head from side to side in a rocking motion; anything that could possibly help her suffer less.

Weekends are not a good time to be admitted into the hospital. There simply is not enough experienced staff to handle the best care of every patient in the hospital. By Sunday night I had had enough. I insisted on having the doctor on call come to Heather's bedside to discuss her increased pain and discomfort. The doctor came and a bedside x-ray was ordered. Heather continued to struggle for every breath. She had been sitting on her bed, hunched over, without sleep for over forty-eight hours. I didn't want to leave Heather's side. Her boyfriend, Rubin, and I continued to share time with Heather so we could both continue over the long haul.

My sister, Shelli, was in town for a birthday celebration. It was difficult to leave Heather late Sunday night, but Shelli insisted on spending the night at the hospital. Rubin relieved her in the morning. That morning I was at my niece's house for a quick visit before returning to the hospital when I got a call from the doctor treating Heather. "Heather has multi-lobe pneumonia, the worst kind of pneumonia that a person can get. One of her lungs is collapsed and we are going to move her to the intensive care unit (ICU) to await surgery to re-inflate her lung."

I felt my switch flip "off" my emotions and my robot kick into gear. "I'm on my way to the hospital right now," I said.

Questioning if prayer made any difference in the outcome of a situation like this, I talked out loud to my higher power, my energy source, whatever it is that I connect with that seems to help me. I didn't know what to pray for, Heather to live, or Heather to die and leave her suffering behind.

When I walked into her room, she sat in the middle of the bed with her legs crossed, a position she had been in for over seventy-two hours. The hospital gown drooped on her thin body. She looked up at me with tear-filled eyes as her voice sobbed, "I don't want to die." At that moment I knew what to pray for: Heather didn't want to die, she was very clear about this. I became clear too. I prayed that Heather would live and recover because that's what she wanted. I prayed she would be made comfortable during her recovery.

Rubin was there, and the three of us were crying together. We were so scared. A man of religion, who wore a white collar, walked into the room and over to the bed next to the window. The patient he was looking for wasn't there.

As he turned to walk by us, I asked him if he could give Heather a blessing as her lung was collapsed and she might die. I wanted all the blessings from all the sources I could find. He opened his Bible and read from the Twenty-third Psalm, words I had only heard in movies about "walking through the valley of the shadow of death." It was as if I was a character in a play. Nothing felt real.

As he read, I looked deep into Heather's tear-filled eyes and tried to create a permanent image of the beauty and aliveness I was seeing, in case I lost her in this battle. I used every ounce of self-discipline that I had to stay right in that moment so I wouldn't miss a single instant. I knew seeing my beautiful daughter alive might not last, and so I clung to every second I could share with her.

After the blessing, the Intensive Care Unit (ICU) Team came to take her to the ICU to await surgery. Rubin and I followed as Heather's bed was wheeled through the cold, green halls.

When she was settled in the ICU, two Mormon missionaries entered the room. They asked if we would like them to give Heather a blessing. Heather and I both agreed. They gave her a blessing that she would recover this time.

We were relieved to have Heather where she would be closely monitored until arrangements could be made for the special team of doctors that would do Heather's surgery. Because of her abnormal anatomy, the surgery had to be performed with magnetic resonance imaging (MRI) so that the doctors could make sure they didn't puncture a vital organ. Because of this delicate situation, Heather had to endure gasping for each breath through another night and another day. Surgery finally took place that evening.

Lynn came to visit in the ICU just before she was to go into surgery. As Heather lay in her bed, oxygen mask over her nose and mouth gasping for breath, Lynn walked over to her and began stroking her forehead. Their eyes met. Lynn's eyes filled with tears as Heather gazed into them with a look of deep affection.

After the surgery, Heather was taken back to the ICU. When we were finally allowed into her room, I was witnessing a miracle: Heather sitting in her bed with the biggest smile I had ever seen on her face. "I am the happiest I have ever been in my life. I can breathe," she said. Her lung had re-inflated after the doctors removed the fluids that accumulated in the lining between the lung and the ribcage, the plura.

A large plastic tube led from her chest to a machine on the floor. The fluids would be draining for the next few days. If they drained out too fast, she could be in trouble again.

Heather was in the hospital for two weeks. It was the beginning of a long, difficult recovery. Logan, Rubin or I were at the hospital every day; one of us was always with her. A nurse assistant was assigned to Heather's bedside around the clock.

When Heather was able to leave the hospital, she wasn't well enough to go home. She still had fluid in the plura, probably infection, but the tube had to come out or there was a risk of infection at the site. She was transported to a nursing home where she stayed for another two weeks. Time was going slowly. We were all fatigued beyond what we could have imagined, especially Heather. She wanted to go home.

Arrangements were made to take her home. Rubin wanted her home too. He was there around the clock to care for her. She was getting IV antibiotics and had lung physical therapy several times each day. I was relieving Rubin regularly, so he could get rest. The IV antibiotics had to be administered in the middle of the night and this was almost too much for Rubin to bear after the long haul.

Meanwhile, I was in the middle of having my new salon remodeled so I could begin working there by May 1. That wasn't all…the trip to Africa for my husband and me had been planned the previous year. We were supposed to leave two weeks from the day Heather went home. I didn't see how I could go and didn't know what to do. There was considerable money to be lost if we cancelled the trip. My intuition told me Heather still had the infection. She just wasn't getting better.

My sister, Shelli, pleaded with me to let her help. Finally, a week before my planned departure in a moment of emotional breakdown, I called her and left a message. "I can't possibly leave for Africa unless you can come to take care of Heather full time. I've accepted I won't be going. Let me know if it's possible for you to come."

She called me back. "Absolutely, I am coming. You need to get away. You need a break for your own health."

Heather pushed me too. "Mom, I want you to go. You can't always put your life on hold because of my health. This is a regular part of my life and your life must go on. You can't always change your plans every time I get sick. I would feel terrible. I will be okay, and Shelli is coming."

Somehow they persuaded me to go to Africa. I don't know how I did everything I had to do to go. I left the painters in charge of the salon and left my salon equipment and tools in boxes in the building to use after returning two weeks later.

My close friends, some of my customers, and people from my old neighborhood came to our rescue. My dear friend Kathy Newton arranged a schedule which included many people bringing Heather and Rubin food, sitting with

Heather to give Rubin a break, doing Heather's lung therapy, and being on call for anything that may be needed. Everyone wanted me to go to Africa. The support was unbelievable. I was so touched by people's generosity. I had never felt so supported in my life. It was wonderful to know so many people were there for me.

We feared losing our luggage because we were traveling to several destinations in South Africa and Zambia. We packed only carryon luggage. Packing was easy because of the limitations. I still don't know how I did everything necessary to go.

Lynn and I left on a Saturday morning. Shelli was scheduled to arrive on Monday. Logan and Rubin were taking turns staying by Heather's side. We had a list which included in-home nurses, friends and family that were on call around the clock. Having a cell phone that gave me a constant connection made it possible for me to go. I left with the knowledge that I could receive a call at anytime concerning Heather's condition.

It's strange that I didn't insist on Heather having an MRI before I left and she didn't either. It's as if we both knew the infection was still there and if we had the evidence of that fact, I wouldn't go to Africa.

I collapsed into my seat on the plane. I slept during the long flight. I had never been so exhausted. All my years of experience compartmentalizing my life made it possible to compartmentalize my life now. I knew I shouldn't go to Africa if I couldn't be present mentally and emotionally with my husband. I was committed to do my best.

Our first adventure was in Cape Town. We had plans to hike Table Mountain. Thick clouds covered all possible views of the mountain. Heavy rain fell. Our first day was a dark, dismal day. We made the best of the day by doing a walking tour of Cape Town. We were staying in a beautiful luxury hotel where they gave us an upgrade to a full suite, due to inconveniences caused by construction taking place at the hotel. We had dinner in a restaurant by the ocean.

In the middle of the night, my phone rang. The sound shocked me awake. I froze. I knew it could only mean one thing. The doctor was on the other end of the phone.

"Heather's infection is worse. As feared, we have to do surgery to remove the infection. I wish I had a crystal ball so I could tell you what to do," the doctor said. "It's a very difficult surgery. Heather will probably do okay during the surgery, but the recovery will be difficult." She put Heather on the phone.

"Mom I want you to stay in Africa.... I am at peace with dying." Her words tore my heart to the core. "Please stay, Mom. The only way I will ever see Africa is through your eyes. Shelli is already at the airport; she will be with me the whole time."

All I knew for sure was that I had to give Heather what she wanted. I had to stay in Africa. I knew I couldn't hang out in my worries and fears, or I might as well go back to Salt Lake. I didn't know how I was going to do it, but I knew I had to accept the reality that I may never again see Heather alive if I stayed.

"For you, I will stay," I said to Heather. "I will take tons of videos so I can bring you to Africa through my photos. I love you, honey." I said before my voice broke, and she returned the phone to the doctor.

"I will email you every day," the doctor promised.

Thank heavens for modern technology. I know I couldn't have stayed without cell phone connections, texting and email. I wouldn't have gone without them.

As I awoke the next morning, I struggled to stay present in my thoughts. We had scheduled an early hike and a tour of the southernmost point of Cape Town. Exerting myself to hike in the rain and fog was therapeutic. It gave me an outlet for my nervous energy. When I am in nature, I feel I am in the arms of my higher power. I couldn't have been in a better place to endure such a difficult emotional experience.

Once off the mountain, we were picked up in a van and driven to the southernmost point where we saw penguins. Taking videos for Heather kept me going. I felt like I was doing something for her. After an eventful, long, physically demanding and emotional day, I sunk into a hot bath in the room. I could barely move. I collapsed onto the bed. I had to sleep.

Lynn felt helpless. He wanted to take care of me, to do anything I asked. He ordered his dinner to be brought to the room as I was too tired to eat. When his dinner arrived, I felt rested enough to sit with him while he ate. After dinner, we stepped outside onto the balcony that overlooked the harbor. It was a beautiful sight. The boats and water were lit with the moon and darkness of the night and clouds blocking a view of anything beyond.

The following morning our guide arrived for a tour of the city. We spent some time in a museum. As if the heavens wanted to give us a gift, the rains stopped and the clouds disappeared. We could see Table Mountain. This was our last afternoon before an early departure the following morning. We left the museum to go to the tram that took us to the top of Table Mountain.

Heather's surgery hadn't taken place yet as the doctors had to make special arrangements with MRI equipment and specialists before beginning. No mistakes could be made.

After visiting Table Mountain, we cleaned up at our hotel and had dinner at the hotel restaurant.

In Africa morning came too quickly, while Salt Lake City was still covered with darkness, as we boarded the small plane that was to take us to a game reserve an hour's flight away. My body was in Africa but my heart and mind were with Heather. As I looked out the window of the small plane, I talked with my higher power and asked that Heather be made comfortable. I didn't feel alone. My soul was comforted.

Upon arrival, deep in the bush, we were picked up by an open jeep and driven to a lodge on the game reserve. When we arrived we were told about a safari that would be leaving in thirty minutes. I was drugged with Dramamine, which relieved my motion sickness from the flight, and felt nervous about such a quick transition. I ignored my hesitation and quickly prepared to go.

Within five minutes we spotted a beautiful honey and black leopard lounging in a tree just around the corner. Seeing a leopard, being in nature, and being in the outdoor air, helped me experience the moment and move out of my worries about Heather. I was busy shooting a video for her as well. We were out for three hours, until well after dark. The sights were amazing.

As I finished dinner and prepared for bed, I knew Heather would be going into surgery as I slept. I didn't have cell phone service in the bush, so I had a phone brought to my cottage in case there were any emergency calls during the night. We had a guide walk with us to our room as there were no fences around the resort. Wild animals could come into the camp at any time. Already on edge because of Heather's health, I was very nervous at the idea of wild animals being so close. My high emotions branded everything I experienced into my memory.

We were awake at dawn and ready when our guide knocked on our door. His defense against wild animals was a flashlight, which he assured us was enough to scare away any unwanted predators. When we arrived at the front door of the lodge, I was called to the phone. It was Dennis, my friend and customer who arranged our trip; he had been in regular contact with the lodge where we were staying and was calling to tell me Heather made it through the surgery and was in recovery. My heart was filled with gratitude. I know post surgery is the most painful, uncomfortable and risky time, and I was seriously concerned for Heather. I had to pray constantly for peace of mind and help to take in the incredible experience I was having with my husband in Africa. Once in the jeep, on the trail, my mind was at high alert looking for wild animals. We saw amazing sights: a pride of lions sleeping in the late morning sun; birds of every shape and color; even the vegetation seemed wonderfully strange and exotic.

A huge breakfast was awaiting us when we returned three hours later. After we ate, Lynn went on a walking safari with the guide. That was more than I wanted to do. I stayed behind.

As I gazed into the bush from the balcony of the lodge overlooking a large watering hole, I prayed for Heather's comfort. I was watching gazelles and wild deer come to drink off in the distance. After an hour or so, off in the far distance, as if a message sent from God, the elephants came. I felt like I was having a spiritual experience. Many elephants were running, their ears flapping in the breeze, to the water hole. The energy, passion and excitement I felt was indescribable. Just God and I were present for this amazing experience. With shaking hands and blurry eyes, I picked up my video camera to film this amazing sight for Heather. Doing this for my daughter gave me peace and calmed my soul.

After two more safaris and dinner, I sat down at the computer in the resort library to receive my first email from the doctor. Heather was doing okay. She was being watched closely; the doctor assured me that I would be notified if anything changed.

The next morning brought another early phone call from Dennis reporting Heather's stable condition. After three more safaris, good meals, and wonderful people, night was here again. Off to the library I went to receive my daily email from the doctor. Again, I received the news that Heather was doing okay so far. Shelli, Logan and Rubin also sent me reassuring emails.

The following morning, our last morning, I was greeted again with a phone call from Dennis. His calls made it possible for me to continue my stay and even enjoy our safari experiences. We saw mating lions, a hunting lioness, mating warthogs, jackals, water buffalos, hippos, a leopard hunting in the early morning hours, elephants threatening to charge our vehicle, a cheetah on a termite hill watching for prey, and playful lion cubs by spotlight at night. This was a magical experience and I was getting it on film to share with Heather when I returned.

The time came to fly back to town for the night. Early the next morning we would board a small plane for the flight to Zambia. Lynn and I were so full from the adventures we had experienced already, we felt as if we should be leaving for home. Once in Zambia, we experienced a river ride on a big paddle boat where we viewed our first giraffes along the shore line. The experience was unbelievable.

The following day we walked to Victoria Falls from our hotel. What a breathtaking sight that was! We flew in a helicopter over the falls to view it from the air. The falls flow into a large crevice so viewing from across the falls is difficult. We hiked along a path created to view the falls from the front, but the water had such great force it created a mist like a torrential down pour. Even with rain gear and umbrellas, we were drenched.

I continued to receive my emails from the doctors every evening before bed that told me of Heather's progress. The recovery was grueling and difficult for her, but she remained stable. Sometimes I was able to text Logan and Shelli from the outskirts of the hotel grounds. I didn't have any reception in my room, but I knew I could walk a short distance and connect. They were protecting me from challenges they were having with Heather's feeding tubes and other scary situations. They did their best to keep from divulging information that would worry me. They were so committed to creating the environment for me to enjoy my trip.

Lynn was amazing. He supported me in every way he could. His love kept me calm. I'm sure he was having a difficult time keeping his mind on the trip too, but he didn't show evidence of his concerns. He wanted to give me a wonderful experience to balance the difficult challenges I face in my life. He is always here for me.

We visited an African village in Zambia. I played with the children because I didn't have any presents to give them. They taught me how to make a helicopter from a stick and leaf. We ran around with our helicopters, pretending we were flying. It was a moving experience for me to visit the village. We bought a few trinkets to take home to Heather and Logan from the village shops.

Our last dinner in Zambia was at the hotel, with small monkeys watching for food to be dropped on the ground which they could quickly steal. As we were walking to our room, we nearly walked into a herd of zebras that were eating the grass by our room. If I hadn't looked up right when I did, we would have crashed right into them. It was dark and their white stripes stood out in the lights around the grounds. We got some great photos to take back to share with Heather.

The doctors decided to keep Heather in the hospital until I arrived home even though she was eager to go home. Rubin and Heather strongly urged the doctor to let her go home to recover instead of going to the care center. With the care of an in home nurse, my help, and the support of many friends, Heather was able to go home the day after I arrived back in Salt Lake City.

As soon as our plane landed, Lynn and I took a taxi home, dropped off our luggage and drove straight to the hospital to see Heather.

Afterword

Heather

Heather is tall and thin and has curly light brown hair. Her blue-green eyes sparkle when she speaks about a topic for which she feels passion.

Heather, now 33 years old, likes to focus her time and efforts on projects and activities that make her feel happier and more comfortable in her day to day life, especially because her disabilities cause her discomfort and unhappiness so much of the time. Her limited abilities, energy and hours in a day make her more conscious of her choices, and narrow her choices of how she will spend her day. She understands why older people don't travel, go on outings with friends and family, make phone calls, or keep their homes as clean as often as they did when they were younger. She understands more about life than she did when she was younger and I believe more than a lot of people in general.

She is a gifted teacher. She enjoys teaching people about autism so she reads personal stories and does research about autism. She wants to write a book about autism that can help people who are affected by it one way or another.

She finds value in herself and sees how she can contribute to other people when she is teaching or tutoring another person. She loves to write and sees writing as a form of teaching. Her passion is teaching about autism. One of my customers has two grandchildren with autism. Heather met with her several times to teach her about the characteristics of the condition.

Heather has been on a few panels to teach health professionals about autism. She wrote an informative paper giving them information that would help them work with people with autism. Her paper was published in the April issue of a news letter called, "Health e Connections", for autism awareness month. She looks forward to future teaching opportunities.

She teaches Logan and me about autism, obsessive compulsive disorder, attention deficit disorder, diabetes, and other conditions that affect our lives. Heather enjoys researching and sharing information so she can teach us to help our lives be better. She has so much to offer and we're excited to find avenues for her to teach.

Some of Heather's health goals are: gaining weight through eating enough healthy calories daily and improving her physical health by exercising regularly on a Rebounder–some people remember this as a "mini tramp." Heather researched the Rebounder design and says it's different from a mini tramp. She decided that the rebounder is the best form of exercise she can do comfortably. She also likes to take short walks on the beautiful walkways around her apartment complex with her partner, Rubin.

Heather feels safe when she is walking with Rubin. She doesn't feel any less safe in this world because of her disabilities than she thinks the average person feels. When she is leaving her apartment, getting in or out of her car, or in an unknown environment she stays alert and notices what's going on all around her. She feels vulnerable when she thinks about her limited ability to defend herself when she is exposed to an unleashed dog, a person acting strangely, or perceives a situation to be dangerous. She recognizes these feelings from childhood experiences; being afraid of falling when riding a bike or rollerblading, or being nervous about being hurt while on the school playground with balls and kids flying everywhere.

Heather's favorite clothes are soft blue jeans, a solid colored T-shirt and a soft jacket. The weight of the jacket gives Heather a feeling of comfort and security. High top, soft, supportive shoes work best for her.

Through her interactions with people, she's learning the value of sharing herself with others: "In social situations where I get to express my thoughts, feelings, ideas, and interests, I experience myself and I leave feeling emotionally full, knowing exactly who I am and what I love. When I focus on what I love and experience myself, I don't feel lonely."

I asked Heather what makes her want to get out of bed every day and face her challenges and she said, "Staying in bed is boring. Being bored makes me unhappy and I don't want to be unhappy, so I get out of bed and live my life. This makes me happier than lying in bed. I get out of bed so I can create happiness for myself and while I am doing that, I also try to help improve others people's lives as well."

She enjoys staying current with the news and politics and uses the information to vote responsibly when election time comes.

Heather loves reading, seeing weather and nature change, and she loves observing and experiencing animals. Diversity in people, belief systems, and behavior are also of interest to her. She enjoys learning about love, kindness and empathy, experiencing pleasures like eating good foods, traveling and connecting with people. She explores topics like mathematics, physics, statistics, science of the universe and words.

"I like to experience other people's creativity in art, culture and other beliefs that reflect the essence of beauty in life," Heather said. "I like growing as a person, and spiritually, so that I know more about love and giving and can assist others in knowing about love. I'm seeking truth, fairness, and peace. I look to Zen Buddhism and the sense of a higher energy of wisdom beyond myself to guide me. I seek to connect. I enjoy connecting patterns between subjects, people, ideas, experiences and I like connecting to these patterns and to people, their souls, my soul and our lives. I find the spirit of the universe in everything."

Television, internet and books give her access to many interests, which include cognition and perception, physiology, biopsychology, developmental psychology, social psychology, nervous system and senses, human brain structure and functions, nutrition, pharmacology, nature, animals, literature and poetry, math/physics, technology, perspectives and social interaction.

The area of Heather's specific primary interests is perception and consciousness. She explains: "I am interested in the construct of individual reality that is influenced by the cognitive processing and integration of information from the sense perceptions and resulting interactions with the environment. I want to know the explanations of a reality perception (the senses would be physiological), the creation for the perception (development exposure to environment and social exposure to people), and the interpretation of the perception (individual cognitive perspective)."

Heather's broad interests are: genetics, geography, weather, philosophy, geology, chemistry, astronomy, astrology, religion, new age and alchemy, music, computers, electronics, fiction and science fiction, expression, culture, and development of language.

She also has a category of autistic fascinations which include: words and writing styles, physics and math formulas, statistical calculation, categorization of knowledge, logic, organization of nature, rhythm of things (ecosystem, music, and social dynamics), economical calculation and probability.

Heather accepts her challenges but still feels frustrated when she wants to do more than she can. She deals with the daily challenges of having bronchiectasis, caused by PCD, and other frustrations she experiences by focusing on her fascination with life. As these categories of interest show, she loves to learn about almost anything and loves to see things from different perspectives. "This is what gets me out of bed. I spend a lot of time reading and thinking. Those two things are what keep me afloat much of the time from being dragged down into negative feelings about my lung disease. When I am sick and laying there coughing in my bed with a fever, wondering 'what now?' I often get back the answer: a new moment. What I am focused on is how my time is spent each hour of each day and how that makes me feel."

Heather's ADHD was discovered and a medication for ADHD allowed Heather to focus much better in social situations, which has enabled her to create and participate more in conversations. The three years Heather lived alone in her twenties were years of self-discovery. Through traveling, sharing quality time with relatives, talking with people online, going to support groups, learning about her autism diagnosis, getting help for her ADHD, taking care of her health and daily living responsibilities and learning to manage her stress, Heather created a life she enjoys.

Until then she focused on accepting her challenges, getting to know what activities would help her health and bring meaning and fulfillment into her life. She was at peace and even enjoying living alone in her own apartment. She created a comfortable environment where she felt happy living and working on her own interests. Successful with that goal, she decided she was ready to find a friend.

Heather found her life partner, Rubin, whom she met in October of 2005, 5 years ago. He is very important in her life. His blue eyes reveal wisdom and maturity; he is someone who looks for meaning in life, and finds meaning with Heather. His light brown and thinning hair is beginning to gray, as is his beard, which tickles Heather's neck when he hugs her. Heather's eyes twinkle with affection when she looks at him.

Together they enjoy watching movies, playing scrabble, Wii, and talking about their personal interest projects with each other. They engage in deep conversations about physics and spiritual topics. Rubin loves to cook for Heather. They stroll through the gardens and view the ponds and ducks together, holding hands and enjoying the beauty of the outdoors.

"I met him at a support group that I would go to weekly for mental health issues," Heather said of her first contact with Rubin. "One week he was the facilitator, as the regular facilitators had another meeting at the same time. I noticed him and watched how he talked and took control of the group. I heard him say he is a practitioner of neurolinguistic programming and I understood then how he thinks, so I baited him. We were talking about something that makes each person happy and when it was my turn, I knew I wanted to say something that would pique his interest. I said that having new insights about myself makes me happy. Later on, I talked about one of the insights I've had and after group, he walked by me and said, 'We should do this again sometime.' I agreed.

"After my appointment with the pulmonologist the following Monday, I was grieving about having a lung disease and how the doctor couldn't help some of my symptoms. I called the regular facilitator of the group and we met Tuesday morning and talked. I told her how my biggest fear is being sick and alone. We were figuring out how I could do more things and be with people and I mentioned that I liked Rubin and thought he liked me. She gave him my number and told him I needed a ride to the group the next night, as I don't like to drive at night, so he picked me up. After he picked me up, we talked awhile in the car before going inside to the meeting and we discovered how much we had in common. We met together a few more times and talked on the phone many nights and then decided we wanted to be together."

Rubin is a very loving, nurturing, kind, honest, intelligent interesting man and connects with Heather like no one ever has. I'm so happy to know she is with Rubin. She learns communication skills and other lessons available for a person in a committed relationship.

I'm happy knowing Heather is spending her evenings and weekends with Rubin and gaining the fulfillment relationships can bring. We discuss the challenges and rewards of being in this kind of relationship. She communicates wonderful insights on exactly what she is learning and why she is with Rubin. She teaches me as she shares what she is learning.

Her answers come in her insights. "I focus on details that people miss or forget about which really can remind us what we are living for, reconnecting us to our humanity and the joy of exploring this life."

"Maybe it is the love between us and how we care about others that makes us hopeful about our lives," she said. "Our challenges have enhanced this love and caring about each other and our lives.

Living with disabilities and lung disease and accepting the challenges these bring help her pay more attention to what is most important to her. "At times I feel like I have a love affair with life in that I am fascinated by all the beauty and expression life has to offer. I am able to see intimate details of life that tickle my soul and make me feel alive. I live for these moments. No amount of differences or struggles in life can touch these or take them away. With my enjoyment of words, I am grateful for the ability to re-create those love affair moments on paper for others to be able to experience as well."

Hearing Heather describe the fullness in her life and communicate what she thinks could bring it more meaning brings me joy. "My disabilities are validated and respected; I am accepted as being a person, not only by what I can or can't do; I am well loved and taken care of; there are people that like to talk to me; I get joy from my interests and being with people and have hope for the future."

Communicating with Heather helps me find ideas to explore for other areas where I may help her create more meaning in her life and my own. Making a difference in her life brings meaning and purpose to my life. The lessons she has learned and insights she has gained shape her into the wonderful human being I am privileged to enjoy in my life.

"When I compare myself to others, in a lot of ways, I come out richer," Heather said. "I am grateful for what I have: positive attitude, acceptance, differences, and unknown surprises. How do I connect in different ways? Here are a few: belonging, strength, endurance, surrendering, connections, gratitude, taking care, perspectives, self growth, and social and cultural growth."

Logan

Today is November 21, 2009. Logan is almost thirty years old. He feels the best he has felt in years. He wants to feel better, but sees his progress and feels more optimistic about his future as a human being and an artist. He has gained many insights. He wrote some of them and collected others. His favorites are written on small pieces of paper and placed around his apartment where he can read them often. Following are a few examples:

"Choose to accept what you can't change."

"If it's not a matter that ends in death, it's not that important."

"Life is hard, but it's our responsibility to make it work."

"If we argue about our limitations, we get to keep them."

"The best decision is the one you've already made."

"Question your thoughts to discover your truths."

"No matter how bad things are, only you can do something about them."

"Self confidence comes when you are accountable."

"You will never control what others think or feel about you."

"What's true for you is the only thing that matters."

Logan is a self taught artist. We discuss the possibility of Logan getting tips from art teachers to speed up his learning process. He's not sure how he feels about lessons. He enjoys learning on his own, even though he does get frustrated sometimes when it takes too long to find the method that works best to create the look he wants. Logan said, "Friends and family tell me that people don't expect of me what they expect of those without disabilities. Believing this results in my having realistic expectations to achieve success."

Logan's previous medium was acrylic. Currently he is painting with oils. His first oil painting is a large portrait he painted as a gift for my sister, Kathy. The portrait is of her son, Brandon, who died at the young age of thirty-one, of cystic fibrosis. While doing this painting, Logan cried. Until then, he was unable to cry. Feeling his sadness for the loss of his cousin and the pain of life by crying was therapeutic. It was a very moving experience for Logan. Kathy was deeply touched by this gift from Logan. The painting hangs in her living room in her home in Florida.

Logan's second oil painting is a brown Labrador commissioned by one of my customers. It is an 8 x 10 inch painting that was ordered when the owner's dog died. His third oil painting is a self portrait He is sitting on a chair with paint brush in hand, thinking about what to paint next. He calls it "Stuck."

Finding peace and contentment alone is important for a person who hasn't found a partner. Logan is learning that lesson now. He knows himself better because he has been introspective for the past five years. He continues to gain acceptance and understanding of his disabilities, limitations, and personality traits one day at a time. He is looking forward to creating avenues to meet new friends and a possible life partner.

His experience of having a regular girlfriend in high school and his friends along the way, give him the confidence to believe he will achieve this goal when the time is right. Knowing himself better helps him know what kinds of personalities in friends and partners work best for him. He is excited to venture out to discover more about himself, communication and relationship dynamics.

Meanwhile, Logan values his friendships. His friend Sara, recently said, "Logan is a truly tender hearted person with a lot of love to give. As his friend, I have always felt blessed to be a recipient of that love. Even though we have had our hard times, we have always been able to get over them because of the true friendship that exists between us. I believe Logan is a very loyal friend and a very honest friend. Sometimes the honesty can be hard but Logan will tell you the truth, even in those hard situations. A lot of people aren't honest enough with themselves or their friends to tell it like it is. I find that is a true blessing. Logan also has a wonderful sense of humor and of course, he is an incredibly talented artist. I have always admired Logan for overcoming the struggles in his life. No one knows what it's like to be Logan and I don't think any of us would come out on top of things the way he has. I really admire and look up to him."

Lifelong friend, Spencer, described Logan this way: "He's defiant. Usually, that has a negative connotation attached to it, but in Logan's case, it was a positive connotation for those around him. Logan never let his disability get in the way of something he wanted to do. Even if someone told him it wasn't safe for him to do it, or it wasn't possible, his defiance would kick in, and he'd set out to prove them wrong. Using determination and his creative ingenuity, he would find a way to accomplish what he set out to do. I recall multiple times, where he would tell me of an invention that he wanted to build to make the currently impossible, possible. His determination set the bar for mine, and the other people around me. Whenever I would feel like I couldn't do something, because it was too hard, or because I was tired, frustrated, or disappointed—all it took was one knowing look from Logan, and you instantly have your motivation back. He'd look at you like, 'Are you really going to try and tell ME that you can't do something?' In the unlikely event that just him giving you that look didn't work, then Logan would use that creative ingenuity to help you come up with a solution for whatever was standing in the way of your goal."

When Logan was ready to love and care for a dog he found, Charlie, a Chihuahua mix. Charlie turned out to be the perfect pet and companion. Charlie loves Logan unconditionally, and caring for Charlie gives Logan structure. He always knows Charlie is waiting at home for him when he returns from a day of errands.

Logan has emerged from his cocoon of suffering and introspection, sometimes punching, cursing, fatigued, and anxious, but at the same time confident because he knows himself better and lives his progress. He is accepting his challenges and knows his strengths and talents. He is exposing himself to people and social situations that he has avoided for the past five years. He is breaking out of the binding restraints of his disabilities. He now has completed building his base camp, a place where he feels safe, where his personal belongings are organized in his apartment and art studio. Everything has a place and he knows where to find what he needs at any given moment. He keeps a daily journal where he writes his thoughts and insights.

Heather and I met with Logan for a few weeks so Logan and I could learn more about autism and ADHD. Heather helps give us the understanding we need to keep moving forward. With this information, Logan understands how autism affects his life and perceptions. He knows why he reacts the way he does in social situations. He understands why it's difficult for him to make decisions about his career as a self employed artist. He knows what to do to create success.

Being independent is one of life's most important accomplishments to Logan. He handles all his responsibilities, and has learned that part of being independent is learning to ask for help when he needs it. Sometimes, obtaining help is what makes independence possible.

Logan's artistic talent excites and stimulates him when he sees the colors, textures, and shapes that are all around him every day. He sees many avenues where he can express himself as an artist. He paints with acrylics and oils, takes photographs, and looks forward to classes in metal art, sculpture, wood carving, interior decorating, and clothing design. These passions keep Logan excited, so excited that it's hard to make decisions on what to do next.

After six months of organizing his home and studio, he had a "painter's block" which kept him from putting brush to canvas. Finishing his fourth oil painting, a self portrait he titled, "Helpless" wasn't coming easily. The dramatic painting, a 48 x 48 inch canvas done in oils, features Logan's naked body on the floor, rolled into a ball with hands on his head. His position in the painting makes him look as if his cocoon is gone but he is still confined to the small space that bound him for so long, as if he feels helpless to open himself up to the unexpected experiences ahead.

The painting sat in his apartment, leaning against the wall, but is now mounted on the rope and pulley behind the shelf he designed to lean his elbows on while he paints. This gives his overworked back a break from constantly using his shoulder muscles to raise his arm to the canvas. The ergonomic table sits in the center of the room, along with the height adjustable tables he found at second hand stores. He has sawed wood, glued, taped, bent and soldered together many materials to create custom tools to use in all aspects of his life as an artist and life as a person who doesn't have a typical body for using the manufactured items for everyday life. I'm impressed to see all the amazing gadgets he has invented to make his life easier and less painful. I'm sure he could patent some of his creative ideas.

I was excited to receive a text from him one week ago that said, "I have finally put paint to canvas!"

After spending months tackling the burden of going to his doctors, at first every two weeks and now once a month, to find the right combination of medications that help manage his chronic pain from scoliosis and other skeletal abnormalities and his autism, obsessive compulsive disorder, and anxiety, Logan has the tools to live a productive and fulfilling life.

Lynn and I recently hired a designer to remodel our bathrooms. When she came to our home for the first consultation, she fell in love with Logan's paintings, which cover the walls of my home. Over the course of two months, she sold five of his prints and commissioned Logan to paint an original for her.

When Logan arrived at the designer's home to discuss the commissioned piece, I saw a tall, slim, young man, with dark blonde hair naturally highlighted with light auburn hues. Along with his striking blue-green eyes one cannot help but notice his distinguished looks. My heart swelled with joy as I watched him walking up the sidewalk lined with the fall oranges, reds and golds of the landscape. I made introductions and said good-bye, leaving them to talk.

Driving away, all the beautiful colors on the mountains and in the landscape that surrounded me—the colors of fall and browns of winter on its way, colorful houses, signs, cars, and everything around me—jumped into my view. I'm looking forward to experiencing all aspects of Logan as he continues to gain acceptance, comfort and peace: his good sense of humor, attentive listening, problem solving, appreciator of beauty and style, lover of animals, charm, wit, depth of character and fullness of wisdom and love.

It is good to have my son back. So good.

Debbie

The real victory in my life is that I have found joy in the face of my suffering. I experience joy many moments of every day. The intensity of my joy equally matches the intensity of my deepest emotional pain. I experience this happiness because of my suffering. As I awoke this morning a scripture came to my mind: "Man is that he might have joy." Perhaps this memory came from my early days of religion. It is perfect for the answer I was looking for to my current question. "What is the greatest lesson I have learned through my challenges?"

Questions, answers, inspirations, direction, thoughts and peace appear in my mind every day, along with a specific feeling. The feeling radiates as a force, a life force, my life source. Several words attempt to name it for me: Higher Power, God, Life Force and Universal Power. It doesn't matter what I call it, this force exists for me and is as real for me as gravity.

I am not a religious person, so it's interesting that a scripture would come to my mind. I don't recall the rest of that scripture and I don't spend much, if any, time reading scriptures of religion. I would love to study all religions, to learn about the many tools available for creating the most in life. Opportunities exist all around me, but I lack the time and energy to take advantage of them all. I spend my time tackling the never ending challenge of being conscious in each moment of every day. I am learning and relearning each moment as it happens, trying to make the best choice possible to create my present moments and my future.

I follow my life force, creating more joy, because the more joy I attract into my life, the more positive energy I feel when I awaken every morning. I live from this positive place. I've discovered that joy acts like a magnet. When I feel joy as I meet another person during my day, they seem to react positively from my energy. This results in my experiencing the positive energy even stronger, as if it builds synergy.

Life keeps bringing me challenges. This is the nature of life as I know it. I have learned that if I accept the new challenge and don't resist it, my successes will be surer and the journey easier. As the challenge appears, I feel the shock, disappointment, sadness, frustration, anger, and all the human emotions that come along with the challenge. After I experience these uncomfortable feelings, and validate them by expressing them through crying, talking, thinking, and any other avenue that helps me feel better afterwards, I focus on what I can do to solve the problem or make the challenge easier. I ask myself and others: "Can I do anything to change this situation?" If the answer is yes, I get busy doing what is required. If the answer is no, I accept that reality and focus only on what can be done, not on the impossible. Usually this takes time. Human emotions are complicated. Because I focus on the joy in my life, it exists to balance all those emotions and make my life worth living, and makes me love living. I focus on the joy and the positive.

I love being Lynn's wife. I love being Heather and Logan's mother, and I love making a positive difference in other people's lives. By sharing their difficulties; through loving them, helping them, supporting them, and always creating avenues to make our lives contain the joy that keeps us inspired, I find my purpose and meaning.

Heather and Logan are still finding their pathways, which lead to their purpose and meaning, and then fulfillment, so they can experience long lasting joy. I am optimistic and hopeful that they will succeed. I do everything I can to help them in every way possible. As I succeed in making choices that create happiness, joy, peace, and contentment in my life, even with my challenges, I am showing Heather, Logan, and Lynn, my family members, friends and other people that joy exists. It is all around us. Believing that joy exists and believing you can have it, even if it is not yet your reality will bring joy to you through your daily choices.

6663325R0

Made in the USA
Charleston, SC
20 November 2010